Lessons in
Grid
Computing

Additional praise for *Lessons in Grid Computing: The System Is a Mirror*

"I really like the storytelling format for communicating these ideas, and I have a strong feeling this book will be uniquely positioned in the volumes of IT advice/offerings. The "Stuart Robbins philosophy" of IT project management is rooted in a genuine appreciation of the human side of technology. This book articulates these important and surprisingly simple (yet all too often overlooked) lessons. The accessible storytelling format will communicate to a wider audience than just IT management."

Maggie Law, User Interface Designer, PeopleSoft

"I was thrilled to read this. It's such an easy thing but most often it is overlooked. It's very true that system reflects the harmony (or the lack of) of an organization. This book explains in plain English one of the secrets of measuring the success or failures in this complicated and ever changing world of IT."

Ruyben Seth, Database Manager, Symantec Corporation (Oregon)

"This is a very complicated and challenging concept and you have raised some serious thought provoking issues."

Atefeh Riazi, Worldwide CIO, Ogilvy & Mather, Inc.

"These stories are easy to read, and good fodder for students!"

Carol Brown, Ph.D., Kellogg School of Business

"You are an excellent writer and [this theory] demonstrates that you are a visionary in our industry!"

Steve Yatko, Head of IT R&D, Credit Suisse First Boston (NYC)

Lessons in Grid Computing: The System Is a Mirror

Stuart Robbins

John Wiley & Sons, Inc.

Library of Congress Cataloging-in-Publication Data

Robbins, Stuart, 1953-
  Lessons in grid computing : the system is a mirror / Stuart Robbins.
      p. cm.
  Includes bibliographical references and index.
  ISBN-13: 978-0-471-79010-5 (cloth : alk. paper)
  ISBN-10: 0-471-79010-9 (cloth : alk. paper)
  1. Information technology—Management. 2. Business—Computer networks. 3. Management information systems. 4. Industrial management—Technological innovations. 5. Decision making. I. Title.
  HD30.2.R627 2006
  658.4'038—dc22
                                                 2006002910

Printed in the United States of America

10 9 8 7 6 5 4 3 2 1

For my son, Max

"We must transform ourselves."

−Steve Yatko
Head of IT R&D, Credit Suisse First Boston
2004

"Language is digital."

−Gregory Bateson
Steps Toward an Ecology of Mind
1972

CONTENTS

FOREWORD

Since 1978 I have worked in the high-tech sector as a sales and marketing executive, a marketing and strategy consultant, an author of books like *Crossing the Chasm* and *Inside the Tornado*, a venture investor, and a public speaker. Before 1978, however, I was an English professor who taught writing and literature at a liberal arts college. What a delight for me, therefore, to encounter a business book that lives at the intersection of my two careers.

This book is an experiment in discourse. It uses the medium of the story to engage the issues and ideas of business. Unlike other such experiments, such as *The Goal*, this book is profoundly intellectual in the very best sense of the term. And it needs to be, for it is tackling a deep idea, the notion that our computer systems replicate our social relationships and that managing either can be improved by learning from the other.

The notion that computer and social systems are ecologically intertwined is at first startling, but within seconds it becomes commonplace. Of course they are intertwined—how could they not be? But then why have we not made more of this in the past? Well, that is what bright ideas are all about: they show us things we are pretty sure we already knew but have never brought properly into focus.

The stories Stuart tells are compelling in their own right. He is a good writer, and it shows. The book is a good read even if you don't care a fig for business or technology. But if you do, it is an even better read, provided you are willing to play your part. This book is not a how-to book. There are no 22 immutable laws of anything here nor any one-minute solutions to your daily problems, though there are lessons to be learned, and techniques that can be applied. This is a book that requires and inspires reflection.

Reflection is largely missing in action in today's business climate. At a time when the fundamentals of technology architecture and business process management are being revolutionized by the Internet and global commerce, we are far too focused on short-term transactional issues. At the opening of the 21st century, the economic torch is passing across the Pacific just as it passed over the Atlantic in the 20th century and the English Channel in the 19th. To reframe our business practices for success in this new environment, we need to reimagine ourselves and our roles. Stuart's book provides a great platform for beginning or extending that exercise.

I cannot say what *you* will get out of this book. No one can. That is the magic of literary form. We each bring our own experience base to the stories we read, we each co-create the story with the author in our unique way. What I am confident of, however, is that you will get out every bit as much as you put into it. Stuart is raising thoughtful issues in a provocative fashion. It is up to you to take the next step.

Finally, I cannot resist the observation that if ever a book called for blogging, it is this one. Books that initiate lines of thinking complete themselves in the dialogs they engender. As Web 2.0 emerges from Web 1.0, readers have the opportunity—maybe even the obligation—to become writers, to take the story to the next level, to participate in the wisdom of crowds, which exceeds the wisdom of any single individual. I hope you have the kind of experience with this book that warrants blogging. If you do, I hope you will hop on the Web to get your voice into the act.

Geoffrey Moore
June 2006

FOREWORD

Having spent the last 20 years teaching information management to C-level executives at the University of California-Los Angeles (UCLA), I am fortunate to consider as friends and colleagues some of the most prominent thinkers in Hollywood. This and the fact that I was fortunate enough to spend some of my formative educational years at Carnegie-Mellon University—whose curriculum encourages the productive collision of computer science and the dramatic arts—have long led me to believe that there is big money in owning the film rights to the unabridged *story* about what really happens in IT.

Stuart Robbins, my friend of many years, may not own the film rights to that story, but he has certainly written the screenplay about IT, each chapter adding to the movie's momentum.

Too many in our society view information management and information technology as the sterile domain of pulse-challenged, math-obsessed weenies and geeks. Nothing could be further from the truth. At the beating heart of our contemporary civilization one finds the throb, whir, burp, hum, scratch, sniff, and hiccup of carbon-based life forms interacting with silicon-enclosed intelligence.

Stuart has written a 21st century book for the world we will soon inhabit.

Technology matters, and it matters deeply. Stuart believes, as do a growing number of industry leaders and policy makers, that the world of the future needs a more tech-savvy citizenry. This book is a vital tool and step along that path.

Too many among us believe that technology and technology decision making is "someone else's job." Who can forget the CEO involved in a white collar fraud case who responded to the question, "You had a computer on your desk didn't you?" with "Yes, but it was just for show." Prison isn't bad enough for this kind of mindset. We should extract his critical organs and donate them to more deserving people higher on the evolutionary food chain. Fortunately, this kind of thinking will soon migrate from being passively stupid to being prosecutably malfeasant.

In conjunction with four business schools (UCLA, UC-Berkeley, Arizona State University, and The Ohio State University), two think tanks (the IT Leadership Academy at Florida Community College in Jacksonville and the Brookings Institution's Metropolitan Policy Program), and two major trade publications (*CIO Decisions* and *Computerworld*), I spent time with approximately 1,500 leading denizens of the CIO Habitat in an effort to distill the essence of leadership success.

Stuart's book brilliantly and, more importantly, accessibly addresses each of these critical areas.

Although Stuart is not a professionally trained anthropologist or sociologist, he provides insights from these disciplines that place him at the *front* of the field of practitioners. Social scientists have long recognized that those who build cannot be separated from that which they build or the world in which they work. Stuart takes this just-below-the-level of consciousness insight, and makes it come alive.

Information systems mirror the people that build them and the organizations that cause them to be built.

I recall research I conducted while working at the University of Amsterdam's Controller's Institute. I was charged with creating an insight-producing shared space for wicked-cheap (i.e., value-focused) Dutch CFOs and monstrously misunderstood CIOs. In one telling exchange, an exasperated CIO, lamenting his fiscal emasculation, exclaimed, "you get the systems you deserve." In that statement one finds the truth and challenge facing us. Here we find the cause and effect of misunderstandings between corporate tribes, in this case the financial headset of the CFO and the "technology isn't free" mindset of the CIO. The way we move forward is via stories.

That is what this book is all about.

Stuart encourages us not to adopt a master narrative from one or the other discipline but rather create an environment in which all points of view are heard and blended.

Thornton May
June 2006

ACKNOWLEDGMENTS

Geoffrey Moore, who is a role model for everyone who wants to be Core, for his encouragement, in so many ways.

Thornton May for the humor and humanity he brings to our industry, for his relentless pursuit of Thinking Differently, and for his many-faceted support.

Sandra Braman for her friendship, and her mentoring on second-generation cybernetics and the systems theory underlying everything.

Mohamed Muhsin, whose organization at the World Bank is an example of how IT should be done (with grace and compassion), for his constant support and friendship.

Sean Moriarty, whose technical understanding of our industry is exceptional, who read the first draft of the chapter called "Virtualization," and who said, "I love it."

Carol Brown, the first to define CIO history (quoted in so many of my white papers), who later became a friend and cherished colleague.

Maggie Law, for many years of unconditional assistance in everything I have pursued, and for her truly exceptional intelligence, a symbiosis of far more benefit to me than I have been able to return.

Mark Forman, who posed a simple question over lunch one day about autonomic computing that, in some very specific ways, led to this book.

Steve Yatko, the first person to call my work "visionary" and the leader of an expert IT team that has, among its many accomplishments, confirmed much of what I have proposed in this book.

Tom Lux, who once told me in 1973, on learning I had published a poem in an Oberlin journal, that I should stick to playing second base.

Bob Linn, for the essential truth of Linwood Eddy's unbelievable story.

Jim Levine, for the insight to see something in the first drafts that was worth his valuable consideration and advice, and for his artful representation as the book turned to reality.

Sheck Cho, from John Wiley & Sons, whose advocacy and guidance has been calm, patient, and specific.

Finally, and most importantly, **Diana and Max,** for their love and their tolerance when I excused myself from the dinner table, so many evenings, and announced that I was going back to my office to work on the book, again and again and again, instead of telling stories to him at bedtime, or falling asleep beside her.

I could not have written this book without their help.

CHAPTER I

THE PRIME THEOREM

These stories are distributed objects on a local network, the perimeter of which is bound by the covers of this book.

Each story/object represents a fundamental concept underlying Grid Management Theory, formulated over two decades of my profession in information technology (IT) and based on a core set of central principles. Rather than presenting each concept in the traditional mode of other management books, or in the accepted academic format of research papers with statistics and an annotated bibliography, I have chosen a narrative format for two important reasons:

1. The central premise of Grid Management Theory is that the people who design, build, and manage our technology ecosystems are an essential component of these systems. Subsequently, concentration on their life stories can provide a more inclusive portrayal of these central principles.

   In this case, fiction offers a more honest picture.

2 The greatest handicap observed in any technical organization, large or small, corporate or private, is the nearly universal inability of technologists to explain themselves adequately—to their executives, their customers, and their spouses.

   These stories provide a bridge.

Each concept is embedded in a story with believable characters struggling with real IT issues, an accessible format that will hopefully engender more fruitful discussions within and beyond our organizations than those normally provoked by academic treatises or business guru-speak. One

1

thoughtful extension of this strategy might be an IT Director sharing a copy of Chapter 3 on Virtualization with her sales/marketing counterparts, to help them understand the impact of this issue on the Director's organization, their morale, and their place in history.

The Internet, viewed from this perspective, is a latticed system of relationships—among libraries, information objects, servers, and, as you will see in the course of these stories, the users of this system. The best example is the lesson I learned more than a decade ago: hypertext is nonhierarchical, and therefore, to be successfully implemented, it requires nonhierarchical (matrix-managed) teams. To manage Internet-based projects properly (software development, eCommerce, publication), one must manage the series of relationships among the people who build and support those projects.

The central proposition of this book is a theme I've observed at every level of the corporation and at every level of our IT architecture: *information systems mirror the people who build them.* Each story in this collection is based on this central theorem and a set of corollaries, derived from the broader discipline of systems theory as it applies to information systems.

The Prime Theorem is this:

We mirror ourselves in the systems that we build. Therefore:

Corollary 1. The systems will not "talk to each other" if the people are not "talking to each other."

Corollary 2. The relationships between systems reflect the relationships between the people who build and support them.

Corollary 3. To correct problems in our information systems, we must first address the problems among the people that build them.

Corollary 4. We must transform ourselves to the same degree that we want to transform our systems.

To introduce this collection of short stories,[1] it is important to emphasize that I have observed examples of this theorem *everywhere.* When I was an IT manager, every company and every project reflected this theme.

During my career as a management consultant, I am frequently asked to perform quiet, background audits of distressed projects for the executive team. The expectation, among most of my clients, is that a *technical issue* is the root of the problem. Invariably, I have discovered that the central issue is nested among the *people*, not the technology.

Most recently, I was asked to review the Services-Oriented Architecture project successfully implemented by a major worldwide firm. They had written a brilliant exposition of the integrated framework of data, applications, and infrastructure transformed to maintain competitive advantage. Their understanding of this transformative architecture and their execution of its initial stages was impressive, a model for others to follow. However, when I reviewed their documentation, there was not a single reference to the *organizational* aspects of the project. I asked whether they had considered the possibility that the IT organization would be transformed to the same degree that they had transformed their environment. One of the directors turned to me and said, "If someone had posed that question two years ago, it would have saved us many months of organizational confusion."[2]

Like an optical illusion in a child's gaze, patterns are subtle and easily overlooked until a parent suggests that the child look for the long tail of a squirrel. The child calls out with delight, "I see it!" and after that moment of recognition, she can never again look at the diagram without first seeing the once-hidden shapes, now in the foreground of her attention, as if the original image of intersections and arcs has become transparent.

Our mirrored image is similarly hidden in the complex constructions of technology we have created during the past two decades. Unlike the optical illusion, there has been less intentional obfuscation, yet the technology is nonetheless a diagram of intersections, arcs, wires, boxes, and closets filled with more intersections, boxes, and wires. We see only what we have been taught to see, disregarding our own reflection until the author suggests that we look for the human element.

Almost immediately, like children at that moment of clarity, changing forever our view of the design, someone says "I see it!" and their comprehension of technology is altered. The original impression, the purely physical realm of circuit boards, coaxial cables, wireless relay junctions, and dumb terminals becomes transparent.

It has been ten years since I first postulated a relationship between information systems and the "people systems" that build and maintain them, in an editorial and subsequent conference paper for the Association of Computing Machinery.[3] Back in 1995, it was only a *theory*, founded on my understanding of the writings of Gregory Bateson and, later, the mentorship of Professor Sandra Braman. In the past ten years, in every company and in every role, I have witnessed its proof. I no longer consider it merely an interesting theory to be talked about briefly in hallways. It is a fundamental concept that underlies everything we do (and cannot do) in IT.

As we move toward Grid Computing and the many related technologies composing the "new IT," this principle becomes more than theoretically intriguing. It must be an integral part of your strategic roadmap. *For success on the Grid, we must transform ourselves and our organizations to the same degree that we seek to transform our architectures.*

As corporations begin to connect their systems, and as their company's networks are connected to other networks, adding to an immense and complex architecture that becomes difficult for executives to understand and impossible for their staff to explain to them in a language the executives can comprehend, an entirely new and daunting challenge presents itself. By analogy, water does not flow easily between the new pipes and the old pipes. In this case, the water is information, and as our companies increasingly become dependent on a transfer of information among customers, partners, vendors, and consultants, the myriad layers of software, servers, routers, repositories, databases, access points, devices, and the ever-increasing volume of information itself, is now a barrier.

In many cases, you simply can't get there from here.

The IT industry finds itself at yet another evolutionary cycle, with new technologies emerging with features and functions that were impossible only five years before. Such trends—web services, open source, blade technology, commodity search, distributed computing, and the Grid—offer substantial benefits. However, we find it difficult to describe those benefits to our executives, who are inclined to say, "Just make it happen," without an appreciation of cost, complication, or risk.

We need a new way of communicating with our executive teams and with the many other significant people who can influence our lives as IT practitioners. I have elected to tell stories,[4] stories that reflect the essential principles we must incorporate into our world of IT in the coming decade. I wanted to utilize a preexisting Application Programming Interface (API): the narrative format, which has already been used successfully to convey important business issues by many others, from Eliyahu Goldratt's *The Goal* to Stephen Denning's efforts at The World Bank and Debra Stouffer's strategic use of storytelling at DigitalNet.

We need a new politics in our industry, with a new vocabulary, one that provides a bridge between companies, between individuals, and between executives and their technologists.

Of course, I recognize the double-edged challenge inherent in this task: I might oversimplify complex themes and alienate the technology professionals to whom the book is dedicated, or I might make the tinsel of computers too significant and thus bore those who delight in narrative, and well-crafted sentences.

Between these two polar challenges (the Scylla and Charybdis of this book) I envision a middle ground, the place where technology is embedded in our existence, where everything is connected to everything[5] and the place where work involving binary logic is like any other work that we do each day.

We are what we build: it is a unified theory that acts prismatically, in which the elegance of heightened prose and the artfulness of "if-then" statements cast similar colors through our stained glass windows as we come home each day.

Short stories *are* distributed objects, and they are situated in this book like services on a local area network, bound by the perimeter of its covers.

The central theories underlying well-constructed narratives mirror the practices we must put into place to implement Grid Computing successfully and to benefit from it. That mirror also offers us an opportunity to learn something about ourselves.

We can no longer focus solely on the relationships between elements in a database or servers in a data center; rather, we must also consider and manage the relationships between the people that build and support them. We, who live in the IT world, are also nodes on the network, each adding value as every phone added value to the growth of the telecommunications industry, as every web site added value to the growth of the Internet, and we will harvest the true value of this networked world only when we begin to manage the people and the technology in a systemic (unified) way.

This book presents several ways to do just that.

NOTES

1. My career spans many years of publication, both nonfiction and fiction, and includes a Master of Fine Arts in Creative Writing from Warren Wilson College in addition to more than 20 years in Information Technology.
2. My work led to a white paper entitled "Grid Management Theory," which includes a case study of this institution's significant achievements. The paper was sponsored by Cassatt Corporation, www.cassatt.com. It is accessible at www.srobbinsconsulting.com/docs/.
3. Stuart Robbins, "Turbulence and Information Systems: The System is a Mirror, (Volume 38, Issue 5; May 1995 " *Communications of the ACM* May 1995). Note: my original essay was printed beside John Perry Barlow's infamous column about the Network and Teilhard de Chardin's notions of an integrated human consciousness. Barlow's essay comes into play in Chapters 6 and 9.
4. John Allen Paulos, *Once upon a Number: The Hidden Mathematical Logic of Stories* (New York: Basic Books, 1998).
5. Kevin Kelly, *Out of Control: The New Biology of Machines, Social Science, and the Economic World* (New York: Basic Books, 2004).

CHAPTER 2

INTERFACES

E very night after leaving his office, Linwood Eddy spent an hour at a federally funded nursing home nicknamed New Dachau by those who reluctantly lived there. Most of the time, he played a simple game of checkers with his father-in-law, or, if the old man was feeling particularly alert, gin rummy for points.

Linwood liked his evening ritual at the home—not for the awkward candor across the checkerboard, or for that inevitable moment when the old man pretended to forget the rules of engagement, but for the cross-town commute between his company's main facility and the home. It was an easy drive, repeated so often that, over the past 18 months since they first convinced the old man to leave his cottage, Linwood drove it in a trance. It was the only time of day when his mind was free to wander, to think randomly.

When the old man could not sleep, when his medication levels ebbed and surged, or when he refused to take the pills, he wandered the hallways of New Dachau, toward an ageless and more lucid path to lullaby, greeting other insomniacs or offering help to the janitorial crew. This was his standard condition when Linwood visited in the evenings, whereas, on the weekends, Linwood came to New Dachau in the morning, when the old man was in his daytime state of feistiness—a very different kind of visit.

Even after Linwood and his wife separated, he continued to visit his father-in-law, partly to bridge the chasm in his family and partly through what seemed a moral imperative—as if the old man's descent into solitude needn't be quickened because his daughter wanted a divorce. The quiet nobility of Linwood's dedication to his father-in-law was not recognized by anyone of significance in Linwood's life, certainly not by the old man himself.

"I don't *know* him!" the old man barked when the floor attendant sang out, "Look who's here." Linwood nodded his thanks, and she left the two men to their checkers.

"I said I don't know him!" he yelled as she closed the door. "Don't you people care? He could be here to *rob* me!" The old man slumped between two pillows on his angled bed. "I told you they treat me bad. Did you see that? Did you see how she just ignored me?"

"Red or black, Pop?"

"I'm not your Pop."

Linwood opened the bedstand drawer. The red box of checkers was worn to a smooth cardboard gray at each corner from years of handling, and it slid open easily, as if it were eager to display the pieces inside.

"So, don't call me Pop," the old man said.

Linwood nodded his agreement, arranged the checkers, and then swung the moving tabletop in front of the old man so he could reach the first row without lifting himself from the mattress.

"We can't play. There's a piece missing, look," the old man said, his pencil-thin finger pointing to an obviously empty space on the board. "Can't play with a missing piece, can we?"

Linwood reached into his pants pocket, as he always did on the evening visits, and produced the 1970 Kennedy half-dollar that served as their missing piece. The old man made his usual remarks about Joseph Kennedy's ruthlessness and John Kennedy's lack of discipline, followed by what a shame it was that the U.S. Treasury couldn't make a real coin anymore and had to resort to cheap, copper sandwich coins. Finally, the old man plopped it hard onto the surface of the foldout board and smoothed out the yellowing tape that kept the two pieces of the board connected.

On that particular evening, Linwood's father-in-law was alert enough to win the first game legitimately. The old man tired by the middle of the second game, and they decided to call it a draw. Linwood realigned the checkers in the worn old box, pocketed the Kennedy half, and agreed to stay for five more minutes so the old man could tell him the familiar story about how long he had owned that same checker set.

"Bought it when your little girl was born, you know," he explained, as if it were the first time. "God, we sat for a long time in that waiting room, didn't we? It seemed like days. She really didn't want to come out, did she?"

Linwood didn't say anything.

"Her momma was a trooper, though, wasn't she?"

Linwood nodded.

The old man looked up, squinting through the neon lights, into Linwood's eyes. "So, why don't they come to visit me? If everything was really okay, she'd come to see her grandpa in this goddamned place, and so would her momma."

"Let's not get into that tonight," Linwood said with a sigh. Adrienne called it the Sigh of Sighs. Neither one of them wanted to be the bearer of bad news, and the old man didn't know about the separation. Linwood wondered how long they would be able to maintain the façade.

"I just asked a question, that's all. Seems the women would come with you, if they cared." The old man pulled the linen up to his chin.

"Long story," Linwood said. "You need to get some rest."

"Okay," he said when Linwood leaned over to kiss his forehead. "Go ahead and call me Pop. Since you married her, I guess it's okay."

"Thanks . . . Pop."

The old man gripped Linwood's sleeve, childlike and desperate, and began the litany of last-minute topics intended to keep Linwood in the room. He grumbled about New Dachau, about the rumors that he was going to get a new roommate in the semi-private room.

"It's going to be the fool next door," the old man said in a whisper, "I just know it. Damn fellow can't remember a thing. Doesn't even know who he is, half the time, I'll have to introduce myself every time he looks over at me. He'll drive me nuts, I tell you."

Linwood told him everything would be fine. They should take things one day at a time, cross bridges when they came to them, hope for the best. Such analgesics were useless at the office, where Linwood's teams were too sophisticated to be so easily distracted, but his father-in-law liked the clichés of their goodbye dialogues as much as he liked talking about the Pittsburgh Pirates, back in the days when Clemente and Mazeroski were young, in the days when baseball wasn't a rich man's game.

"I'll see you tomorrow, all right, Pop?" Linwood said as he two-stepped past the tiny inlet that served as a bathroom and supply closet, filled with the last remaining possessions of old age.

"Once a week would be *fine*!" the old man yelled for the nurses' benefit as Linwood opened the door and headed into the mustard-and-beige hallway. "Don't make any efforts on *my* account!"

Linwood stopped at the front desk to thank the attendant for his late-night attentions. The young man was preoccupied with an uncooperative computer. Linwood watched as the man turned it off and on, then off and on again, and continued to reboot the machine, even as he spoke to Linwood about the old man's feistiness. The evening staff of the home was mostly university graduate students; they rotated through the grave-yard assignments in two- or three-month intervals, hoping to complete a thesis during the night shift and then quitting when they discovered that many of the residents did not sleep. That night, the attendant thanked Linwood for the five-dollar tip and promised to look in on the old man in 17A regularly. Linwood left, saying "Goodnight" and "Thanks again."

Back in his commuter trance, he drove past a construction site that had sprung up by the road during the past few days. Incandescent yellow spotlights highlighted two immense tower cranes, their necks criss-crossed to form a giant X in the eerie light.

Linwood slowed to look at the solitary cranes in the haphazard construction site and thought about the relationship between people and their machines. The site looked like a neighbor's backyard scattered with toddler's trucks. Our mechanical world might be radically transformed every ten years or so, Linwood thought to himself, yet our machinery continues to reflect who we really are: our discarded cars, our uncooperative computers, our lonely construction cranes, and though we may organize them into new patterns, Linwood thought, we rarely remember that they are mirrors of who we have become.

Linwood Eddy had liked the Army—its routines, its procedures, a new relationship with computers. After two years he returned to the States from Germany for a job as the only punch card processor in a small but very industrious company called Sounds, Incorporated. The company's business was built on residual income from the distribution rights to most of the noisemakers in the world.

Sounds, Incorporated didn't make the actual devices, except on the rare occasions when they were forced to acquire the manufacturing facilities in order to obtain the patents. Usually, dozens upon dozens of tiny companies throughout the United States and Asia manufactured the products. Sounds, Incorporated simply negotiated for, purchased, retained, and resold the patents for the devices, as well as the rights to re-use the sounds. In some cases, they retained the rights to the sounds. It was primarily a legal and marketing proprietorship, a kind of holding company for countless contracts and copyrights on behalf of hundreds of investors who, over the years, were willing to sell future uses of their tiny sound machines for some present-day cash. Each time the sound was used in a device, Sounds, Incorporated made a few pennies. Those pennies were tracked on punch cards, and the cards and the pennies added up.

Beginning in 1985, the company began to convert all the buzzers and doorbells and chimes into memory, tiny electronic cells that over the course of the next two decades would become embedded in birthday cards and novelty socks and bedside radios of every shape and size. The electronic cells were easy to reproduce and cheap to manufacture, and each one paid handsomely because each one required a license to use the sound, and each license brought royalties.

In the old days of the company, when Linwood knew each person by name and they all had lunch together on Fridays, Linwood's best friends were the room-sized computers with the reels and sorters. He still had a particular knack, learned in Germany when he was working in Field Operations, for looking at any punch card and recognizing the pattern of the holes.

"This one is out of order," he'd call out from the computer room, holding one aloft to the amazement of everyone else on the floor.

The first time he performed the feat was for the manager of the company's computer room, a university-trained scientist who saw conspiracies everywhere, and believed that Linwood had been sent by Washington as a corporate spy. *It must be some kind of trick, computer sleight of hand,* the man would say whenever Linwood demonstrated his ability to locate a punch card that was out of sequence.

Everyone else in the small company grew to trust Linwood's special relationship with the large machines.

They knew he had a particular understanding of the machines' binary language, and he was eventually promoted to lead the training team when IBM personal computers began to appear on employee desktops. As those same personal computers began to appear in their homes, as the card-processing behemoths became smaller and faster, Sounds Incorporated promoted Linwood, first to manager of the entire computer room when the university-trained scientist became too paranoid and was fired, and later as director of the Computer Services division, when the company had grown large enough to employ a team of technicians to manage the systems that managed their data—data about customers, data about contracts, data about the sounds themselves.

After all, Linwood understood what others thought was either sacred or slightly arcane, like tea leaves or tarot cards. He also understood people.

Linwood was their connection with a computer system that was otherwise foreign. They didn't need to know any more because Linwood was always there to translate the problem in ways they could understand.

"Just put your hand on the keyboard," Linwood said whenever one of the secretaries was afraid to use the new computer that had appeared on her desk.

"I can't," she whispered, "what if I accidentally erase something?"

Linwood took her hand and pressed it against the keyboard, and dozens of random letters appeared on the monitor, yet nothing happened. He pressed her hand against the keys again, smiled, and explained to her that a computer cannot do anything unless you tell it. He explained that most errors were retrievable and that she would have to be an expert—and intentionally try to erase data—to do any harm.

The first secretary to become proficient, because of Linwood's calm and helpful assistance, was Cicely Thompson.

Sounds, Incorporated eventually merged with an audio software group that helped to automate much of the manufacturing process. The company changed its name to Digital Sounds, Inc. and grew from the original 27 employees to more than 700 employees in six buildings in the United States and one facility in Taiwan.

During the company's expansion, as the Computer Services division grew, Linwood no longer had the time to talk to the computers in the basement of their new headquarters and talk to the employees about them, because there was simply too much work for one man, even one good man. So the budget was adjusted, and he was given a team of engineers to work on the machines.

Linwood Eddy did not like the task of managing people as much as he liked managing machines—people were less predictable and less reliable, and much more time and effort was needed to keep them synchronized.

However, he had just married Adrienne and his new promotion to management seemed to offer much-needed security as they began to plan a family. Later, the higher salaries allowed them to save enough money to pay for Rachel's first year at Stanford, so he always tried to keep the benefits of his management position in mind.

At the end of his first week as the new manager of the Computer Systems team, Linwood realized he needed to teach his new team how to connect with other staff, so he could attend to the managerial duties that were quickly building up. The new, very technical employees understood the technology (Windows, Unix, and something that had just begun to capture the industry's attention, Linux) better than he did, yet they did not understand how to communicate with important people in the company, like Cicely Thompson. Cicely had told him that his team was annoying the very people they were meant to support.

So Linwood did what no other manager in the company had ever done before: he organized a field trip.

First he treated the team to a hearty dinner at a local Red Lobster restaurant, to cement their relationship, and then he brought them to the university campus for a lecture from a visiting professor who had recently published a book on the Computer Human Interface (the CHI).

He was expecting a presentation from the researchers at the Princeton Engineering Anomalies Research (PEAR) program, which measures the effect of human consciousness on machines using random event generators. As the team settled into their seats at the back of the auditorium, a very different lecture began, one about corporate communications. Linwood smiled at the irony. It was a lesson they sorely needed, and it would become their theme as the company around them became more sophisticated. The lecture began like this:

"Throughout my consulting career at the executive level, I have used a simple metaphor in the course of my work with two groups of people who are not communicating.

"To begin, I draw three rectangles on their whiteboard, because there is always a whiteboard. I need only add a handful of terms to make the image recognizable to any engineering audience. It is the role of the Application Programming Interface (API).

"If you were to ask an engineer for a definition of an API, it would sound much like this:

> API is the virtual interface between two interworking software functions, such as a word processor and a spreadsheet. This technology has been expanded from simple subroutine calls to include features that provide for *interoperability* and system *modifiability* in support of the requirement for data sharing between multiple applications.

"However, in most of my engagements, I have found it useful to describe an API differently, for reasons that will become apparent to you.

"First I draw a picture of the standard application stack, that is, the three basic architectural layers of software. Remember that this is a conceptual diagram only. The uppermost layer is what we call the Presentation Layer, the user interface, where commands and instructions are given, where functions need to be well understood, and where everything has to fit together. The user interface is *what we all see*." (See Exhibit 2.1).

"The second layer is the Middleware, situated between the user interface and the databases below. It is responsible for integration, coordination, and rationalization. As the instruction set becomes increasingly complex, the need for this layer of software increases. Middleware performs a very specific translation so that the tables and fields in the database layer can

EXHIBIT 2.1   *Communication Protocols: Example 1*

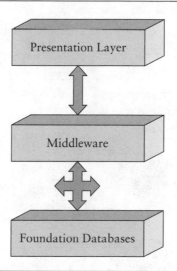

understand the instruction and respond with the correct piece of data or the correct relationship between sets of data elements.

"I can see that most of you in the audience understand this concept, so I will move on. Note the arrows in Exhibit 2.1. These are standard communication protocols; without them, every engineer knows what can happen to even the most artfully written software programs.

"Naturally, there is an interface between many or all of these major software layers."

Linwood watched as the team slowly responded to the man's lecture. One by one, from the expressions on their faces, he could see the metaphor register and take hold of their imaginations. The lecturer continued:

"For those of you who are technologists, I will admit a certain simplification of your domain, for the purposes of drawing an analogy. However, I am sure you have each seen a complex software architecture simplified in such a way.

"Now, let us, for the moment, draw three more boxes, and consider, conceptually, a company as a similar system, with similar layers: Executives, Middle Management, and Individual Contributors." (See Exhibit 2.2).

EXHIBIT 2.2   *Communication Protocols: Example 2*

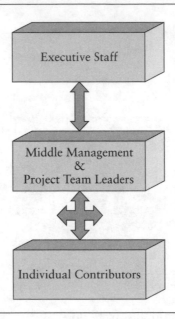

"I can already see, by your facial expressions, that this idea, barely conveyed, has triggered several of you to jot this down in your notes or whisper to the others around you. Before I even had the opportunity to explain the connection, the metaphor accomplished its task. I probably don't need to explain further, although I will.

"As you have already discovered, our 'conceptual company' functions in much the same manner—without protocols to communicate data clearly between levels.

"We are left to our own poor efforts, our hallway and even bathroom conversations as well as our, voicemail, each a 'custom call' that is hardly dependable. Without APIs in the software, data is lost, and actions lose any coordination. Without APIs in our organizations, knowledge is lost.

"In the many companies I have visited over the course of years, I have rarely observed an effort to attend to 'people APIs' like software APIs are attended to. In fact, miscommunications, scheduling problems, synchronization issues, and even difficulties with passing on the simplest instructions often go unnoticed until severe problems occur;

even then, few recognize that this simple, missing interface has caused the furor.

"We learned it as engineers and we forgot it as individuals in our organizations, as if we are unable to transfer lessons from one area of our lives to another, as if our memories are altered when we walk in the door at work, and they do not return until we come home each evening. Sometimes when we leave work each night we forget everything we have learned there and do not remember any of it until we return the next morning.

"We have lost our ability for *metaphor*.

"What is metaphor other than the moment of wisdom elicited from a comparison of unlike objects?

"Without metaphors, our literature would be flat and unevocative. I would even suggest that literature would long ago have ceased to be a discipline of interest.

"So, too, our engineering discipline will cease to be of interest if we do not refocus our attention on the necessity for well-articulated interfaces. (This will take an effort of will because we will face the resistance of an entire system.) With an excellent library of interfaces, even the most complex layers of software can communicate. Without interfaces, even the simplest and most benign shell scripts would lose their capacity to make things happen.

"This lecture is an interface—between disciplines, between distinct areas of our experience that have much to offer each other if we relearn the capability of passing information by means of standard protocols. What we know in one area can help explain away the darkness of the other. However, most of the practitioners (in both the humanities and the sciences, I'm sorry to say) have not only forgotten the benefit of such APIs or metaphors, they have been taught to avoid them.

"What a fine mess we find ourselves in, ladies and gentlemen."

Linwood's team returned to work the following morning with an enthusiasm that no previous manager had been able to trigger. It was as if the metaphor of "people APIs" had given them a vocabulary to communicate with their business partners within the company, and, beyond that, some specific information about how their company behaves and why. Linwood's plan for the coming week was to help them understand the next interface lesson: what the company needed, instead of temporary links between permanent teams, was permanent links between temporary teams.

For now, it was enough that they understood themselves in the context of the larger entity. They knew information systems. Now they understood that the company itself was a system, not unlike the systems they knew. Each of Linwood's new employees seemed suddenly transformed by this understanding. Their company's darkest corners had been illuminated, and they maneuvered in these corners with sudden confidence.

They were connected.

Whenever he could not sleep, Linwood kept himself in bed until 3 a.m. If, by 3 a.m. he had not fallen asleep or grown tired enough to believe he'd be dozing soon, Linwood chose one of two alternatives: either drink himself to sleep or do some work, starting the next day a few hours early.

There was always something to drink, and always some work he could do, so the choice was not always easy. That night, however, his insomniac's dilemma was simplified—he had to prepare for an early morning meeting.

Earlier that night, Adrienne had fallen asleep beneath the quilt they had purchased for $6 in Mexico on their honeymoon and then spent $40 shipping north. He carefully pulled away from the covers and stepped slowly to the bedroom door, a practiced kind of stealth. Sometimes he would make it all of the way out of the bedroom without disturbing her, but more often she'd lift herself up to ask if everything was okay and he would say "Yes, go back to sleep," and she would. Adrienne never remembered their 3 a.m. conversations, but Linwood liked her sleepy concern and his quiet knack for sending her back to her dreams.

In his flannel robe and thick hiking socks with extra padding in the soles, Linwood turned the corner of the hallway and headed toward his tiny office without noticing the two-tone Mustang through the huge plate glass windows that looked out over the lawn. Nor had he heard the noise of the Mustang arriving in the driveway, several minutes before, because he had been thinking about the meeting, about his presentation, about what he should say and not say. He was thinking about the ten supervisors that had come and gone since he began at the company 19 years before.

Linwood didn't realize his daughter was home until he found her rummaging through The Room of All Things.

"Hello, College Student," Linwood said in an upbeat whisper. "I didn't know you were coming over tonight."

Silence. Rachel's ability to ignore her father was prodigious.

During elementary school, her contempt became so problematic that Linwood was forced to preface anything he said to his daughter with the phrase, "Your mother told me to tell you . . ." if he wanted to get her attention. Adrienne had suggested family therapy before high school and again before college classes started. She wanted her daughter to begin the next part of life on the right foot, but Rachel had refused to attend. She thought her father was an imbecile. She pronounced the word with a French accent, am-beh-seel. This single word was capable of ending any family gathering or conversation. Linwood had long since learned to accept her rejections as an amputee accepts the loss of a limb.

Linwood turned toward the kitchen. He poured himself a glass of milk, measured three tablespoons of coffee and three cups of water, and flipped on the electric coffeemaker they had originally bought for Rachel to take to college. On the day before classes, she had informed her parents that caffeine was one of the tools used by the capitalist classes to keep the Third World in third place and refused to take it with her.

While the coffee hissed, Linwood turned on the tiny kitchen TV and watched CNN with the sound turned off. He ignored the captions, concentrating instead on the Up/Down symbols in green or red that displayed how the Tokyo markets were performing. The overnight markets were usually a good indicator of executive morale on the following day. When business had been good overseas on the night before, meetings invariably went smoothly, even those with the controversial agendas.

Rachel appeared in the kitchen door. No *Hello* or *How Are You*.

"Do you have any idea where mother keeps my old school things?" She was wearing army fatigues. Beside her, like a suitcase on the floor, was her first computer, now an antique that belonged in the Tech Museum in San Jose.

Linwood said no.

Rachel muttered something under her breath and abruptly disappeared. He knew she would leave without saying goodbye. She never said goodbye, and these unspoken departures always left a kind of sadness in their wake. That night, the feeling was a mixture of grief and relief because, at least for one evening, they had avoided the argument, avoided the word "imbecile."

The front door closed, and the Mustang grumbled out of the driveway a few minutes later. Headlights splayed brightly across the walls of the kitchen as she turned up the street.

CHAPTER 3

RELATIONSHIP MANAGEMENT

Perhaps it was the funeral. Or perhaps it was the second latte she drank before her flight from Florida.

Whatever the cause, Deanna found herself in a candid conversation with the passenger in the window seat. She rarely spoke with anyone on her frequent business trips, opting instead for the solitude of e-mail (she was always a day behind in her responses) or reading one of the many technical journals (such as the one in her hands that morning). For some reason, on this particular airplane on this particular day, she was startled by her own willingness to chat with a complete stranger.

". . . And what do you do professionally?" the fellow asked as the flight attendant reminded everyone to keep cell phones off for the remainder of the journey. They both reached into their briefcases, to double-check their phones.

"I'm an IT Director, information technology, of USA Financial," she said. "I manage teams of programmers for the firm. Lots of travel. And you?"

The fellow in the brown jacket, eyeglasses perched atop his thinning gray hair, seemed remarkably easy to talk to. His response explained it to her, or so she thought at the time.

"Psychologist," he said with a smile, "though now I seem to spend a lot of my time on airplanes between lectures." He turned on the overhead air and asked if she was traveling on business.

Fork in the road. Deanna could easily answer *yes*, and keep the conversation on an impersonal level. She considered doing so—after all, her flying time was usually business related. She hopscotched from the bank's data centers in Austin and Chicago, to their New York headquarters, where most of the back-office operations were located, or to Bangalore, where much of their new technical support was located. For some unexplained reason, she chose the more honest reply.

"We buried my mother yesterday in Boca Raton," she said quietly.

"I'm *sorry*," he interrupted, as everyone seemed conditioned to reply when they hear about the death of one's parent. It was a reflex statement, like *That's wonderful* when hearing of a baby's birth, or *Bless you* when you sneeze.

There was an awkward silence. Both were faced with the choice of opening their laptops, now that they had reached the proper altitude. He didn't want to pry, she thought, and he would certainly be aware of the emotions in play on the day after her mother's burial. Then, breaking the momentary ice around them, he blurted out his recognition of the irony.

"On Mother's Day!" he quietly exclaimed. "My God, you buried her on Mother's Day."

She forced a smile and briefly looked down at her copy of *Communications of the ACM*, an issue celebrating the work of Peter Chen. Her Database Manager had circled a section from one of Chen's earliest essays for her attention.

Information Concerning Entities and Relationships (Level 1)

> At this level we consider entities and relationships. An entity is a "thing" which can be distinctly identified. A specific person, company, or event is an example of an entity. A relationship is an association among entities. For instance, "father-son" is a relationship between two person 'entities.' It is possible that some people may view something (e.g., marriage) as an entity while other people may view it as a relationship. We think that this is a decision which has to be made by the enterprise administrator. He should define what are entities and what are relationships so that the distinction is suitable for his environment.[1]

Deanna reread the paragraph about entities and relationships, but the man spoke again before she could determine what aspect of the article seemed so important to her staff.

"Did she understand your work?"

Deanna was relieved by the question and realized that, indeed, she wanted to talk, not necessarily about how it feels to lose a parent, but simply talk. "My mom? No, no, she didn't understand why it was so complicated, managing technologists and computers."

The man turned sideways in his seat. He didn't say anything; he just turned ever so slightly. It was a subtle invitation to say more, if she wanted to. This guy is good, she thought to herself.

"Let me give you an example," she began. "I work with very talented staff, from many cultures and geographies. The diversity of the staff is fascinating. Anyway, last December, when I was visiting my folks . . . I think it was on my trip back from the Caymans where we were considering new facilities . . . My mom asked me what my biggest problem was at work. I'm sure she was just making conversation; she was good at that. Like you are, I suppose. I think she expected me to talk about how hard it was, being a woman manager among a bunch of white executives. She was always concerned about it because she read so many magazine articles about the glass ceiling."

The man nodded in interest, and it seemed genuine.

"Instead I told her about two of my managers. One of them, brilliant, PhD from UC Berkeley, grew up in Korea, where most of his family still lives. The other, my database architect, is an H-1 from northern India."

"Is it important for me to know what an H-1 is?"

That, she thought, is a terrific maneuver: showing that he is listening without interrupting the train of thought. I Do This with My Own Staff, she considered, paused making a mental note about it before continuing with her story, hoping she would somehow remember it when she got back to the office the next morning.

"It's not important to the story, but it's easy to explain. Work visa, he's here in the States because he can't find employment elsewhere."

When he nodded his understanding, she continued. "I told my mom that both of them were good workers, excellent technologists, but that

a recent project was many weeks late and their manager was on sab-
batical, so I brought both of them into my office to ask the reason for
the delay. Both, in unison, pointed to the other and said, "I'm waiting
for him to finish his part."

The man laughed, not loudly, but with enough strength that his glasses
jumped from his head, flying over the seat in front of him and into the
lap of a shy 15-year old who seemed quite undone by the sudden appearance of glasses from above. The man apologized to the girl, then to
the girl's mother, and as he negotiated for the return of his eyeglasses,
Deanna returned to the article about Entity Relationship Diagrams:

> The database of an enterprise contains relevant information con-
> cerning entities and relationships in which the enterprise is inter-
> ested. A complete description of an entity or relationship may not
> be recorded in the database of an enterprise. It is impossible (and,
> perhaps, unnecessary) to record every potentially available piece of
> information about entities and relationships. From now on, we shall
> consider only the entities and relationships (and the information
> concerning them) which are to enter into the design of a database.[2]

"It's classic, isn't it?" she observed when he had retrieved his glasses, realizing that the girl's inability to speak to an older man was not unlike her
two engineers' inabilities. "Both had completed their portion of the work
weeks before; they were simply waiting for the other to say something."

"It wasn't in their cultural make-up to be the assertive one," he observed.

"*Exactly*," she said, "and it happens for lots of reasons. I spend a lot
of time with people in their one-on-ones."

"One-on-ones?"

"Ah, yes, not important to the story but again, easy to explain," she
said. "I actually spend at least half of each week meeting with individual employees."

"Of course," he said, recognizing the obvious, "one-on-ones. I have
those, too."

Deanna glanced back at the journal on her lap, to the diagram illus-
trating Chen's point about entity definitions (see Exhibit 3.1).

As she turned down the corner of the page for future reference,
Deanna thought about her employees, how much they needed to talk
about their families, their co-workers, the unfairness of corporate life.

EXHIBIT 3.1 *Data Structures and Entity Relationship Diagrams: Peter Chen*

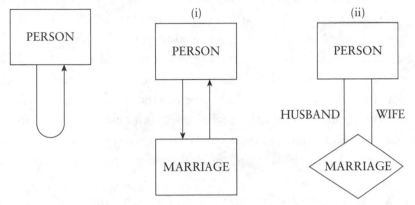

Source: Association for Computing Machinery

Actually, the "people" side of her business was more difficult than the technology. She knew that if her direct reports stopped telling her what was on their minds, it would be a sign that she was becoming too removed. Deanna hoped she never became the kind of manager who refused to listen to the people around them.

"Your employees," the man said. "They worked on two different elements of a system, is that correct?" he asked. She nodded.

"Well," he said, in the kind of matter-of-fact tone that is common when someone states a blatantly obvious truth, "it seems fairly obvious to me that your computers won't talk if the people aren't talking."

"Now *that*," she said, "I'm going to write down."

Deanna was writing this truth in the margins of the journal on her lap, next to Chen's description of husband-wife entities, when the man in the brown corduroy jacket said something even more useful.

"Pardon me for suggesting something about your work," he began, "I usually bristle when someone in another discipline offers a suggestion to me that is often completely out of context."

"Please, go ahead."

"Well . . . if I were you, I'd stop doing one-on-ones, and start doing one-on-*twos*." he said with the gentlest confidence she had ever witnessed.

"Excuse me?"

"It seems to me that anyone in a supervisory role in business should manage the relationships *between* people rather than the individuals *themselves*. I think how they behave as individuals is less of an issue to the business than how they are capable of working together."

Deanna stared down at her journal, absorbed by his simple but very relevant suggestion. It was certainly true of servers and data elements—so much of the technology had reached a level of abstraction and the interactions were so sophisticated that the true value of the objects on the network or in the database lay in their relation to other objects or nodes or pieces of information.

If it was true about the hardware and software, could it also be true about human capital?

Whatever the reason for her absence from the office—conferences, vacations, or funerals—Deanna's return was always turbulent. Just getting into her office was an experiment in chaos theory. Problems seemed to increase exponentially as soon as she came into the building, and she had learned to judge the situation by the number of interrupts that occurred between the time she parked her Volvo C70 and the time she arrived at her desk.

On that particular Tuesday, seven people came to her holding contracts, or an Ethernet cable, or a Palm Pilot, each with an extremely urgent problem requiring immediate executive attention. Of course, on that day, everyone also wanted to offer their condolences before they divulged their very urgent issues, which doubled the length of each interruption.

She lifted her bulging briefcase onto the more orderly of the two desks that formed an L at the end of her oblong room and heard her secretary's footsteps behind her.

"It's going to be a very long day, Sherry," Deanna said without looking back.

"I've already cancelled your one-on-ones with Paul and Alec," Sherry said, referring to her leather-bound day planner with dozens of yellow post-its lining the margins of most pages, the closest thing to a Bible that could be found at USA Financial. "You have a Special Topic IT staff meeting at 11. Don't ask me what it's about, there's been nothing in the e-mail and none of the other admins have a clue . . . and remember, you've got Oracle here at lunch, I've ordered Italian."

Deanna raised her hand.

"What?"

"Tell Paul and Alec to come in *together* at 10," Deanna said quietly, careful not to seem unappreciative of Sherry's busy morning, "and cancel the Italian, just coffee and sodas. I want the new guy from Oracle to think we're in an expense management cycle."

"Aren't we *always* in an expense management cycle?" the woman quipped as she spun on her heels out the door. It was a rhetorical question.

Sherry was already in action, but before Deanna could unpack her computer and even attempt to catch up on the weekend's e-mail, her Quality Assurance manager knocked on the partially open door.

"*Sorry* to hear about your *mom*," he said, with the same inflections everyone used that morning, equal parts empathy and protocol. "Anyway, if I'm interrupting just tell me, but there's something you might want to know before . . ."

"Come back at 10, Alec," Deanna nodded. "Sherry's re-sending the meeting request right now."

"But I thought maybe *before* you meet with Engineering . . ."

"See you at 10," Deanna said, crossing the room and putting her hand on his shoulder, "and thanks for the condolences, it was sweet of you to mention it."

They sat on opposite sides of the table, both men with their arms folded, both with a list of open issues to be addressed in what they thought was going to be their private one-on-one.

The dissonance between them was mutual, and also obvious to everyone in the department. Of course, some of the struggle was built into their job descriptions—one was responsible for the engineering team that *built* the software, and one was responsible for the testing group that identified *mistakes* in the software. She'd often discussed Paul in her meetings with Alec and Alec in her meetings with Paul, offering suggestions about documentation improvements and error messages, process improvements in version control, best practices in the development life cycle.

Manage the relationships, she thought to herself. She wondered why she hadn't thought of it before.

"I don't think the two of you like each other very much," Deanna began.

Stunned silence vacuumed the room.

Then, simultaneously, both men began a litany of sins the other had committed in the short time Deanna had been in Florida. One had cancelled a meeting without explanation, the other had misinformed marketing about a new feature. The two men were behaving as if their families had been at war for six generations.

"Let me ask you a question," she said, more like a professor than a boss. At that point, the two were temporarily quieted by her indirect response to their defensive behavior. "Don't worry, it's not a trick question. You can both be right."

Deanna was improvising. "Let's use our network as an example, so that neither of you will feel criticized. When we're in triage because one of our subnets blinks, where does the support team look first—I mean, if the monitoring programs don't point us in a very specific direction, where do we look?"

They both considered the question. Then Alec unfolded his arms, leaned forward with his elbows on the table, and asked Paul about an outage that had occurred on the day of the funeral. Paul agreed it was a good example and turned to Deanna with their mutual response: it was the closet on the second floor near the Chief Information Officer's office, because it had the oldest equipment.

"What equipment, exactly?"

"Well," Alec said, "all I know from the engineering report we got Sunday night is that the first closet we built out has 3Com *and* Cisco gear, and a lot of improvised stuff connecting them."

Deanna nodded. "Okay, good. How's the gear? What I mean to say is, how are the hubs and routers, working okay?"

This time, Paul leaned forward to double-check his answer with Alec, and they both nodded. One of them said something that sounded like an acidic poke at Jay Ravelli, their network guru—long hair, Harley T-shirts, and a virtual Houdini with netgear. Then Paul answered that the 3Com hardware was still working, even though it was off maintenance, and the Cisco gear was also working fine. However, something unusual was happening beyond the immediate comprehension of the software team with that particular subnet when the two were connected in a certain way. Therefore, on Sunday night, Ravelli's team needed to tweak both of them in order for the very rapid I/O to remain consistent. Deanna wasn't entirely satisfied with their answer, so she decided to make another attempt to get the two to think as one.

"OK, so let me ask about our new hypermedia prototype for the Equity platform."

Silence. They knew they were being led down a path. It was so obviously they wondered whether there was a hidden undercurrent to Deanna's ploy other than the simple explanation that two systems can be working quite well in "stand-alone mode" but seem to misfire in combination.

"OK, boss," Alec was the first to respond. "We get the analogy. We're fine by ourselves, but we have to work harder on the team thing."

Deanna recognized the "median." It was her term for the point in the conversation at which she had accomplished what she wanted and should leave it there, at the midpoint, the median of the curve. However, she was rarely satisfied with the median and was well known in the company for pushing the outer boundaries of anything significant, two lessons instead of one, two examples instead of one, two rewards instead of one. It was not her desire for perfection, or even excellence; it was merely a desire to take full advantage of every opportunity before the window closed. Her CIO had counseled her, in her last performance review, to be less insistent, more willing to accept a bit of mediocrity every now and then. She often ignored the man's advice.

"C'mon, guys, we aren't in Little League anymore," she said, "and it isn't just career development. There is something more at stake, something about the technology *itself*."

More silence, interrupted like a gunshot by Sherry's firm knock at the office door. Deanna looked at her watch and then held up two fingers before concluding her first experimental relationship meeting.

"OK, we have to wrap up, so let's finish with a quick recap of the Hypermedia project. Paul, I asked you to come up with a methodology for the prototype."

The two men sat up straighter in their seats, and Paul admitted he hadn't found time to complete his research, chagrined because he prided himself on responding quickly to Deanna's requests.

"Well, Mr. Engineering, today is your lucky day, because I happened to come across a very useful approach on the plane last night."

Alec scanned the one-page tearsheet that Deanna slid across the table (see Exhibit 3.2), and Paul winced. He didn't like being reprimanded, even delicately, in front of Alec and he didn't like Deanna's microman-agement. The Hypermedia project might have been the most complicated of their new initiatives, but it wasn't the only thing on his plate, and he felt it was more than a little unfair to be semipublicly directed, marionette to Deanna's strings.

"So here's what I want the *two of you* to do. Take this methodology[3] as a starting point, and adjust it for our team, for the particular needs of our project."

"Then I want you to present it to the entire Hypermedia team for their feedback."

"Both of us?" Alec asked.

"Yes, Alec," Deanna said firmly. "It will be a *joint* effort and a *co*-presentation, and the outcome will either be a joint success or a joint . . . *lesson*."

Then she scooted them out of the office and into the neon-lit hallway where a line of other managers had formed with her next series of urgent issues. She jokingly ordered Sherry to get a "Take Your Num-ber" device from the delicatessen.

"Sorry guys, but The Boss is due in the principal's office in four min-utes," Sherry called down the hallway, scattering the crowd. Then she handed a blue folder to Deanna enclosing the agenda for the CIO's Staff meeting and a post-it that her father had phoned from Boca Raton.

Deanna looked up quickly.

"Don't worry, *not* urgent," Sherry reassured her, "I think he just needed to hear a friendly voice. I told him you'd call him tonight on your commute home."

EXHIBIT 3.2   *Entity Relationship Management*

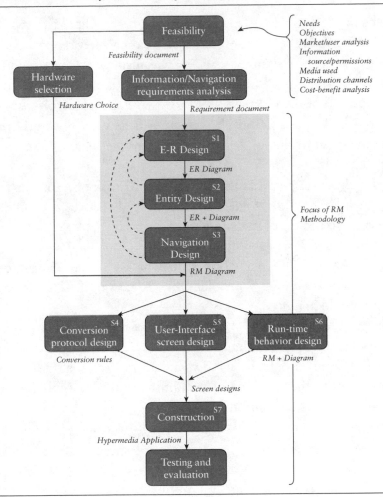

Relationship Management Methodology (RMM) focuses on the design, development, and construction phases. Here we concentrate on the design of access mechanisms, which is achieved through the first three steps of the methodology (shown in the shaded area). Although feasibility, requirements analysis, and testing are undeniably important phases in software development, they are beyond the scope of this book.

The labels on the arrows represent the various intermediate artifacts generated through the use of the methodology. Although they are present in the methodology, we do not show the feedback loops among the remaining stages to avoid cluttering the exhibit. Feedback loops between the RMM design stages are shown by dashed lines.

The RMM data model provides a strong prescription for choosing the nodes and links in the hypermedia application. However, many design issues must be decided independently by the designer.

Source: Association for Computing Machinery

Paul reluctantly brought Alec back to his office, where the two men were unanimous in their low opinions of Deanna's new approach. This had been his special assignment, and he was insulted to share it with the one fellow in the entire department who caused him trouble. Similarly, Alec felt that he already had enough to do without taking on tasks that had been Paul's responsibility. It seemed as if he was constantly cleaning up after Engineering and this was just another example of the unfairness of it all.

"We might as well face it," Paul shrugged, looking for his Deanna folder amidst the amazing pile of folders and printouts that covered his desk.

"How do you find *anything* in here?" Alec asked.

"And here it is, just where it is *supposed* to be," Paul replied with a deep appreciation of the irony. Of course, he knew that his lack of organization was becoming a problem, but Alec was the last person to whom he would admit it.

"What is it, exactly?"

Paul explained that Deanna had given him a printout from a recent book that examined data flows in financial institutions. He was supposed to identify the portions of the illustration that applied to USA Financial and propose solutions for each.

Alec opened the folder and looked at the illustration it contained (see Exhibit 3.3).

Alec recognized the institutional processes in the diagram, but, like Paul, he did not understand the connection between this particular diagram, and the Entity Relationship document she gave them in today's meeting. "Look, Alec," Paul said, "she's obviously trying to tell us something. Let's *pretend* we understand the connection. What next?"

The two men looked at each other for one startling moment, both recognizing that it was the first time in more than two years that either of them had started a collegial conversation without a critical remark. It was a scene one expected to see in the movies, with two lifelong enemies suddenly brought together by a greater threat, only this wasn't the movies.

Alec's first impulse was to underscore the obvious: his Quality Assurance team was always left out of the requirements phase of a

EXHIBIT 3.3   *Hypermedia Event-Driven Structural View*

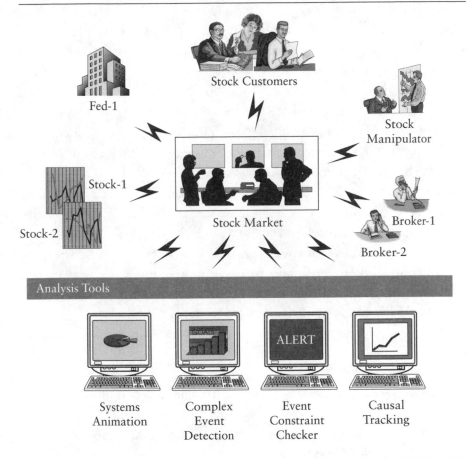

Stock Customers

Fed-1

Stock Manipulator

Stock-1

Stock-2

Stock Market

Broker-1

Broker-2

Analysis Tools

| Systems Animation | Complex Event Detection | Event Constraint Checker | Causal Tracking |

Exhibit 3.3 shows a multienterprise financial trading system. These systems are distributed over various networks worldwide and often use the Internet as one of the networks. When viewed at a macro level, the various enterprises and organizations are simply components of the system. Each of them has its own internal information processing system. The exhibit shows these components, including the stock market information system, brokerage houses and online customers (or, more accurately, their workstations), the Federal Reserve, investment banks, and the networks through which all these components communicate. Messages (or "events") flow across networks between these enterprises. They react to the events they receive and issue new events that are sent to other components. The system is *"event driven"*—it lives or dies on the basis of the messages flowing across its IT networks. This is a rather large system with high volumes of messages flowing through its networks. For example, in 2001, 5,000 or 10,000 messages per second flowed through a single large brokerage house's information technology layer. Soon, that number will be higher.

Source: David Luckham, *The Power of Events,* Addison Wesley, August 2002.

project and was included only at the end of the project cycle when it was too late to offer useful suggestions. Here was a perfect example: first he saw the RMM article and only later had he been shown the initial document. But the significance of their moment, in Paul's office on that day, wasn't the right time to lecture his new partner on the trials and tribulations of Quality Assurance.

So Alec decided to avoid the lecture and simply think out loud.

"I think the diagram from Luckham's book is the *problem* statement— every one of those illustrated end points is a potential View in our project. And the RMM diagram is a *solution* statement—as if we can best identify the end points in our Hypermedia project by developing relational models for each outcome, giving us both a view of the common data model and the specific points where each one might be unique."

He went to Paul's whiteboard, which was covered with squares, circles, arrows, and other engineering notes, and, in the only empty corner, sketched a timeline, using the Luckham diagram as the starting point and the RMM diagram as the method to deliver results.

Paul was impressed, so much so that, despite his intuition that he would someday pay for this moment of honesty, he said so. "Actually, I'm impressed, Alec."

Alec nodded, once, and was willing to take the compliment at face value.

"No, really I am. So, let's go with your analysis," Paul continued. "Maybe our presentation to the team tomorrow should use your problem– solution analogy. I'll take the Luckham diagram and highlight every area that applies to USA Financial media, and you take the RMM diagram, with specific tasks for applying it in each category. We can get together tomorrow to compare notes . . . you know, connect the dots."

When Alec returned to his office, mind filled with possibilities, Paul closed his door, and in an historic moment of catharsis, decided to organize his desk. If they had remained together for even a few minutes longer, if they had taken the time to analyze the sudden transformation in their relationship, the two men would have realized that they had that day become an entity.

NOTES

1. Peter P. Chen, "The Entity-Relationship Model—Toward a Unified View of Data," ACM *Transactions on Database Systems,* 1 (March, 1976), 10.
2. Ibid., 10
3. Tomas Iskowitz, Edward Stohr, and P. Balasubramanian, "RMM, A Methodology for Structured Hypermedia Design," *Communications of the ACM,* (August, 1995), 5–6.

CHAPTER 4

VIRTUALIZATION

— The Company —
Corporate Headquarters
1100 Story Road
San Jose, CA 92032

EMPLOYEE MEMORANDUM: Lucid Kollinger, #4127
DATE OF TERMINATION: October 15, 2005

In The Company's ongoing efforts to reduce expenses and create efficiencies in all operational functions, your position (System Administrator Level III) has been eliminated, and those responsibilities will be reassigned to other departments. The Company appreciates your commitment during your period of employment and welcomes you to seek other opportunities within The Company, as they become available.

Your Human Resources representative will be available to assist you with arrangements for possible transfers to open positions in other departments, or to coordinate your severance benefits and plans.

If no other position is determined and approved by that department's hiring manager, your final date of employment is October 15, 2005.

Sincerely,

Dieter Kahn, Ph.D
President and CEO

Within a week of receiving his letter, Lucid began to display symptoms of the "One Foot Out the Door Syndrome," the curious corporate malaise in which once-loyal and enthusiastic workers slowly realize their current company isn't the exceptional workplace they thought it had been. For Lucid, his commute now seemed longer and more of an annoyance, his co-workers seemed less intelligent, and he was noticing broken processes in every department—inefficiencies that prevented completion of almost any endeavor. It was as if he had been wearing special lenses that had filtered out these observations; his layoff notice had simply knocked the lenses out.

For Lucid, who was prone to analytical observations, it was the logical consequence of separation. At some point, children no longer view their parents as super-heroes, students eventually view their professors as people, not as geniuses, and ex-employees no longer view their companies as examples of excellence.

He, himself, had shifted. He realized he had been a perfect example of IT professionals who hold on to the Old Way of Doing Things.

The layoff had another, more personal and more specific, impact. He needed to pack his office files and bring them home. This meant he had to look through all his boxes in the crowded hallway closet at home, to see what could be thrown away, as there simply was not enough space to hold everything.

The closet, nicknamed The Shrine, also stored his father's possessions.

Lucid's father grew up in Danville, Illinois in the 1930s. He had died more than four years before, but several boxes of personal items remained that Lucid had never looked through. There was always one excuse or another. Initially, it seemed too emotional to filter through the detritus of his father's life, almost disrespectful, as if by storing the boxes unreviewed in his closet he had created a modest temple for his father's keepsakes, a man of modest accomplishment whose greatest joy was to extol the heroic adventures of those around him.

"I cleaned out my closet last night," Lucid told his sister when she called on Saturday, as she had done every day since their parents had passed away.

"You finally *did* it?"

Lucid offered the handiest rationale, that his pending layoff was forcing him to consolidate belongings from the office, and the only spare space available seemed to be in The Shrine.

"Well? What was it like? I mean, dismantling The Shrine?" She asked, always inquisitive about her older brother's sudden breakaways from routine. "Was it like the time you dismantled the stereo? God, Lucid, there was stuff spread out all over the living room floor for days."

"Oh, I'm keeping most of it," he said shyly, because she had never been an adoring daughter and she didn't understand football, so she wouldn't be much of an audience for Lucid's epiphanies.

On the night that Lucid decided to go through the boxes of his father's belongings, he was still distracted by The Company's decision to eliminate his job and further distressed by the feeble attempts of the Human Resources department to help him manage the change in status. Therefore, his first epiphany, when it occurred, seemed entirely haphazard, for surely nothing so arbitrarily coincidental could have been manipulated by anyone's Grand Design.

He was thumbing through his father's many news clippings, artifacts of a previous era. The only theme that linked the clippings was his father's respect for individuals who had achieved something never done before: mountain climbers, inventors, the survivor of an alarmingly long parachute fall (it did not open, yet the man walked away). Several articles described Red Grange, the famous college halfback nicknamed "The Galloping Ghost" from the University of Illinois who revolutionized football with his apparent capacity to elude any tackler. Lucid's father had attended the University of Illinois for two quarters, before the Army suspended his collegiate life. The family rumor was that Lucid's father and Red Grange actually attended class together, a doubtful but enjoyable myth, passed on to the next generation, until the children lost interest because Red Grange was no longer a household name.

One particular article, from the *Danville Commercial-News* sports section, discussed the concept of "The Grange Eye," the name given to

Red Grange's apparent capacity to make adjustments in his movements on the field even before the opposing team had made their moves, as if he had the uncanny ability *to recognize change before it happened*, and adjust in advance, thereby appearing to be always "where the other team isn't." Lucid was charmed by the metaphor, even to the point of realizing that "The Grange Eye" was, indeed, a special skill that would be highly useful in business. *Perhaps I could have seen the layoff coming*, Lucid thought to himself.

But it was on the other side of that page, in a Letter to the Editor, that Lucid's second and more quintessential discovery was made. When he tossed the Red Grange article aside, it flipped over to display the editorial page. The headline was "Hotel Changes Draw Worker's Ire," and the letter was from a woman named Betty Kardon:

> Kind Editors, I must disagree with your article about the Hotel Wolford's progress. Of course, everyone in Danville is proud of the new telephone systems, these marvels of engineering, that allow an entire hotel phone system—yes, 100s of lines, to be managed by a single person in front of a single special machine.
>
> But for those of us who used to work at the Wolford until they brought in the new system, those of us who imagined retiring after twenty-five years of service as telephone operators enthusiastically operating the many wires and cables for our many callers, those of us who are having a difficult time finding similar work in such a small town with few other hotels of equal caliber, this is not progress.
>
> For us, a very big phone company has created a way for a very big hotel to save money by replacing very many loyal workers with impersonal machinery and wiring. The company and the hotel make money, which makes the banks happy, and those of us without a salary are left to wonder how we are going to feed our families next week.

Lucid was overcome by what he read, and he read it again, out loud, as if someone 40 years before had discovered the words to articulate what he had been unable to say when someone asked him about virtualization in the high-tech industry.

At that moment, Lucid realized virtualization was *not* something new.

Virtualization of computing environments was merely the latest example of a standard economic development: the adoption of new technology eliminated the need for manual expertise, even exceptionally delivered expertise. Lucid didn't know Betty Kardon, although his father probably did, yet he understood her anxiety, her depression, her alarm.

History, with its inexorable progress, had trampled on both of them, and he was simply an example of a constant historical trend.

The next day, during his last week "on the job," he began recording his observations in a work journal, noting broken processes (for example, the countless number of unnecessary steps required to provide new employees with their I.D. badges and cubicles, or the obvious constraints in manufacturing that occurred between shifts when nearly an hour was spent by the incoming specialists simply to determine what had been done by the previous shift). He also recorded quotes from newspaper articles of interest, or lunchroom conversations, quotes that seemed to capture the essence of the moment, the underlying truth of an exact point in time.[1]

"Maybe I'll write a book," he told his sister when she asked why he was suddenly keeping a journal.

The most unusual symptom of the "One Foot Out the Door Syndrome," for Lucid, was his increasing capacity to understand virtualization, in context. His understanding seemed to increase exponentially as he accepted the fact that he would be leaving The Company and looking for another job, as if his anxious grip on his current employment had prevented him from learning what would have allowed him to remain. By the time he had understood the concept well enough to explain it to his Human Resources representative at their next session, he no longer wanted to remain at The Company. He was ready for his exit interview.

Q: "How would you describe the relationship with your current supervisor?"

A: "I got the letter, didn't I?"

Q: "Yes, Lucid, and I know this is difficult, but I'm actually asking about your relationship with her."

A: "I'm not much of a relationship person, frankly. I do a good job. I work long hours. I do what I'm told. As for my boss, she does her job, too, I suppose. She leaves at 5 p.m. every day, crisis or no crisis, but when she's here, she does her job. Oh, don't get me wrong, I still think she's in way over her head and causes more problems than she solves—which is not what a manager should be doing, particularly in IT, where it's our *job* to solve problems.

Q: "Tell me what she could have done differently."

A: *"Her* job isn't in jeopardy. *She* doesn't have to worry about rent and student loans. It would be one thing if she really understood the changes and after trying to teach them to me for a few months decided I wasn't up to the task. No, she told me I'm unwilling to change and that my job was at risk because of it, yet she can't tell me how I can change, because she doesn't understand it."

Q: "Perhaps if I understood your job—could you explain it to me?"

A: "Five years ago, when I graduated and joined the Help Desk, each primary server was the responsibility of a specific administrator. Only that administrator had the password to run utilities on it, and when someone in the business needed to bring up a new application, or add a new feature to an existing set of tools, they put in a request, and the assigned system administrator would run the Make."

Q: "The *Make?* Is that something I should know?"

A: "Sorry. It's a command that compiles software on the server, and the Make command isn't open to anyone, only someone with root permissions. Root, that's the primary password on our computers. There's a reason they don't give just anyone access to root, because people—even people with good intentions—can make a mistake. They can bring a server down, or the entire network."

Q: "So the system administrators were important when you came to the company."

A: "I don't mean to say that we were more important than a Director of Finance or the VP of Sales, but a lot of what they do depends on the servers, so they need us. Or rather, they used to need us."

Q: "I don't understand what has changed. We still have lots of servers."

A: "Yes, I think we have 800 servers in the data center, and dozens of others on the network. But the technology is changing, and everything is becoming *virtualized*."

Q: "OK, I know you need to explain *that* to me. How can something physical become virtualized?"

A: "Well, that's the big question, isn't it? We're in the process of changing our data center, moving toward The Grid."

Q: "Which is...."

A: "The Grid, or rather grid computing, is one of our new objectives, a way to take advantage of resources on a network."

Q: "Yes, but what is it, exactly?"

A: "Right, sorry. The best example is the alien thing, you know, the Search for Extra-Terrestrial Life (the SETI)? Tens of thousands of home computers are connected to the SETI network, and when they need to compute something very large, they can access these computers to do some work for them."

Q: "Oh yes, I think my daughter's computer—she's at Illinois State—is part of that project. Is that The Grid?"

A: "It's an example. All along The Grid are resources that can be accessed for specific computing needs."

Q: "I think I understand. What is it about this that worries your manager? It seems like you do understand it."

A: "Oh, that's not really what she's looking for from me."

Q: "So you *do* know what she's looking for."

A: "Here's the problem. Remember how I described what system administrators do? Well, we don't really have responsibility for a set of servers anymore. Instead, we're being asked to become some new kind of system developer, someone who writes software that manages all these networked computers. Instead of a person with root permissions, it might be an automated script that configures the servers. Some of us just don't trust software alone. There's too much risk for failure and no accountability. I mean, if everything is automated, than my servers—the ones that used to be up all of the time because I was good at what I do—are now going to be managed by some software written by someone else, and maybe they won't work as well. It all becomes pretty vague. Virtualized."

Q: "Yes, I think I'm beginning to understand the problem. I imagine that fewer people are needed to run our 800 servers in this way."

A: "That's what they say. They say they can keep the data center running efficiently with 30% of the staff that we currently have. I just don't buy it. I mean, these things still dump cores, they still freeze, or a disk goes bad. Now, someone's fancy monitoring software finds the problem and temporarily switches the activity to another server until the repair is done, but, it isn't repair really, we don't take servers apart any more. Now, it's blades that slip in and slip out. If one fails, just put another blade in."

Q: "Fewer people, yet much more complexity."

A: "Complexity. That's the word that my *manager* used. But if things are getting more complex, how can we be using fewer people to keep it going? I guess I just don't believe in the concept, and she thinks that means I'm resisting change."

Q: "Ah."

A: "Hey, I've shown that I can change. I mean, during the whole outsourcing nightmare two years ago, I was one of the most cooperative guys on the team. I found something else I could contribute. Now I have to do it again, if I can find another position."

Q: "It does sound a bit unfair."

A: "Listen, I'm not some kid stamping his foot. I'm the one in the back of the room saying that the Emperor doesn't have any clothes. I mean, what if this *big change* is just about *saving money*? All this virtualization talk is just a fancy way to say we're going to lay off half of our infrastructure team, and the other half will be forced to figure out a way to make everything work. And it won't. Later, some executive will be considered a genius for adding new staff positions."

Q: "You think they aren't being honest with you."

A: "I don't think they're being honest with themselves."

Q: "So, if it isn't team relationships, what keeps you motivated in your job?"

A: "The machines."

Q: "Excuse me, did you say the machines?'

A: "Yes, the machines. I prefer the company of machines. I took apart radios when I was a kid, my parents used to hide the good ones or they'd end up in pieces on my bedroom floor. I'd take them completely apart and then try to put them back together again to see if they still worked. I'm still the same, with our servers and our network. My machines are "up" all the time, that isn't true for most of the other system administrators."

Q: "You mentioned being *virtualized* earlier, and your other colleagues who are being transitioned are talking a lot about Virtualization, but frankly, I'm still a bit confused about just what it is. Too vague. Could you help me understand it?"

A: "I know. Techies talk to other techies, and we're comfortable doing that, but we don't do a very good job of explaining ourselves outside the *club*. In this case, though, it's more of a history lesson."

Q: "History. Very well, try me."

A: "Well, I have two examples. First one: let's pretend this is 1953 and my job has been to operate an elevator in a large department store. Bergdorf's or I. Magnin, or, even better, remember the old Sears building downtown?"

Q: "*Yes*, it was *wonderful*, my mother used to take me shopping there when I was a little girl. They always had a huge tree in the lobby at Christmas."

A: "Well, let's imagine I was the fellow who sat on the little fold-down chair and operated the levers that moved the elevator from floor to floor. I wear the uniform, understand the mechanics. Let's even imagine that I've become very, *very* good at my job, one of the best. Not only can I bring the elevator to an exact and gentle stop, *perfectly level* with the floor so there's no risk of customers stumbling on their way out, but let's imagine that I have also learned what is on each floor so I can help newcomers decide if it's the fourth floor or fifth floor for washing machines or lawn furniture. I've done the job for so long that I can practically predict what the customer needs when they step into my little elevator world. I am the ideal elevator operator for the department store."

Q: "Ok, you are doing this job very well. And?"

A: "Naturally, there are improvements, over time. Industries begin to automate some of the elevator functions. Eventually, any customer can press their desired floor, and the elevator even remembers multiple requests. Eventually, the doors are sensitive enough to reopen if someone gets in at the last minute, and they've added some security features, too, cameras and secure ID cards for certain floors. And of course, there is a directory of services at every floor so that customers can navigate by themselves."

Q: "I see. The elevators improved, and the role of the elevator operator, even the exceptional operators, was no longer necessary."

A: "Now, let's look at a second example before we draw conclusions."

Q: "I think we have time for Example 2. But we need to stop in a few minutes, as I have another meeting. Some of your peers are having a more difficult time adjusting to their transitions than you seem to be."

A: "OK. In this second example, imagine I'm a phone operator in that same department store, early 1950s. In those days, the saleswomen were still using vacuum tubes to send receipts to the upstairs accounting office. And in the basement, there is an immense wall of switchboards, staffed by fairly competent operators who individually answer each incoming call, unplug the wire connection, and insert it into the requested slot, eventually becoming so proficient that the really good operators can handle dozens of calls simultaneously. Imagine that I'm a switchboard operator with such a knowledge of the business that I can even recognize familiar voices, know the schedules of the upstairs executives, offer assistance, and pass on useful information while plugging and unplugging the telephone wires."

Q: "The same thing happened to them, didn't it? The telephone companies automated the switchboards, and even the best operators were no longer necessary."

A: "That's right, of course. Even the best operators. Because, you see, manual expertise doesn't matter if, over time, the technology has become more sophisticated, multifunctional, more useful. In both cases, it was simply a matter of time until telephone and elevator manufacturers recognized the repeated actions, found ways to accomplish the task electronically, sequenced in proper order, and built the actions into an advanced product."

Q: "And that's the story behind Virtualization?"

A: "I think so. The manual tasks, the way we used to manage our computers, are becoming inexpensively automated. Now layers of software are capable not only of completing most of the tasks I used to do by hand, but also doing them in a coordinated fashion. Even the *best* system administrators—*even the best*—just aren't needed to do their old jobs any more. We're like the old elevator operators, or phone operators. The industry is moving past us, and I think we're on the verge of becoming obsolete. It doesn't *matter* if I can manage dozens of servers and databases without any problems; that was heroic five years ago, but now we're at a stage in our industry where *thousands* of servers can be managed with only modest problems.

Q: "And what do you imagine became of that old elevator operator who was such a nice guy, liked by everyone, and one day, he wasn't there anymore?

A: "I don't know. I'm not a fiction writer. But I can imagine lots of different stories: in one, he becomes an alcoholic; in another, he learns a new trade; in a third, he finds a job in a company that isn't making advances and still does things the Old Way. Somehow, he had to change, or just kill himself."

Q: "That sounds a bit ominous. So tell me what you plan to do, and how I can help."

A: "I think I need to find work where my contributions can be appreciated; that's all, a place where IT still means something."

It was Lucid's fourth interview for a new job, and so far, none of them had been very productive.

His Human Resources representative suggested that he seek *any* opportunity to interview, with as many companies as possible, because it was important to practice how to interview correctly. She prompted him on the basics, but he already knew that the best way to learn how to do something was to do it, correct the mistakes, do it again, and again correct the mistakes.

On this particular day, for the position of IT Program Manager at the Nature Conservancy, he truly prepared for the interview.

First he phoned an old company friend who had been an excellent Program Manager for several years. She explained that the key to her success was *Planning* and *Detail*. She told him a bit about Risk Management Scenarios (specific plans for unplanned events, which made Lucid think again about "The Grange Eye") and Critical Path Scheduling (tracking changes that will directly impact schedules). Then she told him about the Project Management Institute, if he wanted to learn more.[2]

Second, he logged onto the Internet and did a bit of research about the Conservancy itself. What he learned was that the Nature Conservancy was established in 2002, as a separate entity from the City's Parks and Recreation Department, to focus on the strategic value of the city's primary landmark resources.

It is a small, nonprofit organization with some of the city's most recognizable and successful people on its Board of Directors, and everyone who works in their various offices and districts is passionately dedicated to the mission of the Conservancy. Bankers, ministers, former executives, accountants—each one is bound to the other by their common Mission: to keep the environment pristine and flourishing, so their children and their children's children could still experience some of the old architectures, monuments, and landmarks.

He also understood that, as a nonprofit, the operational emphasis must be on cost containment and efficiency. So he brought along several white papers from Gartner, to support his contention that the new technologies—his reason for leaving The Company—could actually be of great benefit to such organizations.

> We regard virtualization as the most disruptive technology the PC has faced in a decade. If adopted and deployed to its full potential, the PC's long journey to commodity status could finally be over. The benefits for users are potentially huge, with enterprise images becoming easier to deploy, manage and secure. The impact on the PC industry could be just as significant, removing all scope for product differentiation and forcing vendors to compete on service and price.[3]

He waited almost 30 minutes before he was greeted in the lobby of their downtown offices by the Conservancy's Director of Finance, a fellow in short-sleeves with immense, meaty hands that conveyed the kind of strength usually reserved for athletes and carpenters. Lucid's hand felt tiny in comparison, and the Director completed the handshake with the same care he probably gave to his young son. When they arrived at the Director's office, Lucid could see that this same son played baseball. Pictures of him stood on the long wooden desk that was otherwise completely covered with folders, papers, and notebooks—all the signs of an overworked manager.

"Does he like playing catcher?" Lucid asked, gesturing toward the framed photo of the young boy in full gear, poised as he readied a throw to second base.

"Not really," the man said with a smile. "He just likes to hit home runs."

Lucid could hear a quiet lilt of pride in the man's voice as he spoke about his son, a mixture of gravitas and joy, and there was something in that simple answer that told Lucid he would enjoy working for this man—for reasons that had nothing to do with technology, or the Conservancy's mission, but for his demeanor. He could not think of a single manager in The Company who so conveyed such humanity.

"I'll be completely honest with you," the Director confided, pulling Lucid's resume from a manila folder. "I know very little about computers, just enough to be dangerous. Usually, our Manager of IT Operations would be conducting this interview and I would only meet the candidates he has previously screened."

"I'd be glad to come back on another day, if that would be more appropriate," Lucid offered.

The Director leaned forward, elbows propped atop the large calendar-blotter that was completely covered with scribbled hieroglyphs. "He's become quite ill," the man said with soft concern. "He may be on extended leave," he continued, "and so I find myself looking for two different staffing solutions. First, of course, the role you are applying for, and now, someone temporary to fill the gaps in management. And there are a lot of gaps. We're a nonprofit, and we're very dependent on Gary, that's his name. I've gotten four calls this morning that he would normally handle without even telling me about them."

Lucid immediately recognized a timely opportunity: the pipes were leaking everywhere, their plumber was out of commission, and, suddenly, a stranger knocks on the front door who knows a little bit about plumbing. No one cares if he is in the Union, or if he's certified by the County, they just need him to get to the basement and stop the leaks.

"But I need to follow the protocol," the Director said, "so why don't you tell me a little bit about your current job, and why you're thinking of leaving."

Lucid was well prepared for the answer, but after a quick description of his various duties at The Company (operation systems, desktop support, e-mail, and telecom), Lucid said something that he did not know was true until he said it. He knew it was the right thing to say at the right time, but it wasn't disingenuous.

"I've decided to look for work somewhere that is *meaningful*," Lucid said finally, "where technology enables a larger mission, you know, something I can be proud to be doing with my life."

Lucid knew it was a good answer, and the man said so.

"I'll tell you . . . Lucid," he said, quickly glancing down to the paperwork, to remind himself of the candidate's name. He explained that the other candidates either possessed exceptional technical skills or compelling program management experience. "You're the first one to mention the Conservancy itself."

Lucid responded, "Actually, I'd like to hear about your IT environment. Maybe you could tell me about the calls this morning."

The Director explained that he had had to answer a whole host of questions about things he didn't understand: there were two questions about lost passwords, one anxious message from a woman in the office whose computer screen had frozen just when she needed to print out copies of an important report, and one unsolicited call from a salesperson who claimed to have the perfect software solution for nonprofit business analytics related to the Sarbanes-Oxley legislation passed a few years ago (deadlines were coming due). The Director shrugged, adding that he hated salesperson calls, even for things the Conservancy needed, because it was a constant reminder that they simply did not have the money for such things.

"Would you like me to help the woman with the frozen computer?" Lucid asked. "That seems to be the highest priority. We could solve her problem, and you could see me at work."

"Now, *that*'s a great idea," the man said.

The Director phoned the woman upstairs to say he was on his way, and as they left his office, he complimented Lucid on his self-confidence. Much later, Lucid learned that his Director didn't expect him actually to fix the old computer. He wanted to observe Lucid with an excitable client. First, Lucid solved the problem by simply rebooting her machine, and then he suggested that she try not to do so much at once.

"How could you possibly *know?*" she said.

"You have lots of files open, ma'am," Lucid said, "too many, all at once. Seems to me that you're juggling a lot."

The woman was charmed by his bedside manner and by his empathy for her workload, so she grabbed the opportunity to list her litany of complaints about the other IT staff and how many times she had to call for assistance.

"Well, in this case, ma'am," Lucid said in his Customer Service tone of voice, "it gave us an opportunity to meet each other."

By the time her system was up and running, he had given her some advice about her AOL account at home as well as the need to back up her important files. He assured her that she was not the only person in the world who didn't like to depend on machines. As they were leaving her office, she whispered to the Director, "now . . . *this* is the kind of help we need around here."

The Director smiled, and when they were safely in the elevator, he said, "The job is yours if you want it. Remember, we're a nonprofit, so

I can't promise I can match what you earn in the corporate world, but I can guarantee you'll go home every night feeling like you've made a difference in the world."

Another handshake sealed their agreement. Once again, Lucid was impressed by the man's hands. He had truly amazing hands.

It was not the simplicity of the work, in comparison with The Company's infrastructure, that made it easy for Lucid to succeed during his first six weeks. In fact, there was an ever-present challenge to deliver consistent improvements in file retrieval, network printing, and e-mail performance while at the same time demonstrating to the Director that the improvements to each project were cost efficient.

In lieu of trivial assignments for a boss who often forgot his name, Lucid was performing heroic feats for a boss who noticed everything: his punctuality, his grace under pressure, and, most important, the quickly rising appreciation of technology throughout the organization. Lucid was taking the time to explain causes and effects to the Conservancy's team, and, in turn, they were beginning to understand the operational challenges.

There was no specific budget for technology. When Lucid first asked about one, the Director laughed out loud and then closed the door for a candid discussion about the delicate balance of nonprofit budgets, Board oversight, and the great difficulty in obtaining any financial support for administration.

He offered one example, from which Lucid learned much about his Director's greatest problem: the Conservancy had recently received a major grant from the Banyan Foundation to provide "hands-on" summer education courses in the local parks. The budget provided enough money for 18 summer jobs and additional support for half-time management oversight of the 18 interns (many of whom were local college Ecology and Environment students). However, no money was provided for administrative operations, applications, background checks, payroll, accounting, video training, cell phone coordination, and so on. All this would have to be "absorbed" by the Conservancy.

During his first two months, Lucid learned that almost all the funding provided to the Nature Conservancy came with this restriction: administrative and operational expenses (technology included) were rarely financed by the donors. Everyone wanted their money to be directly connected to the group's mission.

"So, how *do* you pay for a new printer?" Lucid asked one day, when the Director had invited him to lunch at the corner deli.

"We receive a small operating budget from the city and matching funds from the county," he said grimly. "It never goes up, and in the past two years it's gone down because of the lack of tax revenues." Then the Director offered a candid example, confessing that he hadn't received a raise in three years.

That was when Lucid was struck by an idea.

It was as if he were the only lightning rod on a barn in the middle of a cornfield. At that moment, he completely understood the Gartner report about virtualization. He understood Oracle's movement to Utility Computing, and Sun's initiative to offer CPU cycles for rent. Motionless, between bites of his Nathan's® hotdog, he suddenly understood more about the direction of Information Technology in the coming decade than he had learned in years at The Company.

"Are you OK?" the Director asked, reaching for Lucid's shoulder. "You look ill."

The man behind the counter looked suddenly concerned, as if he would lose his job if one more customer complained about the food, but Lucid waved OK to both of them, swallowed his last hurried bite, gulped his last hurried bit of soda, and began scribbling frantically on his placemat.

"It seems to me that the *entire world* is a nonprofit," he said. The Director seemed to appreciate the poetry, but not yet the reasoning. "It operates just like the Conservancy, using more resources than it has been given, thriving on the heroism of people, such as our staff, who find innovative ways to produce $2 of result for every one donated dollar."

"I'm not sure I'm following you on this, Lucid."

Lucid turned around the placemat, which in simple terms, was a "Before" and "After" sketch of the Conservancy's IT operations: technology, facilities, little boxes for their servers and printers.

Before (see Exhibit 4.1) . . .

EXHIBIT 4.1 *The Old Way of Doing Things and After (See Exhibit 4.2)*

"What would you say if I told you that we could *expand* the use of technology throughout the Conservancy—better printing, improved interoffice collaboration, web sites with information updated on a daily basis by our field agents with wireless devices—while *reducing* the overall cost by 50 to 60% over the next two to three years?"

The Director stared over the rim of his glasses with an expression of doubt so obvious that it conveyed, in an instant, the man's powerful level of disbelief.

"I know it sounds insane," Lucid said, undeterred. "I can just imagine your possible reactions: if it was so easy, why hasn't anyone done it before? Who would risk their career presenting such lunacy to the Board? Am I close?"

"I'm going back to the office," the Director said, but he waited for Lucid outside the deli.

EXHIBIT 4.2   *The New Way of Doing Things*

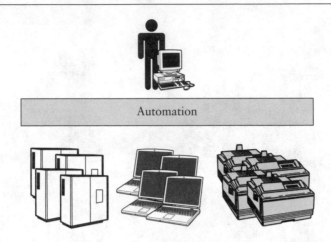

"Look, boss," Lucid said as he double-stepped to keep up with the quick-moving man, "I know I'm the new guy with almost no understanding of the hidden skeletons and dead-ends and screwy politics and paperclip-and-chewing gum solutions that are holding everything together."

They stopped to wait for the light to change, from the orange flashing hand to the white striding man, and then Lucid continued.

"But this is what I believe: I believe that the entire technology industry has come to a moment in history, a transition point, and that there are some new ways to solve old problems—incredibly difficult for large companies like my old one to embrace, but eminently within reach of the Conservancy, because there *hasn't* been a big investment in out-of-date systems. We can leapfrog into the present tense, and I really believe what I said before, I think we can start delivering exceptional technology for much less money than you're currently spending."

"Just tell me what you want, Lucid," the Director said, glancing at his watch.

Lucid used ten seconds to gather his thoughts in silence. It was not the time to explain co-location facilities, Voice Over IP, distributed computing, or hosted applications. It was not the time to outline how major IT vendors might be excited to demonstrate their value in such a setting, purely for the public relations value of the experiment. It was not the time to explain the value of enterprise architecture or grid computing.

"I need two things from you, sir," Lucid said. "First, I need you to pull together the actual figures for the past three years, buried inside the operational dance you have to do every year just to keep us going. I need the actual spending on technology. I'd like to attend an upcoming conference on The Future of IT, sponsored by some companies like IBM and Hewlett-Packard that might be willing to help."

Lucid knew, by the look on the Director's face, that he was actually considering the proposal, considering it seriously.

For the next five months, Lucid Kollinger was entirely occupied with the "as is" portion of his project. To determine what was currently being spent (for how can you save money if you do not know how much you are spending), weeks were required to sift through hundreds of purchase requisitions. Then he needed even more weeks to meet individually with each employee and perform an inventory of the Conservancy's technology assets. Of course, he was also responding to complaints, replacing printer cartridges, rebooting servers, and retrieving lost files. With each visit to someone's office, he casually inquired about their work: what they needed to do, how they were currently doing it, what they wanted and did not have. When he finally reported the results of his detailed asset inventory and the hidden cost of their invisible IT environment, his Director was paralyzed by the resulting data.

"Excluding staff costs," Lucid said, "the Conservancy has spent $137,000 on computing in the past two years."

The second phase of what he called The Memex Project was an evaluation of the wide variety of alternative approaches by designing a thoroughly divergent strategy. He projected a first-year cost at the same level of spending as in each of the two previous years, during which time all software and hardware (e-mail, calendaring, financial applications, and databases for fund-raising) would be hosted by managed service providers outside the Conservancy who guaranteed specific support levels for a basic monthly cost. By year two, he projected a reduction in spending of 20% per year and by year three, 30% per year on an ongoing basis. Organized, outsourced, and optimized—they would be doing more with much less. "We will be strongly linked to them," he explained, "shared cost and shared success."

"I like your math," his Director told him when he presented The Memex Project in their weekly meeting. He seemed to appreciate Lucid's vision sincerely. "But our Board will have questions I can't answer, so you'll need to attend the meeting with me if we are to have any hope of getting them to approve this."

And that is how Lucid Kollinger came to be invited to the annual budget and planning session of the Nature Conservancy's Board of Directors. His sister wisely advised him to wear a tie. His Director wisely suggested that he prepare for a great deal of resistance, because they never knew they were spending so much money and were bound to have a negative response.

So Lucid accepted their advice. He bought a handsome silk tie with nature scenes woven into the pattern, and he composed an introductory slide for his presentation to overcome their wealthy patrons' concerns, using a selection from his journal of useful quotes.

On the night of the meeting, after an elegant dinner and while the Board of Directors was being served crème brulée for dessert, Lucid projected his introduction onto the screen at the front of the room:

Introducing The Memex Project

A memex is a device in which an individual stores all his books, records, and communications, and which is mechanized so that it may be consulted with exceeding speed and flexibility. . . It is an enlarged intimate supplement to his memory. . . the basic idea of which is a provision whereby any item may be caused at will to select immediately and automatically another. This is the essential feature of the memex. The process of tying two things together is the important thing.[4]

Immediately, the Chairman of the Board interrupted the presentation. He was an impressive fellow, a former Mayor and successful trial attorney, and he was emphatic in his message to Lucid and his boss: the Conservancy is *not* a cutting-edge organization, and they can ill afford to invest in "the latest and greatest technology." No budget would be approved that included such futuristic experiments. Period.

Lucid's boss winced, but this was precisely the response that Lucid had hoped to provoke. He waited for the murmurs to diminish. Then he explained that the author of the quote, and the original proponent of the "memex" principle, after which this project was named, was Vannevar Bush, the Director of the Office of Technology in Washington in *1945*.

The Chairman of the Board gasped. Other board members looked to one another in amazement.

"Respectfully, sir, I am not proposing *anything* bold or expensive," Lucid said to his surprised audience, very careful to avoid any jargon that might sound too modern. "However, it does seem to me that saving 20 to 30% of your projected costs over the next five years by implementing an idea that is *60* years old seems quite conservative."

Lucid then explained, at only a modest level of detail, the idea of IT as a service provided by technology partners.

By March of the following year, through partnerships and lease agreements with various service providers and software companies, Lucid Kollinger had modernized the Conservancy's technical infrastructure, improved their customer service and employee satisfaction with that service, and reduced projected IT spending by tens of thousands of dollars. In short, he had *virtualized* the IT environment of the Conservancy, a strategy in which almost everything was rented, fixed quickly, available from home or from the office, and easily managed as a *utility* by a small technology staff.

Gone was Lucid's dependency on The Company for stability without meaningful work, day after day.

Gone was The Shrine to his father.

Gone was his reliance on the Old Way of Doing Things in IT.

Without planning it, Lucid Kollinger had become the future, a time when partnerships and communication will be more significant than owning the information systems themselves, a time when business ecosystems will require a new approach to technology, and a time when the process of tying things together will be of utmost importance.

NOTES

1. Example: "It is not the smartest, nor the strongest, but the most adaptable to change." Charles Darwin.
2. Project Management Institute, www.pmi.org.
3. Brian Grammage and Michael Silver, Gartner Group Study, July 9, 2004, www.gartner.com.
4. Vannevar Bush, "As We May Think," Atlantic Monthly, 1945 (Original *Atlantic Monthly* article, 101–108. www.theatlantic.com/doc/194507/bush).

CHAPTER 5

ORCHESTRATION

They were invisible.

This quality, among so many others, was their greatest asset. Since the company's inception in 1991, they had been quietly responsible for some of the most remarkable technology events of the decade. Invisibility was also their greatest curse, for when they were entirely successful, few of the hundreds of people attending those events knew who was behind the complex systems, multimedia demonstrations, precise and flexible security, and problem-free computing zones erected in less than 24 hours, flawlessly executed, and then dismantled in six hours, loaded into two semitrailer trucks, and driven away without incident. They never lost a cable, router, or lapel microphone. They disappeared into afternoon traffic like the Special Forces "black ops" teams in Vietnam or Israel, who just blended into the jungle or the sand when their work was done.

"I remember the day I conceived of the company," Eleanor Teller said once in an interview for *Women's Wear Daily*, in a column highlighting the best women-led businesses of 2003. "I was attending a huge conference at the San Jose Convention Center in 1990."

You know the type of event, she went on to say in the interview: hundreds of tech vendors filling an immense auditorium with demonstrations and marketing giveaways, thousands of attendees wandering between exhibits with little white cards. One of the vendors at this particular conference was a small team of firewall designers from Israel. The company was called Checkpoint, and no one had ever heard of them at the time. They offered to build a firewall system around the entire network that had been constructed by the Conference Center, and the organizers decided to allow them access. "Within minutes, they had quarantined hundreds of direct hacker attempts to access the Conference Center. Everyone on the floor was huddled around their two-machine booth. It was a magnificent marketing coup for the company," she recalled, "and I thought to myself, this never should have happened."

Eleanor resigned her position as the Manager of Technical Operations for Stanford University, obtained a small business loan with her modest Menlo Park home as collateral, and launched her company with the idea that thousands of business conventions every year needed equipment and coordination for their events on a temporary basis. She remembered filling out the application at a Wells Fargo desk. Almost as a joke, she entered the words *Systems on Wheels* in the box entitled "Name of Business," thinking of the small, dedicated group of people, Meals on Wheels, that brought food to ailing seniors.

In their first year, they leased equipment on an event-by-event basis and did nine events, a good first year, but it quickly became obvious that she could not work out of her home with temporary staff and little event-by-event expertise, so she renamed the company, partnered to refinance the effort with a local venture capitalist (who has since received exceptional support for his own annual conference on Emerging Technologies, at stunning discounts), and then went about the task of hiring truly exceptional experts in every area of IT, program management, communications, and facilities operations.

"I believe we have some of the most talented employees anywhere, in any company," Eleanor said in the interview, and it was true.

That they were all women, in an industry dominated by white male executives and pony-tailed systems experts, was part of her strategy. She believed that women were better problem-solvers, more collaborative, and far more capable of staying out of the spotlight, although in most cases, they were the ones who were turning the spotlight on, aiming it in the right direction, and making sure there was always a backup halogen bulb nearby. She established multiyear alliances with most of the major event organizers, ensured that her teams were trained in the latest technologies and risk management strategies, and in 1997 created a subsidiary force (male and female) that specialized in systems integration of business parks and new shopping malls. In 1999 she spun that business off from her core company at the height of the Internet spending frenzy. That single divestiture provided enough capital to establish offices in Chicago, New York, Atlanta, and Paris—and she now owned (fully amortized) most of the equipment, the real estate, and even the primary trucking and warehouse assets used for all but the most specialized events.

They were invisible, so she didn't receive the kind of attention reserved for Carly Fiorina from Hewlett-Packard or Meg Whitman from eBay (both were clients, of course). Until the article in *Women's Wear Daily*, followed by a front page Column One focus piece in *The Wall Street Journal*, few understood her incredible success, and even fewer truly understood the "special forces" teams she had hired and trained over the years.

These were exceptionally talented women, cross-trained to fulfill multiple tasks, intuitive, adaptive, and capable both of preventing problems and of solving them quietly in the rare instance when something unpredictable happened, before a crisis arose for the sponsors or the guests.

"The women in my company would probably have been burned at the stake in Salem," Eleanor was fond of saying. "I personally recruit each new employee, and I look for intelligence, grace under pressure, and something magical in their spirit, a kind of spark."

"Why haven't you gone public?" the interviewer asked.

Eleanor always smiled when that question was posed. The profit-sharing plan at Teller and Associates was generous, and her staff was very well paid. "Oh no," she said in the interview. "I've never been an advocate for public ownership, the pressures of quarterly numbers, the emphasis on style over substance." What she didn't say, but what was the essence of her philosophy, was the invisibility of her associates. They are always in the background; others are successful because of their efforts. "No one knows we are there," she said in the interview, "and we prefer to keep it that way."

The woman in a tailored black suit and beige sweater, wearing a subtle David Yurman silver chain around her neck,[1] was poised at the back of the empty room, entranced, attentive.

Moments before the first attendees arrived for the complimentary breakfast, after the tables and nameplates had been arranged, attendance verified, notepads and engraved pens aligned at each seat, Sulema Shalom stood in the back of the room and checked for alignment.

She stood exactly in the middle, along the rear wall, staring from side to side, to verify the symmetry. In a manner not unlike the entanglement principle in particle physics,[2] it seemed as if each of the objects arranged in the room emitted a kind of echo, one to another, and she needed only to listen to the objects, in a room empty of other human beings, to know whether they were ready to open the doors to visitors. If something was amiss, it would seemingly call out to her, its absence having a voice like no other for her ears.

On a good day, when she was particularly receptive, Sulema believed she could accurately predict the outcome of the event—the averaged scores provided by the attendees in their concluding evaluation forms—at that precise moment before the doors opened, when the orchestration of every element sang its song for her.

Her attention to detail, while useful in her profession, was not a welcome talent during her childhood or in her marriage. Although it was the subject of so many books and made-for-TV movies, such intuition was, for many years, a burden. As a child, she had combed the fringes of her mother's Turkish hallway rugs so they would all be aligned. In class, while other students were occupied with passing notes and gossiping about each other's wardrobe, Sulema was keenly aware of the number of students in the room, the patterns of their interactions, and the arrangement of reading books on the library shelves.

When she joined Teller and Associates, the CEO offered to send Sulema to Program Management training, but Sulema had a sixth sense, like the psychics and profilers on popular television, and she explained to Eleanor Teller that it simply wasn't necessary, an insight Eleanor came to appreciate over their years together. Sulema respected those who believed in proper planning, coordination, and risk management scenarios, but the subject was academic for everyone else, whereas it was intuitive to Sulema. She knew the answer before the questions were entirely posed. She simply recognized linked relationships and could predict outcomes without pen and paper, Excel spreadsheets, and Project Planner.

For Sulema Shalom, it was never a matter of preparing for every possibility; rather, it was a matter of listening. She experienced each broken link or disrupted pattern as an alert, the way dogs respond to whistles that are soundless to humans.

"Trends in Enterprise Computing: IT in the Next Decade and Beyond"

The sign was posted on a tripod positioned at the top of the stairs, with an arrow pointing to the hotel's conference room that had been reserved months in advance. The number of registered attendees exceeded the number of seats at the U-shaped conference tables, on the theory that there are always last-minute crises preventing 100% attendance.

"My name is Alec," the man said when he arrived at exactly 8 a.m. The first arrival always feels a bit awkward, wondering if he or she is in the right place at the right time.

"Yes," Sulema said without having to refer to the list. "Alec, here you are. You came from downtown."

"That's right."

"I hope the hotel room was comfortable," she said, simultaneously checking his name on the list, peeling his adhesive name tag from the printed sheets, and handing him his name card for the table. "Please help yourself to the complimentary breakfast. I'm sure the others will be here soon."

Soon the moderator arrived with his last-minute requests for an additional flipchart and a different type of table for his paperwork. Sulema ensured that the arriving participants were greeted with the proper respect. Her experience in the technology community at such events was that many come with their egos on a leash, whereas the truly valuable participants are often the most soft-spoken. On this particular day, most of the participants were on time, the moderator seemed prepared, and the speakers demonstrated only a modest level of anxiety, in whispers when the participants were in another room.

"Do you think it's going all right?"

"Are we going to have enough chairs?"

"The eggs were cold last week in Charleston; could we double-check to make sure everything is warm?"

"Do you think it's going all right?"

Sulema was often reminded of a wedding coordinator she had met a decade before at the Stanford Chapel in San Jose, California. If absolutely everything was executed on time and correctly, the doors would open with the bride at the top of the aisle, just as the setting sun was hitting the stained glass windows. That afternoon, at precisely 4:30 p.m., there was an audible gasp from the guests when a burst of radiant colors suddenly appeared behind Sulema's cousin in her long white dress, holding daisies. What seemed to the guests like a near-religious, once-in-a-lifetime moment was actually the result of precise planning by the wedding coordinator, who said later that the only thing that gets in the way of a well-orchestrated event is the people who participate in it.

When everyone had arrived except for one fellow from the University of the Pacific who was caught in traffic and called by cellphone to apologize for being late, Sulema nodded to the moderator, who nodded to the speakers, and the session was under way.

"First of all," the moderator said, most graciously, "I would like to thank all of you for taking time from your busy schedules to come to this conference on The Future of IT. Whether it is Grid Computing, Blades, Linux Clusters, Wireless Remote Access, Virtualization and Orchestration, or . . ."

"Excuse me," said the very tall man at the end of one table. His name was Sheldon Delaplane, from TeleDynamics International. Sulema had known when he registered that he was an *interrupter*. "I'm sorry to interject, but I have to tell you that as soon as you use terms like Virtualization, you lose me. Our customers are the federal government, and if we use terms like that, their eyes just glaze over. Can you redefine that in ways I might be able to understand?"[3]

The moderator reddened, recognizing the classic Moderation Paradox: one cannot detour from the agreed-upon discussion guidelines without distressing the sponsors of the event, and yet, one cannot ignore a question from a participant so early in a session without discouraging later dialogue. He elected to pursue the path of least resistance, for the moment, by thanking the attendee for his question and apologizing if he appeared to be ignoring the question, but he first had several administrative details to address, before the roundtable could actually begin.

"These administrative issues may not seem important, but I have found that it is best to address them before the session begins," he smiled. *The* smile. This man had a smile that could calm a cranky baby.

"First, let me explain the microphones. Even though we are taping this session, it is candid, off-the-record, and not for publication. However, we are often asked for transcriptions, so we provide that service for you. Second, I will not ask you to turn off your cellphones because many of you are front-line IT staff; however, if you could simply turn them to "vibrate" and take the call in the outside lobby, that would be much appreciated. Finally, . . ." he said, lifting a pink sheet of paper, a copy of which was placed at each table setting.

"Do you want us to fill out the evaluation now?" the man in the sleeveless sweater asked. Everyone laughed.

"No," the moderator said, smiling that This Is Why You Hired Me smile again, "I just want you to know that we take these evaluations seriously and hope that you will try to complete them at the end of the session."[4]

The next 40 minutes was consumed by individual introductions, with participants explaining their roles at their companies, the reasons they were attending the session, and their expectations for the outcome—what they hoped to learn. On that particular day, only 2 individuals of the 20 required more than five minutes to explain their roles:[5] one was not articulate, and another enjoyed the attention he was getting from his colleagues, clearly something he did not enjoy in his own workplace.

The final participant, hurrying in from his valet parking and ruffled by the traffic, simply greeted everyone as he took his seat, saying "My name is Allard Cohen, and I am the Chief Technology Officer for an international law firm with offices in 42 countries. The rest is commentary," he said, glancing in all directions to see if there was another Jew in the audience who might understand and appreciate the Talmudic reference. There was not.

"Thanks," the moderator said, glancing at his discussion list for the next topic.

"I'd like to ask a question of the other participants, if I might," some-one said from the corner of the table. The moderator waved for him to continue. "I work for a major financial institution in New York, and we've adopted many of the technologies being described as 'the future' here today. But I'm here as a representative of another group, a consortium of academic and corporate IT teams throughout New York that are working to leverage each other's environments and provide shared servers for redundancy and replication of data stores for high availability. It seems to me that our biggest problem, well, the biggest challenge for any large effort . . . is *complexity*."[6]

The Marketing Director on the speaker team moved to the front of the room, and in the void created by the moderator's passivity, explained that Alec's issue was going to be the single greatest challenge of the coming decade, an increasingly complex technical environment, along with an ever-shrinking IT budget.

"It isn't simply a matter of doing more with less," she said, indicating that one of her staff should begin to distribute the handouts. "You've been doing that for the past four years. It has to do with a completely different approach to infrastructure, to your staffing resources; the white paper we are distributing will perhaps give us a starting point for discussion."

Alec was not impressed by the event; however, the white paper included some useful statistics and architectural diagrams that he knew his friend Paul's university group would find interesting.

> In a computational grid, community resources come, go, and change without warning. In such an environment, programs must have rich methods for finding communities that meet their needs. Once placed, they must be able to determine their membership in a community. During execution, they may need to find resources outside of the community in order to bring them inside . . .[7]

Alec found the term "communities" to be thought provoking, as well as the further discussion of discovery, in which classic programs provide matchmaking services to locate the proper CPU or storage unit to execute the function. According to the white paper, by organizing resources in appropriate I/O communities, simple questions (where is the data?) are answered automatically by the system.

What he found most interesting was the notion that a great deal of understanding about the environment must exist in order to create the proper communities and that this understanding can come from analyzing the organizational communities within the business, the communities of people that are bound together not by hierarchical assignment (we both have the same boss) but by role-based projects (we both have the same task to complete).

He pulled his Blackberry from his belt and e-mailed Paul that he should search the ACM online library for the 2001 article on Creating Communities. Paul responded immediately.

> Paul: I'll get the article and distribute it to the team later. I had to come back to work to deal with an outage. How's the conference going?
>
> Alec: I wondered where you went after the keynote. This roundtable is OK, but the moderator is a corpse. Hopefully, the speakers will have something useful to say.
>
> Paul: Should I forward the article to Deanna?
>
> Alec: No, but maybe your university group would be interested. Will you be back for the dinner speaker?
>
> Paul: Maybe. Save me a seat.

"Does anyone in this damn room have a suggestion for someone who has inherited an absolute mess?" a bald man said from the corner, standing to stretch an obviously aching back. He was wearing a bright blue sport coat with an olive green vest, a combination that was not appealing but definitely drew attention. "We've got nothing but *spaghetti code* and hundreds of servers where there should only be 25 or 30, but how do you get from a mess to something as coordinated as you are describing today? I mean, none of us has a 'green field' implementation available."

The sponsors looked at each other, hoping that one among the team had an adequate response. The moderator busied himself with recording the question on the Open Issues list, thereby avoiding any direct responsibility. Sulema knew the answer, of course, but it was not her place to offer a suggestion, and as happened so often in the course of her work, she resisted the urge to tell supposedly smarter executives how to manage their businesses.

Finally, Alec raised his hand.

"I can tell you what to do," he said. "The next step is quite clear, regardless of your business, or your vendors. *You must separate the layers.* Once you have clarified the server level, and the presentation level, you can focus on the software that will either become a standard middleware implementation or a business process engine distributing services. But you've got to start by pulling apart the spaghetti, strand by strand."

The sound of pencils scribbling on notepaper could be heard from several directions, and the primary speaker stepped forward, now that the correct answer had been given, to explain how their company could assist with such an effort. Alec smiled but said nothing; he could not imagine engaging a firm that could not answer the question yet volunteered to assist in the solution.

Sulema gathered the evaluations and distributed the gifts to the participants as they left the conference room, heading for one of the four "Birds of a Feather" sessions that were scheduled before lunch. She hoped their keynote speakers would keep them engaged, but she could tell from the evaluations that some of them were already bored and weren't likely to remain for the entire day.

Alec, was lingering at the registration table, shyly asking one of the speakers for an extra giveaway package for his son. Sulema walked over and offered her own.

"I have plenty of these back at the office," she said.

Alec stuffed it into his computer bag and looked as if he was leaving the hotel, so Sulema asked him to offer some comments, to help them prepare their next conference better.

"Well," Alec said, "you could find a moderator who is comfortable in front of a group of smart people, for starters."

She laughed.

He glanced at her name tag. "If you don't mind my asking, can you tell me about your name? It's unusual."

Sulema was always charmed when strangers asked about her name. It was a part of her heritage that she rarely inserted into her daily business efforts. "It means Woman of Resistance."

"Really?"

"Yes, my father gave me that name."

"You seem so organized," he said, "you know, efficient. Resistance doesn't come to mind."

Sulema thought about explaining her rationale, that life was chaos and that her path of resistance, in a life of chaos, was to provide a structure that allowed progress to be made. She thought about his earlier statements, how he struggled with complexity, and she knew he would be interested in her theory. Orchestration was not easy to explain, except to those who understood the effect of its absence. She wondered, as she gathered the remaining evaluation forms and packed her registration box, why most technologists find this so difficult to understand. She turned to offer her more sincere explanation, but Alec's attention had been caught by the man with the aching back.

"I'm damned interested in that opinion of yours, son," the man said. "Pulling apart spaghetti isn't easy when the only people you have are the damned people who wrote the spaghetti in the first place."

"Make it a contest," Alec said, only half-seriously.

"Excuse me?"

Alec realized the man was going to take his suggestion back to his company and recommend it exactly as he described; for a brief moment, he wondered if he had indicated which financial firm employed him— his Risk Management team wouldn't like it if they knew he was giving out technical advice. He excused himself for a brief moment and leaned toward Sulema, asking very quietly if his contact information or corporate background had been provided in any of the conference materials, and she reassured him that such information was kept confidential; it was entirely at the discretion of the participants to provide it or not.

Alec exhaled his relief, asked her to wait for one more minute, and returned to the fellow who seemed overwhelmed with his problem of customized, undocumented software and the re-architecture it was calling out for. He imagined that the man had learned the true nature of his IT environment only after he had accepted the job.

"Well," Alec said finally, "what I would do is present it as a challenge to your programmers, you know, offer a bonus to the one who can provide the most efficient strategy for separating the current code into a three-tiered architecture. It's been my experience that programmers like to solve problems, even if the problem is the software they originally wrote."

"I like your style, son," the man said, nodding his head as he walked away, thanking him again from several steps away. "I might just do that."

By the time Alec returned to his conversation with Sulema, she had completely dismantled and boxed the materials, gathered the glasses and plates, returned the unused pencils and notebooks to their cartons, and turned off the lights to the conference room. Hotel employees were carrying the boxes back to their central office, and Sulema looked back to Alec, hoping he might ask her to have a drink or, even better, dinner.

He did not.

The keynote speaker at the luncheon session was a well-known figure, an author of several books on wide-ranging subjects, the winner of Inventor of the Year. President Clinton had once described him as one of the finest thinkers of the modern era. He was the "big name" that conference organizers always strove to attract. Although his speaker's fee was more than the budget allowed, and despite the less-than-adequate attendance to pay the difference, Sulema was pleased to see that the ballroom was filled for his presentation.

The meal was standard fare, a salad with small olives that defied definition, chicken or salmon, and the promise of chocolate mousse during the keynote presentation. Until the speaker arrived, the luncheon attendees were expected to "network," which, to Sulema and the other organizers, simply meant trading business cards.

Sulema hoped for something more dynamic at her table. Again, she was the only women with seven men from various companies. One was the Chief Technologist for a company that made virtual machines, another was on the IT team for the St. Louis Cardinals. A third man, seated to her immediate left, was very bald, quite shy, and seemed content to butter his roll without dialogue.

"Tell me what bothers you most about your job," she asked.

The man seemed to sense that she was speaking to him, rather than to the more extroverted at the table, but he did not seem to mind answering the question.

"They think we're plumbers, most of the time," he said, biting into his roll.

"They?"

"Excuse me," he said, "I'm Henry Soloff, and I manage the IT group for a mid-size insurance company on the East Coast. We're about 40 people, and we spend most of our time fixing the things that the business people break because they aren't paying attention."

"Maybe electricians would be a better analogy than plumbers," Sulema suggested.

The man looked up at her, unsure whether she was insulting him, or simply offering a more articulate method of explanation. She continued, "It seems to me that most information systems professionals are treated like electricians—they are expected to keep the power on, despite the wind or the rain, but no one takes the time to have a significant conversation with them."

"Yes," the man said. "That's right, but we're much more than electricians."

Sulema paused before her next statement; she had noticed that everyone else at the table was listening to their conversation. They had dispensed with the usual pleasantries and, feeling awkward, were pleased to listen to someone else's disagreements. "The electrician for my condo complex is one of the finest men that I know, very smart, a good problem solver, always makes you feel like your problem is significant. I don't know why the comparison would bother *anyone*."

The man across the table from the virtual machine company CTO suggested that, unlike her electrician, who seemed an honorable and self-assured man, many of his peers (and indeed, most of those at the table, although he only insinuated this thought) lacked the humility that comes with professional excellence. "We want to be constantly recognized for our wonderful work, although there are thousands of us around the country and around the world doing the very same thing we do, and few of us ever truly offer anything of significance, anything that truly improves the quality of people's lives."

"Insecurity," Sulema suggested.

"Perhaps so," the CTO shrugged. "We like to think we are more important than we actually are. But not without good reason. We work very long hours, often sacrificing time with our families. Perhaps it is the absence of recognition."

"We just leave a $20 tip at Christmas for our electrician," she said, "and he always seems quite thankful for that."

Just then, they were interrupted by the moderator of the conference, a fellow who looked like he worked for Anderson Consulting (and in fact, he had, which was why his wardrobe still reflected the starched solemnity of the firm). He briefly introduced their speaker.

"He has constantly reminded us that we live in a world of complexity," the moderator said, "and our job is to simplify the world, to orchestrate it so that it is livable. His book, *Intelligent Design*, has been recognized . . ."

"*Problems of complexity require orchestration*," Sulema thought to herself. Finally she was going to hear someone worth listening to, so she quietly thanked the waiter as he filled her coffee cup. Seymour Glass took the podium.

"I must first apologize," Glass said. "For those of you in the audience who expect me to be speaking about the debate between Darwinians and New Christians, I am sorry to disappoint." Laughter interrupted him. "In fact, current debates in various classrooms around the country have forced my publisher to reissue my book with a new title, *Designing with Intelligence*,[8] to help new readers understand that my area of expertise is not the creation myth, but how we blunder when we build the world around us."

He touched the remote button, and a picture of the conference room doors was displayed on the large screen behind him.

"Elegant doors," he commented. "Probably very expensive. Yet the handles are constructed for their look, not their function, and I counted at least 20 of you, as you entered the room, who pulled instead of pushed when you came into the room. I am sure, in the very near future, they will be adding the words Pull beside each handle so that we can all be instructed how to use those very expensive doors properly."

Just as the speaker was giving homage to the work of Donald Norman[9] and the teams at IDEO in Palo Alto,[10] whose expertise had led to breakthrough products in human design, Sulema's cellphone vibrated. She flipped the phone open and a text message said simply, "Code Red—Control Room—come immediately."

She sighed, for too many months and too many events had passed without an opportunity to listen to someone who actually had something interesting to say. Code Red events were nonnegotiable, however. She quietly excused herself from the table and took three steps out of the auditorium. She always sat near a door, ready for just such an occurrence, although Code Red messages were rare at Teller, and she was instantly intrigued.

Teller and Associates always constructed a Control Room with their own badge access supplanting the conference facilities security. Here they housed state-of-the-art server racks, failover systems to ensure 100% uptime, multivendor security suites, and a triage desk with monitoring systems capable of tracking all facility network traffic, content management for the various presentations, and wireless access for the main exhibits. The Control Room was always staffed by two or three of Teller's best operational staff. Sulema had worked with this particular threesome on at least a dozen conferences, and nothing had ever gone awry before.

Also in the room, which was unusual but not unprecedented, was the Chief of Security for the Hilton Renaissance Center, a very large muscled man, suitcoat stretched to the limit around his shoulders and biceps. He reminded Sulema of the actor Ving Rhames. A look of intense concern was etched on the man's sculpted face.

"Status," she said, pulling up a chair beside the monitors where the three Teller Associates staff and the Chief of Security were gathered.

"Jumper in Room 2101," said the man with the jacket that could not contain him.

"It began about an hour ago," Randee Smith-Daley began. She was the Teller Project Lead for the conference.

"We monitored an attempted hack of the hotel systems and traced it to that room," another woman said. It was Jennifer Breland. Her claim to fame was that she had once dated Phil Zimmerman, the creator of PGP (Pretty Good Privacy) who was on the board of several well-known security firms in San Jose.[11] "It was a pretty sophisticated hack," Jenny continued, "and, with apologies to our new friend here," she said, nodding to Will, the man with the sculpted face, "it easily poked through the hotel's wireless backbone and reconstituted itself on the hotel's kiosk system, which is fairly unguarded."

"We never thought to secure the kiosks," the big man said, unapologetically.

"The man tried to post a rambling note about the unfair labor practices of one of the sponsor companies, nice idea actually, would have been fairly embarrassing to everyone, but we quarantined it and called Will." Jenny was duly proud. Once again, she had intervened before the note was posted in 30 kiosks throughout the facility. "It was actually Debbie here who noticed the last few lines of the hacker's posting, so Will took another security guard and went up to the room."

The man looked squarely at Sulema with an odd expression as if he was silently asking her for reassurance that she could fix everything with a wave of her hand.

"No answer, so we had to bust in, and the guy just went for the window. I don't know how he squeezed through, they're not designed to open, kids, you know, liability . . . Anyway, my man's up there with him, and our usual policy is to call the police. We let them handle it, but someone said to call you, too."

Sulema looked back at Jennifer and Randee. They explained that they'd phoned Eleanor in Seattle. "She said that, if time was of the essence and the man seemed really intent on doing himself harm, we should call you. She said you'd know what to do."

"How long before the police arrive?" Sulema asked. Will explained that in normal Friday traffic they'd have a car here quickly, "but the Crisis Response team that handles these things, well, sometimes it takes a while."

"I'll talk to him," Sulema said, and Will led her to the Employees Only elevator that had been locked down for the emergency.

"You do this a lot?" Will asked her on the very fast elevator up to the 21st floor.

"Hard to explain," she said. "What do you know about him?"

"Not much," Will shrugged. "Seems he worked for Elan Microsystems for 11 years, although none of their marketing team here at the conference know him. He said something about getting laid off six months ago."

On the 21st floor, the NYPD Traffic Patrol Officer had arrived, and he waved Will and Sulema into the room, where she immediately noticed the laptop on the desk, connected to an unusual, custom-made router (no encasing, LED lights blinking inside). Another police officer was at the window. Unmade bed. Suitcase and briefcase open on the floor beside the desk. Towels on the bathroom floor.

Sulema leaned through the open window and recognized the bald man from her breakfast session that morning, the fellow who complained about spaghetti code. He was in red and green striped pajamas. They looked like an old Christmas present that no one actually wears.

"This will make an awful mess," she said to the man on the ledge. He recognized her and smiled.

"Why did they call you?" the man asked, voice heightened by the adrenaline.

"Oh, you know, I'm very organized. Maybe they thought I could help you clean up your room before all the official people show up."

He laughed out loud. "That's *good*. I *knew* I liked you, you and that fellow from the bank." Then his voice changed. "Too late though, can't back down now, can I?"

Sulema wanted to get out on the ledge with him, and she told him so, but the angle of the open window made it difficult, and she couldn't understand how he had navigated it. Then she found the right thing to say.

"Never too late, Charles," remembering his name from his registration sheet at the breakout session. "Besides, you've got a darned good skill with *windows*," she said, hoping he'd understand the joke.

"That's *good, too*. You're a sharp lady, windows in a hotel, security gaps in Windows software. That's *funny*."

"Really, Charles," she continued, "you figured out how to hack the kiosk system, pretty snappy idea, great mass communication vehicle, and then you figured out how to get out of this blocked window . . ." she paused to check if the man was listening. "You should be consulting *for* hotel chains, teaching them how to make their systems more *secure*, not flying through the air like the Daring Young Man about to make a daring splat."

Charles looked over his right shoulder, real eye contact. A good sign.

"*Really*, Charles," she said, as matter of factly as possible, "you've done an excellent job at identifying not one but *two* breaches in their systems today. You come in, and I'll get you that job."

"You may be good, but you can't *do that*, smart lady. Nice idea, really, but you can't promise that, not now, they're going to lock me *up*,"

Sulema looked at the Police Officer, who nodded and whispered it would be at least a 72-hour hold for putting himself in danger.

"Oh c'mon, Charles," Sulema said, "a 72-hour hold is *nothing*. Gives you just about the right amount of time to draft a report on the system breaches if they let you have a computer."

She paused again as the formal Crisis Team arrived. After a hurried consultation, they acknowledged that she had developed a positive relationship with the man and that she should continue, with their counsel.

"You come out, and I'll go with you to the station, Charles. Heck, I'll even go to the meeting with the hotel people and tell them that instead of pressing charges for the hack, they should hire you to help them prevent other hacks. This could be positioned as a great *publicity stunt* to educate everyone on the need for better security systems. It'd be a shame if someone else gets hired to do that work, instead of you. Don't you think?"

Charles nodded. They kept on talking over the next ten minutes.

Then the man, with Sulema offering him a helping hand, voluntarily returned to the hotel room by acrobatically twisting himself through the window, where NYPD allowed him to change into street clothes before being handcuffed and taken to the hospital for examination. Sulema then convinced Will not to press charges. (Teller had prevented the actual disruption of the kiosk network).

Will asked her *what*, in God's name, gave her the idea to offer him a *job*?

"Complexity needs orchestration," she said. "His room was a mess, his thoughts were a mess. I knew he'd inherited a lot of unorganized code at work and couldn't figure out how to undo it. He needed someone to organize his thinking, just for a moment. Seemed obvious," Sulema shrugged. "It's what I do."

Of course, the newspapers wanted to interview her, but a quick call to Eleanor reminded her it was always best for Teller to avoid the publicity. *We're best when we're invisible*, Eleanor said.

Sulema thanked Eleanor for suggesting that she get involved. She was glad to be able to help. It was an example of why she preferred Teller and Associates to any other firm. Her talents, diverse, difficult to articulate, and wide-ranging, were not only appreciated, but put to good use on a regular basis. She couldn't think of another company where that would be true.

"Seemed obvious," Eleanor explained.

Nothing else remarkable occurred during the remaining sessions of the conference, which was notable, to many of the attendees, more for its impeccable operational efficiency than for the content of the sessions. Within hours of the final presentation, dozens of servers, routers, projectors, cables, and other miscellaneous equipment had been inventoried, returned to their cushioned positions in the Teller trailer (which also housed the alternate UPS power supply that had not been needed that day), and driven back to their New Jersey warehouse.

Sulema Shalom lived in Brooklyn Heights, only a subway stop away from Manhattan, and her upcoming work schedule didn't require travel for two days, giving her the much-appreciated opportunity to sleep in her own bed that evening, a rare and very welcome luxury. She threw her black suit on the pile of other suits destined for the dry cleaners in the morning, glanced through her mail for anything that deserved immediate attention (only bills and advertisements, and one letter from an old college roommate).

She pulled on her silk pajamas, the ones she kept for home and never took on the road, primarily because she never wanted to be seen in public wearing something so self-indulgent, and there could always be a late-night interruption. As she brushed her teeth and admired the mother of pearl pajama buttons in the bright bathroom light, she remembered something.

She climbed into her warm, comfortable bed—always friendlier than even the finest hotel mattress—with a copy of the most recent *McSweeney's Enchanted Chamber of Astonishing Stories*,[12] edited by

Michael Chabon, open across her belly, thinking of the one unexplained anomaly of her entire day.

Why did Charles change into his pajamas after attending their morning session?

She fell asleep to dreams of that imagined story appearing in a future issue of *McSweeney's Stories*: "The Mystery of the Hacker's Pajamas."[13]

NOTES

1. The platinum chain from David Yurman and Company had been a gift from her company as Employee of the Year.
2. In quantum theory, the principle of entanglement proposes that two or more objects may reference each other although they may be physically separate. This leads to correlations, relevant in this context because it has been learned that the state of one object can immediately impact the state of another object, although the information cannot, at this time, be proved to travel faster than the speed of light. "Entanglement—the weird quantum property in which one particle instantly knows what has happened to a distant partner particle. . ." "A Cosmic Conundrum" by Michael Turner and Lawrence Krauss, *Scientific American*, September 2004.
3. Sulema knew the answer to his question: the discussion was about concepts, not marketing terminology. She made a note to herself to draft a short list of Best Practices for their moderators, including terminology issues.
4. Sulema wondered whether an electronic format for the evaluations would be more convenient, allowing the individuals to enter notes throughout their sessions and scoring the event in progress, so the results could be tallied at the end and discussed during the closing remarks. Automation of the paperwork would increase participation, and also add to their ability to make improvements mid-stream.
5. Sulema noticed that, once again, there were no women in the room, and only one African American. It was not for lack of marketing. Indeed, they had made particular efforts to recruit a broad constituency, which often leads to a more dynamic dialogue. However, she had learned that most women and minorities simply do not feel comfortable taking time away from the workplace, an indirect result of the inequalities that continue to exist in the corporate world

6. Sulema understood Alec Michaelson's issue, a theme that had emerged in many of their roundtables, and she also knew that it was a classic demonstration of Complexity Theory. The real issue was not technology, just as the wedding coordinator had stated ten years before. People get in the way.
7. Douglas Thain, John Bent, Andrea Arpaci-Dusseau, Remzi Arpaci-Dusseau, and Miron Livny, *Gathering at the Well: Creating Communities for Grid I/O*. Computer Sciences Department, University of Wisconsin-Madison, ACM, 2001.
8. Seymour Glass, *Intelligent Design*, 1992. Reprinted as *Designing with Intelligence* (Human Press, 2004).
9. Donald Norman, *The Design of Everyday Things* (New York: Basic Books, 1988), originally published as *The Psychology of Everyday Things*.
10. www.ideo.com.
11. Among them is Encentuate, a provider of token-based, two-factor authentication, founded by Peng Ong, who had founded Interwoven, one of the products Teller and Associates frequently used for content storage. Also on the board with Phil Zimmerman was Guy Kawasaki, from Garage Technologies; According to this story, Eleanor Teller had supposedly known Guy since his days as a Fellow at Apple Computer.
12. Michael Chabon, *McSweeney's Enchanted Chamber of Astonishing Stories* (New York: Vintage, 2004).
13. Author's note: if this were detective fiction, the odd event of the character's intentional change into his pajamas after appearing fully dressed in her workshop that morning would be an indicator of subplots not fully realized. In technical mode, as this book proposes, viewed as a reflection of an unexplained event accidentally captured by network monitoring tools (necessary for the orchestration of complex infrastructure), such an oddity would never be overlooked by the systems team: the observer would file a "trouble ticket" or "bug report" noting the unexplained phenomenon. On the network, it might simply be a corrupt file misrepresented by the monitoring tools: they were not pajamas, but the data corruption caused them to be interpreted as such. In the other form, detective fiction, the oddity could instead be an indication that the entire security breach had been designed to mask other, more serious, crimes being committed at the hotel at the same moment as the character stepped out onto the ledge, pajamas being the external reflection that he could not have been involved in the other, more serious crime. Neither perspective has currently been examined by this author.

CHAPTER 6

COMPLEXITY

The Professor cared not one iota for the difficulties he caused at the university.

Had he not broken ground, along with Robert Coover of Columbia, with his version of the Hypertext Hotel, The Labyrinth,[1] years before anyone else in the academic world considered the network as a learning tool?

Hadn't his graduate students, one after another, moved on to remarkable achievements in the arts, humanities, and business?

Although he had been widely recognized for his thoughtful and innovative contributions to literature and technology, he had little in common with his colleagues and the department warlords who would rather argue about finances than discuss the relationship of narrative theory and second-generation cybernetics.

The Professor opened the window of his cluttered office and stared across the city's sprawling urban nightmare, chrome skyscrapers wrapped in neon advertisements that would surely trigger an epileptic seizure if one stared too long. The brickwork of the university building where he'd lived and worked for almost three decades was a stark counterpoint to its metropolitan surrounding. The Professor was enamored with the matrixed pattern of the bricks. (He had used the metaphor in more than one poem to demonstrate the ardor of intersections.)

That day, on the ledge outside his window, a small green caterpillar inched across the dark red surface, slowly examining crevices, crossing the mortar between the bricks without regard to patterns or gravity.

The caterpillar paused, lifted its head (the Professor assumed it was the head) to survey the next challenge with apparently careful consideration, and then patiently resumed its version of the Pilgrim's Progress.

I have more in common with you, bug, than with any human in this institution, the Professor thought to himself.

Then he leaned forward with cocked forefinger and flicked the caterpillar from the ledge, watching the tiny green worm fly in a high arc, past the branches of the only tree in the neighborhood, and into oblivion, toward the street below.

The Professor returned to his Royal typewriter. As he thought how he might compose the request he had avoided all afternoon, he grumbled to himself (only because there was no one else in the room) about the university's Management of Information Systems (MIS) team. This group could troubleshoot networking protocols and laptop wireless configurations but refused to maintain his typewriter. He was a pioneer of computing systems in his research, but he did his finest thinking on an old Royal. Once, at a conference on the Next Generation Internet on the Berkeley campus, he was accused of typing manuscripts and asking his interns to transcribe them digitally, so they could be archived by the University. He remembered his ardently eloquent denials that day and smiled at the recollection of the accusation that was, after all, so close to the truth of it all.

```
To:     Dean Gerhard Lindstedt

From:   Dr. B. Maimon

Re:     Systems Support

Date:   October 10, 2005

Dr. Lindstedt:


As requested at the faculty meeting of 10/7, I
met today with the university MIS team responsi-
ble for systems support to determine what, if
```

> any, steps can be taken to ensure more timely re-
> sponse to computing issues of our Fine Arts stu-
> dents, compared with the level of support given
> to the Smiley Research Lab and to our esteemed
> colleagues in the Mathematics department.
>
> I am sorry to report that we were unable to reach
> consensus on improvements, given current bud-
> getary constraints. I have learned that the small
> MIS team currently provides system administration
> services to more than 10,000 students, a ratio of
> 800 to 1. While I am sensitive to our current
> fiscal crisis, a clear symptom of the overall
> economy, the drastic reductions in federal fund-
> ing, and the cascading drop in donor participa-
> tion, I must once again raise the issue of
> inadequate systems support for Faculty review.

The Professor leaned back, reread the text in progress, and reached for his spiral notebook. He wrote: *Relationship between Bad Economy and Philanthropy: A Polemic*, to serve as a reminder, guardian of memory, that he was two days late for his guest editorial for *The Columbia Review*. He was leaning back toward his typewriter with the goal of completing his mild complaint with an additional, angry (i.e., truthful) conclusion to the Dean's letter when the silence of the office was shattered by a knock at the door. It seemed that no one cared to read the note on the door asking visitors to Knock Softly.

"Professor?"

He recognized the young man in the partially opened door—the fellow from MIS had attended their meeting earlier in the day on the subject of systems support—but he did not recognize the woman behind him. She seemed too well groomed to be in MIS.

"I'm sorry for the interruption," the young man said, with so much sincerity that the Professor was already waving them in, rather than barking at them for intruding after office hours had officially ended. "I thought you might like to meet Esther. We were talking about the funding issues and she had a great suggestion."

The woman smiled, just a wisp of a smile, really, and carefully removed the stack of graduate papers from the only chair in the office before sitting in it. She held the papers in her lap with appropriate respect, and the Professor decided he liked her, he liked her ideas, and he would say yes to anything the twosome suggested. This was his greatest fault, as a tenured faculty at the University: his inclination to approve projects on the basis of intuition, with only the smallest amount of relevant data at his disposal. It had caused more than its share of problems, over his years, but he dared not intervene in the process that he likened to the creative act of composition. If one began suppressing natural instincts, soon the imagination would be lost, and before he knew it, he would become just another college professor with too many papers to grade and too little appreciation for the subtleties of life.

"So," the Professor said, like a banker reviewing a young couple's application for a home equity loan, "tell me the idea, and be quick about it. I'm working on an important piece of prose, Pulitzer quality really."

The young man made sounds about coming at a better time, but the more discerning young woman did not even acknowledge the Professor's condescension. Instead, she quickly offered a background explanation for their visit. It was certainly more interesting than the memo to the Dean, and he listened intently as the woman explained her thesis.

"It's only preliminary, but perhaps it's related to your current situation," she said melodically. "I am interviewing ten academic IT teams about the impact of distributed computing requirements on their strategic plans. We've held several joint meetings, once a month, each session chaired by a different IT team."

She was going to ask for his help. He was preparing for her invitation to speak at the next meeting when the young man broke in.

"It seems to us," the man said, "that all the MIS teams in schools across the city are burdened by inadequate resources, yet most of us are addressing the same problems. We haven't done the analysis yet," he apologized, "but it seems to us that if we combined efforts, we might be able to increase our productivity and increase our response rates."

The Professor understood the principle at work. He knew that, as systems become more interdependent, the teams that support them must also become more interdependent, and that the notion of shared resources was entirely synchronous with shared compute environments.

"You know, a Native-American tribe . . . the Miwok, I believe, lived in very small clusters," the Professor said to himself. This time, there were other people in the room who could hear him. "They traded surplus supplies with other small communities, so that each group would have enough to endure the winters."

Sensing that he understood their concept, the two students crossed the distance to his desk so quickly that, had this been cinematography instead of prose, their movements would have blurred on the screen. The young man pulled a chart from his knapsack, and, as he unfolded it, the woman explained.

"More specifically, Professor," she said in a matter-of-fact tone that would serve her well in her Orals, "we propose that our existing infrastructure is more than adequate to provide 100s of megabytes of unused disk space and processing time to several teams who have the reverse of our problem: they still have IT staff but do not have a capital budget to expand their compute farms."

"Don't you see?" the man said, excitedly.

"All I see," the Professor said, grimly playing the role of Older Person, "are are two well-intentioned students trying to do the right thing, but very little business thinking, statistics, validations."

The woman responded to his critique. "As I said, I haven't finished my research, but it is my contention that institutional boundaries actually limit our ability to maintain an agile computing environment. I believe that, by the end of this year, I will have very clear results proving that, by sharing technology resources, and I mean both the hardware and the technical resources to support the hardware, we can actually improve our compute capacity enormously, at no cost to the participating institutions."

The Professor wondered, silently, how enormous was her definition of "enormously," and, as if she was reading subtitles of his thoughts on a background office screen, she answered the unasked question.

"Perhaps by 50%."

The Professor returned to his office the following morning, after his lecture on the Inevitability of Patterns in the Work of William Gass. Even as he stepped across the threshold and before he closed the office door, he noticed the half-completed memorandum upright in his

Royal, wedged between perfectly balanced black rollers, awaiting his return.

```
...economy, the drastic reductions in federal
funding, and the cascading drop in donor partic-
ipation, I must once again raise the issue of in-
adequate systems support for Faculty review.
```

He knew that any request for funding, howsoever passionate on behalf of the overworked MIS teams supporting dozens of departments in multiple campuses, would be greeted with bemused detachment by his department chair. However, it might be phrased differently. . .

```
Toward that end, I would like to propose a six-
month study, in conjunction with ongoing research
in the graduate Economics Department, of a Theory
of Shared Capital applied to Internet-based sys-
tems. With your approval, I would like to sponsor
a joint program with several local colleges, an-
alyze the impact of this theory on our university
systems, and hopefully improve systems support at
the same time.

I am not requesting any budget increase, only the
approval to add this to the already long list of
approved duties as a guest lecturer on Internet and
The Arts for the remainder of the academic year.
```

"Authoritarian regimes will always approve additional workloads for the working poor," he had explained when the young man from MIS had asked whether the idea would work. As if to prove the predictability of hierarchical management practices, the Dean actually came to the Professor's office later that same day.

Dean Lindstedt was widely published, an administrative genius with the political stamina and acuity of a successful presidential candidate. He also had a wardrobe that immediately placed him in a salaried category far beyond that of an Assistant Professor. Today's tweed jacket matched the man's socks, belt, shoes, and watch band. "I *like* this new development," he said, holding a copy of the letter in his hand like a conductor's baton. "You know I'm sympathetic, and my hands are so often tied by the damned budget, but *this* . . . this has *potential*, Ben."

"Yes," the Professor said, "I thought you would appreciate the multi-college partnership aspect."

The Dean said it was always beneficial when the university offered services to the broader educational community. He suggested an article in the *Review*, when it was time to announce the project; then he spun out the door like a dervish and down the hallway. The Professor detected a slight aroma of Bay Rum.

Esther knew that even the combination of a well-respected novelist as Executive Sponsor and the reprovisioning of several Linux clusters in the University's data center did not ensure success.

She also knew about the consequences of a Fundamental Attribution Error: that her own subjectivity—after all, she was already convinced that innovation would increase in direct proportion to the capacity of individuals to share workloads—might cause her to overlook important details, hidden anomalies, variations in analytical patterns, and minor discrepancies in Likert scales.

It was midnight, and she was still in the library, hers the only lighted carrel in the second floor wing. She never felt entirely safe on campus after dark, and she decided to take the remaining work to the Union coffee shop, which was 24/7.

Down two flights of concrete-reinforced stairs, through the main floor reading room where two other women were packing their books and heading for the front door, past the sleepy security guard at the information desk, and into the cool night air. It was almost Halloween, and grotesquely carved lanterns could be seen in the windows of some dormitory rooms as she walked across the quadrangle to the coffee shop. Even before she entered, she noticed her MIS partner through the windows. He was troubleshooting the computer link at the coffee shop register.

"Don't you *ever* stop working?" she asked, though she knew the answer.

He shrugged without looking up from the tangled LAN wires that wrapped around the cash register and absorbed two phone lines in a twisted braid that disappeared into the cabinetry. "Good thing everyone appreciates tech support," he said, exhaling loudly as he finished the connection and tested the keyboard, which chimed like a credit card machine. Then he joined her with a Styrofoam cup in his hand.

"Don't *you* ever stop working?" he parodied, sliding into the seat across from her.

She didn't know him well, not even his last name, and she was fairly sure he was at least two years behind her, even more. His brown ponytail was held together by a single rubber band that had broken and been tied together; she commented that he was obviously familiar with the reuse of legacy materials. He laughed, though somewhat shyly, as if she had breached the boundary of their very new acquaintance by commenting on his appearance. She decided to reroute the conversation to their new ally in the project.

"He's not so bad, really," the man said. "He hates that I won't touch his precious typewriter, but he's pretty technical for someone from Lit."

Then she apologized. "I'm sorry, I realize I don't even know your last name."

"You can just call me Frank," he said, sounding suspicious.

"And how would I get a hold of you, call the college operator and ask her to be connected to Frank, just *Frank*?"

He stood slowly from the table when his pager vibrated on his waist, sipped the last sip from his cup, and said, yes, she could just ask for Frank.

"They'll find me, if you need me," he said with confident resignation. "They always find me."

There were 40 people at the meeting, although half of them were in the hallway on cell phones, responding to the latest crises. Esther tapped the microphone and asked everyone to take their seats while Frank worked with the Professor's laptop and the overhead display. Font problems.

A few more attendees came into the room, pausing at the table for bottles of water before taking their seats near the rear. Even when there are empty seats in the front row, students avoid sitting too close to the speaker out of fear, reinforced by too many years in classrooms, that they will be called on for the answer to an unanswerable question.

"As I explained in my group e-mail last night, we have a proposal to create working groups that would operate among our various schools. Yes, it's a research project and I think we'll come up with some remarkable stats, but today isn't about statistics. I think you're all here because you were hoping someone might be able to help with your overwhelming workloads."

Someone named Geoff in the back, wearing a black Led Zeppelin T-shirt from the 1977 World Tour, joked that he was *always* appreciative when someone offered to do his work for him. The woman next to him in a Stanford jacket tugged on the T-shirt, and the man sat down.

"To launch our project," Esther continued, "I'm very pleased to introduce Professor Ben Maimon from The University of San Francisco, the creator of The Labyrinth,[2] one of the university's most treasured projects . . . Professor?"

Esther stood away from the podium at the same moment that Frank completed his repair of font discrepancies, and the Professor's presentation appeared on the white wall behind them. Esther's shadow crossed his on the screen as they took seats in the very empty front row.

"Good morning, everyone," the Professor began.

Then he mumbled something about preferring his old Royal typewriter to his IBM Thinkpad, and one or two people laughed.

Frank nestled close to Esther and whispered that they wouldn't think it was funny if they were the ones who were called at 2 a.m. when the ribbon got tangled with his errant e key.

The Professor began.

"Did you know that atoms smashing into other atoms at the CERN[3] facilities in Europe produce patterns remarkably similar to the patterns made by the exchange of files on organizational networks?" It was his favorite ice-breaker.

The audience murmured an appropriate level of interest.

The Professor looked across the room at the startled expressions in the audience, and Paul noticed that the man was wearing mismatched socks. "Particles and waves and strings," the Professor added, "are the basic pieces of biological systems, and I think they have something to do with the systems all of you are managing."

"It seems to me that we, in the arts and sciences, need to change our understanding of structure and form. We'd rather build computers manually than struggle with the challenge of managing the more dynamic spirals as the structure interacts with the real world. Our ability to shift, to begin to manage complexity, is the broader challenge."

Esther looked at her watch.

9:20 a.m.

If the Professor was allowed to continue on his philosophical path, they would never have time for the rest of the agenda. Already, some in the audience were asking questions about his concept of a *unified theory of everything* on their networks. They were fascinated by the notion of gravitational forces in academic institutions, students and faculty as particles in collision, generating new particles in the form of published papers. Esther whispered to Frank that she would have to refocus the conversation, and Frank asked her to give the Professor 20 minutes.

"We need a faculty sponsor," he whispered, "and ours likes to talk theory."

"OK," she whispered in return, "ten more minutes. Ten, and then I cut him off."

What occurred in those ten minutes demonstrated for Esther, who had never attended one of the Professor's lectures, why his classes were always the first to be filled each semester. Some students took the same course again, without credit, because he never repeated the same syllabus or lecture exactly, and they found a repeat of his course more intriguing than most of the graduate courses on information and systems theory. As the Professor continued, she also noticed that the audience was enraptured by the cadence of his voice.

"Excuse me, Professor," one of the attendees said. She raised her hand from the back row. "Is your analogy best understood in relation to service-oriented architectures?"

"Go ahead," he said, encouraging the woman to continue.

She ignored the protests of her companion in the Led Zeppelin T-shirt and stood up to complete her question. "Well, it seems to me that what you are saying demonstrates the complexity of the systems that the business world will present when we graduate."

"Alas, my young friend, do not be fooled," the Professor said, paging down to a PowerPoint slide of a service-oriented architecture from The Actional Corporation (see Exhibit 6.1).[4]

"This is what you have in store for you, upon graduation. Very complex issues, layers of interrelated systems, and executives who simply will not understand that complexity. You will all be very busy with employment after graduation, with little time to think creatively. If you do not give yourselves time to think creatively now," he said, "you will not have the time when you enter the workforce, despite what your new boss promises, because most of you will still be doing tech support in large companies, and you will be tackling an infinite list of complex problems. You simply won't have the time to innovate unless you find a different way to work . . ."

Esther recognized the opportunity, stood up, and faced the audience.

"*Time* is the reason we are here today," she announced. "We would all like a few hours each week to work on something interesting, but none of

EXHIBIT 6.1   *Service-Oriented Architecture: Simple and Complex*

These requirements can all be encapsulated through abstraction, an absolute requirement for all SOA environments. Architects and analysts have varying names for this requirement, including service virtualization, service facades and service views. Through the use of an SOA-Ready abstraction layer, common infrastructure elements can be shared across all services resulting in reusable services that are simpler to manage and built for change.

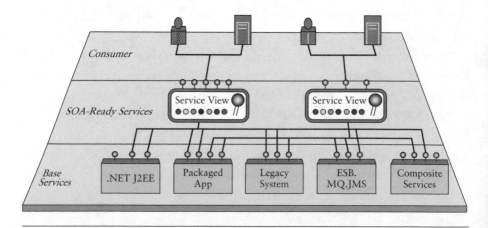

us can find it, correct? However, if we employed some load-balancing, if we pooled our technical support teams to help each other, my guess is that we could each find two to three hours a week for what the Professor calls the creative thinking . . . If you multiplied that productivity. . ."

Before she continued, the debate was on, a rapid dialogue initiated by the nay-sayers, who complained, of course, about politics in their universities.

Too many password problems.

Too many permissions to be obtained.

Too many password problems.

Too many intellectual property constraints.

Too many password problems.

Too many heterogeneous environments.

The room was filled with "too manys," the sudden hesitation of workers who were simply afraid to try something out of the ordinary because of the risks imposed by governance committees, college policy boards, and faculty guidelines that protected unpublished work from reaching broader audiences. The validity of the idea was being pushed aside by the litany of reasons why the status quo could not or should not be challenged.

Frank waited until the right moment.

He had been noticing lately that groups of people behaved much like the old pulse systems for telephones, wherein surges prevented new calls from being initiated, and that the only way to manage a pulse system in the face of faster communications devices was to employ what Frank called the "Comma Comma Space" insertion in the dialing processes. He paused until the exact moment when the surge seemed to dissipate before he offered a suggestion.

"Professor," Frank asked loudly, "I'd like to suggest a pilot program, with only two schools involved. We can monitor the pilot, and if the results are successful, then we can try to take on these more complicated issues, one at a time."

"Yes, Frank," the Professor nodded, "that's the right approach, and you've just volunteered *your* school and *your* time. Does anyone have a suggestion for the actual focus for such a prototype?"

The murmurings surged again, each MIS team proposing their own crisis as the one that most deserved attention. One team had eLearning platforms to be built without any budget for applications, another proposed joint negotiations to lower the cost of Cisco routers, and a third proposed Directory Services for information dissemination between institutions. Esther was writing them down as fast as they were being suggested, but none of them had the necessary element she sought for the first pilot: high probability of success.

Finally, a young man in the far corner introduced himself.

His name was Paul Michaelson. He apologetically explained that he was not from academia but worked in a San Francisco brokerage firm and had received the broadcast message because he was on the alumni tech support alias from his school in Sacramento. He explained that the major financial institutions often faced this issue as they constantly sought to experiment with emerging technologies while also working to maintain the viability of their production systems. He further explained that he had worked on a similar cross-institutional pilot for three firms that were merging but had not yet completed the reorganization and therefore were constrained by various rules of engagement and Securities and Exchange Commission guidelines from actively combining forces.

"We stumbled across a problem that all three firms were experiencing," Paul said, "and that one pilot project drove such a high degree of ROI that the executives demanded we continue the collaboration efforts."

"Excuse me," the Professor interrupted. "ROI?"

Esther smiled at the obvious turn, roles reversing in an exchange of domain knowledge. Paul explained "Return On Investment" and then suggested that the room consider Disaster Recovery as their first experiment.

"This is what we learned," he said. "First, none of us had sufficient budget to truly back up all our data offsite. All of us had enough disk space to copy our own files onto our own second servers, which addressed High Availability but did not resolve Disaster Recovery. If the power grid blinks, it blinks for our entire data center, so we need archives in other geographies."

Frank had already guessed what the fellow from Wall Street was going to say, and he liked the idea immensely. He leaned over and told Esther that this was the one and that she needed to get the Professor's immediate endorsement before adjourning the meeting.

Paul continued. "What we decided to do was provide cross-institutional backup of everything except the most proprietary information. Yes, there are intellectual property issues. You think your faculty has issues with sharing research, you should see what an Equity Fund manager thinks about his latest investment research being leaked to our competitors. The impact could be in the billions in lost revenue."

Even the Professor was impressed by the numbers, far beyond university finances, even the largest universities with substantial trust accounts.

"So we used each other for backup," Paul concluded, hands gesturing for emphasis. "There was a rotational and nightly schedule, with scripts for most of the work, and everyone provided Unix and Oracle support for each other, which allowed us to accomplish the first phase of Disaster Recovery requirements—think of it, complete failover and recovery, without a single additional dollar being spent for new systems."

He shrugged, and apologized for the interruption. "Anyway, I thought it might be an idea for you to consider."

He took his seat as his Blackberry asked for attention.

Earlier that morning, Paul's Blackberry had vibrated with a message from his own Unix administrator with the news that the primary mail server for the company had been hit by a Trojan Horse and needed to be disinfected, patched, and rebooted. Downtime for company e-mail would be approximately two hours, but they could not send out a warning message for fear of spreading the malware. Paul responded with a reminder to queue all incoming and outgoing messages, so that nothing would be lost during the downtime, and had cc'd Deanna so she was aware of the crisis in case her SAP project was in a "critical path" juncture. Then he sent a private e-mail to his Unix team, suggesting a voicemail message announcing the downtime.

He could have gone back to work. The trains ran every 15 minutes, but he had wanted to hear Esther's ideas about sharing resources, so he had clipped his Blackberry back into the plastic holster on his belt, stopped for a Starbuck's latte, and arrived at the university meeting just as the Professor was thanking everyone for attending on short notice.

"Did you know that atoms smashing into other atoms at the CERN facilities in Europe produce patterns remarkably similar to the patterns made by the exchange of files on organizational networks?"

"I am inclined toward commonalities between disciplines," the Professor was saying. "A truth that applies to both gardening and archery, a truth that applies to humans and to systems. In this case, we are creating a community, and it occurs to me that this new community of people is not unlike the new community of servers you propose to study."

From the Professor's Notebook (1990):

> Laid by one thousand bricklayers, mosaic patterns interwoven in complex combinations, alignments, intersections,

> the original Story Road lies underneath modern pavement outside this office, old roadways constructed of bricks in perpendicular dimensions and different objectives,

> similar patterns of lines and squares, each brick positioned to form a framework joined with mortar by the skill of the architects and masonry specialists,

> 100 years before such patterns were discovered, in similar construct and design in Inca homes and Leningrad plazas, in Roman fountains & the Watts Towers,

> the interconnectedness of all things becoming real in the hands of bricklayers, now a lost skill, this world having long since moved beyond such alignments,

> patterns formed over centuries, cultures, geographies, and disciplines, repeated patterns that are most notable for what they tell us about ourselves.

Esther was stunned, simply stunned, by the wildfire success of the prototype. Within days, the first two schools had completed a full backup of each other's primary databases. Within weeks, six additional schools were added to the matrix, and by the end of exams in December, 18 universities and colleges were participating in their program.

She completed the diagram (see Exhibit 6.2)[5] and bundled herself up for the long walk to the Professor's office.

"Few of us plan for unpredictable success," the Professor told her on the coldest day of the year, as she was completing the Discussion section of her thesis. She had come to his office to show him her list of Open Issues, which he had read thoroughly before she finished removing the coat, scarf, and two sweaters that she'd layered for the walk across the Quad.

"The bloggers have been very helpful in documenting our processes and listing issues," she explained, "and there hasn't been one single problem with downtime. We've also been contacted by the Southeastern Universities Research Association (SURA),[6] a group of institutions in the southeast using Internet3 as the backbone." She gave him the crisscross diagram (see Exhibit 6.2).

"Teilhard de Chardin," he said.

"Excuse me, Professor?"

"Christian mystic and philosopher, early 1900s. He had a theory called the Noosphere, in which the spirits of all beings would be connected in an entity that would mirror the mind of God. Our criss-cross looks like his Noosphere, to me. John Perry Barlow wrote an essay in the early 1990s on Chardin and the Internet.[7] I have it here, somewhere . . ."

EXHIBIT 6.2 *Community of Communities*

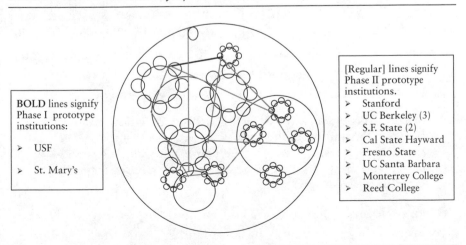

BOLD lines signify Phase I prototype institutions:

➤ USF

➤ St. Mary's

[Regular] lines signify Phase II prototype institutions.
➤ Stanford
➤ UC Berkeley (3)
➤ S.F. State (2)
➤ Cal State Hayward
➤ Fresno State
➤ UC Santa Barbara
➤ Monterrey College
➤ Reed College

Source: Maggie Law, "The KM Conundrum," KMERA Corporation, 2004.

He realized that Esther did not appreciate the symbolism or the bibliographical assistance, so he tried a more subtle form of guidance, something to soothe her obvious anxieties about starting something that had grown too large to manage. He explained that Complexity Theory requires a different approach, at all levels, and the apparently chaotic nature of constituent parts isn't a lack of organization, merely a type of organization unsuited to standard management theory.

"Someone once said it was akin to flocks of geese in flight," the Professor said with the most soothing voice his aged vocal cords could muster at the end of a long day. "Any specific goose need only follow the basic rules: don't bump into anything, keep up with everyone, and stay in close proximity to the formation."[8]

Esther finished shedding the outer layers of clothing and sat down at the edge of the same chair she always chose when she came to his office, arms folded tightly, as if she were hugging herself for comfort.

"This makes you nervous, doesn't it?" he asked.

"Yes, Professor." She was quiet, as if asking permission to speak the unspeakable.

"Spit it out, woman," he said boisterously. "God, you've single-handedly solved a major business problem for 18 institutions of higher learning, written a thesis that deserves broad acclaim, and you look like one of the engineers before the Shuttle disaster."

The office was completely silent. She stared at his Royal typewriter.

Finally, she pointed to the last item in her open issues list and asked whether he had clarified it specifically with the Faculty Committee. She did not want a political problem to occur in the final days before she presented her thesis to her Committee, and she also knew that the Professor was not well known for his exceptional communication with his colleagues.

> Item 12: Proprietary research for Institution A now resides on servers in Institution B. Proprietary research for Institution B now resides on servers in Institution C. This is not well understood by the institutions, beyond the IT organizations that have designed and maintained the matrix.

"No, my dear," the Professor said humbly. "I prefer to ask for forgiveness and make innovative progress, rather than to ask for permission and wait forever for the paralytic bureaucracy to prevent that innovation. Didn't that finance fellow say they had the same problem?" the Professor asked. "*They* developed guidelines and received approvals. *We* did *not*. They tested their systems before, using actual corporate research, but we're using real intellectual property from each of the participating schools. If *your* department chair learns that *his* own research now resides . . . let me see, on University of Illinois servers, he might have some concerns, don't you *think*?"

The Professor enjoyed the idea that his Dean would be undone by this knowledge and, for a moment, toyed with the idea of phoning him from the office, just to hear the man's reaction. But he liked Esther, and she was not protected by tenure. She was as nervous as a seer on the verge of an unfriendly visitation.

"You expect us to be hacked, don't you?"

"Yes."

"Well," he said, leaning back in his creaking chair, clasping his hands behind his head, and thinking out loud, a sure sign of his trust in her, though she had no way of knowing so.

". . . There are two approaches to the problem, both eminently available to us, it seems to me. The first is to attack before we are attacked—I don't mean to hack our own systems, I mean to publish our success and receive such excellent recognition that the Faculty will, in their infinite egos, want to take full credit for the success, thereby limiting our political risk. For this, I am sure that SIM (that's the Society for Information Management) would be very glad to consider your thesis in their next competition. An award is always good in politically murky times, don't you think?"

Esther recognized the tactic, and she was also flattered by the Professor's suggestion that her paper could possibly win a SIM Technical Paper competition. "You said there were two approaches . . ."

"Ah yes," the Professor said. He liked Esther. He wished he were younger. "The second approach is to get ourselves a damned good security geek and have him . . . or her . . . audit the crisscross and put some extra layers of security in before hackers force us to do it."

"Do you know anyone?"

The Professor agreed to make some calls. He hoped she was reassured by their meeting. He leaned forward and wrote himself a note to call his venture capital friend in Palo Alto to ask for a reference, and he put the note atop his Royal typewriter, standing at attention like a little soldier, guardian of memory.

She was right. This was a train wreck waiting to happen.

As he always did, when presented with contradictions, the Professor went home and had a drink, a tall crystal tumbler filled with ice and good whiskey that warmed his mind, all the way to his fingertips, fuel of his digital engine, elixir of his muse.

Then he turned to his typewriter.

NOTES

1. Beginning as an online writing experiment, the Professor wrote a short story about a family who lived in a small Midwestern town suffering from economic recession and racial conflict. He then invited students to select a character or building or event and link the original passage to one of their own stories. In theory, the reader would decide which plot line to follow, depending on which links they chose to read and in what order they chose to read them. The Labyrinth became an annual assignment, accumulating hundreds of nested (interrelated) fictions and remains an active online journal that currently occupies 400 megabytes of text on university servers.

2. The Labyrinth became a topic of academic interest in the mid-1990s when one of the school's doctoral candidates noted that the complex of random relationships of independent writers linked over decades was a pure example of Social Network Analysis manifested in networked fiction.

3. "CERN is the European Organization for Nuclear Research, the world's largest particle physics centre. Here physicists come to explore what matter is made of and what forces hold it together." www.cern.ch.

4. "Critical Infrastructure for a Service-Oriented Architecture," Actional Corporation, 2004.

5. Maggie Law, "Community of Communities," The KM Conundrum. KMERA Corporation, 2002.

6. Southeastern Universities Research Association and SuraNet, www.sura.com.

7. John Perry Barlow, "The Great Work," Association of Computing Machinery, *Communications*, January 1992.

8. Megan Santosus, "Simple yet Complex," *CIO*, April 15, 1998.

CHAPTER 7

DISTRIBUTED RESOURCES

"Jonathan, are you even listening to what I am saying?"
Whenever she asked her husband that question (at least a dozen times during the past year) he always offered a sincere response. If he had been completely honest, however, he would have confessed that endless stories of dying e-mail servers and minor corporate intrigues were simply not very interesting to him.

Yes, they loved each other, but they didn't understand each other's work. They feigned interest whenever they talked about their jobs at dinner. Gillian nodded politely when he talked about his students, and Jonathan struggled to remember the key differences between NT and Unix, or between IT as a "cost center" and IT as a "core competency," though she had explained the terms to him many times before.

"Not listening doesn't mean not caring," he said, wincing even as he said it because it sounded like something from *Psychology Today*.

Jonathan always knew when Gillian was angry, because she became immediately quiet, not just wordless but entirely soundless, with not a single clink of silverware as she cleared her plates from the table and noiselessly moved away from him. Jonathan knew how the rest of the evening would unfold: she would bury herself in work until 2 a.m., and he would fall asleep waiting for her to come to bed, Bill Clinton's autobiography splayed across his chest.

Her term for this uncomfortable evening ritual was their "standalone mode." Sometimes it lasted for several days, the two of them living together but behaving as if they were completely independent of one another, not married, not struggling with their parents' illnesses, and not thinking about having children and the impact of that decision on their careers.

On many such evenings, Jonathan retreated into his solitary corner of their home with few regrets. He, too, had a great deal of work and never enough time to do it all; he, too, needed more time to think through some particularly difficult faculty meetings scheduled for the following day. But on that night, as she noiselessly closed the upstairs office door, he regretted his inattentive response. He had just returned from a three-day conference in New York and he wanted to talk to his wife about it; also, he knew she'd just been given a new project, and he wanted to hear more about it.

Melting ice cubes chimed in his water glass. Their staccato song was the only sound in their house.

The engineers at CERN[1] study massive amounts of data generated from atoms smashed in their Large Hadron Collider, and the types of software being used at their facility involve some of the most complex programming in the world. This is where the World Wide Web was born, out of necessity, to enable scientists around the world to study the origins of the universe.

One particularly unique example of this programming is based on the notion that atoms are objects, monitored by their systems. The CERN researchers soon realized that files on networks can also be considered objects. By running their complex algorithms against various lists of information transfers (e.g., departmental e-mail and FTP logs), they have been able to generate graphs of the information flow within and between their departments (see Exhibit 7.1).

Gillian Meachum first learned about these visual maps of information transfer when she was still an undergraduate at the University of California, Berkeley. She was so fascinated by the notion of information mapping that, in 1995, she returned to UC Berkeley's School for Information Management Systems and extended this notion as the topic of her graduate thesis. Gillian's theory proposed that the flow of freely distributed information follows certain specific patterns, regardless of the

EXHIBIT 7.1 *Information Mapping: Results Sample from Kronodoc Oy*

Communication Matrix													
partners	1.	2.	3.	4.	5.	6.	7.	8.	9.	10.	11.	12.	13.
1. mikko — 2													
2. tku — 4													
3. et — 2													
4. ilona — 2													
5. marko — 3													
6. mikael — 5													
7. judit — 8													
8. kaisa — 9													
9. rainer — 9													
10. sami — 6													
11. krono — 4													
12. fuki — 3													
13. juhaot — 1													

The shaded areas indicate the intensity of communication between individuals. Similar displays can be drawn for any group, or interactions between groups, providing visual cues for areas of priority or neglect.

Source: www.kronodoc.fi

media or nature of the content. She believed that the patterns would be similar, based not on content, but on the social navigations of the individuals exchanging the content, over time.

Every other student in her class yearned to jump into the New Economy. They wanted to join startup technology companies, raise millions of dollars in venture capital, and become multimillionaires when their young Internet companies went public. More than a few did so, although many others were left with collections of worthless stock option certificates useful now as wallpaper, or drawing sheets for their children.

Gillian was the only one in the entire graduating class who had a different dream.

Since the second day of her Internet Programming class, while everyone else was aiming to build the next "killer application," Gillian had been fascinated with information itself, its behavior on the network, and how it flows between us. In the library that day, unable to locate a copy of *The Beginner's Guide to Visual Basic*, and waiting for someone to return the book to the stacks, she stumbled across Dr. Carol Brown's 1993 study of successful Chief Information Officers (CIOs).[2] This article put her on a course that would later make her the first woman CIO in her firm.

In those days, the role of CIO seemed a perfect blend of business and technology: this person was the gatekeeper of information in an information economy. Of course, at that point she could not have learned two lessons that her future would offer: first, that CIOs are, by all accounts, members of a troubled and unappreciated profession, the last to be consulted by their management and the first to be blamed when something went awry; and second, that in times of crisis, what matters most is not only what you know, but who you know, and whether they will remember you, when the time comes.

CIOs want to be architects and visionaries, but their fellow executives treat them like plumbers. They want to be the gatekeepers of information in an information economy, but they rarely are noticed until a compute problem affects corporate revenue streams. Although they might understand their industry, they are usually excluded from critical business meetings. Never consulted, always blamed.

At the end of each day, the only truth about her job was the sign posted on the door of her office: We are not to blame, we are here to serve.

However, her UC Berkeley internship—more than her training in Visual Basic—provided the inadvertent foundation for her later success. The graduating class was in a flurry to find good positions. Gillian was accepted by Stefan Bricknell, an alumnus of the university (he had completed his MBA at the Haas School of Business) to complete her thesis while working on IT operations for his investment firm in San Francisco.

She often thought about her first day as an intern, when he casually inquired about her thesis topic, and she explained her theory of information distribution patterns, independent of their content or mechanism.

"You're suggesting that there is an underlying principle that guides the flow of information," Bricknell said thoughtfully.

She drew her basic information theory on a Post-It, indicating the commonalities, intersections, diffusions.

Years later, Bricknell credited Gillian's concept for his own development of commercial exchange patterns, applying her notion of information flow in society to his specialty, commerce, with fluctuations in currency and market directions driven, not by the standard factors, but by an underlying principle of flow, independent of the medium. Stefan had become very successful over the years, and Gillian often recalled his declaration that he "owed her a favor." It was a favor she would eventually collect.

Gillian was eventually recruited to run the worldwide IT division at Perkins Global Partners, and her first 18 months as their CIO were filled with the standard operational and managerial issues that confront an incoming executive: undoing the mess left by her predecessor, in this case a little Mussolini who governed by loud proclamation and delivered little, undermining morale and eventually the quality of the division's work. As a result, few in the company took the role of CIO seriously, nor did they believe her organization offered anything of substance.

With the success of her recent SAP project for one of Perkins' strategic accounts, she was able to get approval for a "Phase 0" investigation of New Computing Trends, and her case study concerned the use of Shared Memory to reduce latency and improve overall performance in a major Enterprise Resource Planning (ERP) project. It quickly became the most intriguing project she had encountered since her student days.

That night, the folder of draft concepts for her presentation was open on her desk and her attention was pulled to a circled topic inside:

> In most cases today, a distributed computing architecture consists of very lightweight software agents installed on a number of client systems, and one or more dedicated distributed computing management servers. There may also be requesting clients with software that allows them to submit jobs along with lists of their required resources.

> An agent running on a processing client detects when the system is idle, notifies the management server that the system is available for processing, and usually requests an application package. The client then receives an application package from the server and runs the software when it has spare CPU cycles, and sends the results back to the server. The application may run as a screen saver, or simply in the background, without impacting normal use of the computer. If the user of the client system needs to run his own applications at any time, control is immediately returned.[3]

Gillian was disappointed that she hadn't been able to explain the new project to Jonathan. When he wasn't being a complete jerk, he usually had some smart things to say. But she knew there would be plenty of time to talk over the weekend—they were driving north to visit his father, who had just been moved to another nursing home—and besides, she was still too mad at him to break out of "stand-alone mode" just yet.

She looked through her folder for a better definition of distributed systems, realizing there was a difference between distributed *computing*, as a term, and distributed *systems*.

> A distributed computing system consists of multiple autonomous processors that do not share primary memory, but cooperate by sending messages over a communications network. Each processor in such a system executes its own instruction stream(s) and uses its own local data, both stored in its local memory. Occasionally, processors may need to exchange data; they do so by sending messages to each other over a network.[4]

Gillian thought the author's definition was overly simplistic but still not accessible. Indeed, a reader with little technical background might simply skim the section and move on to the next without due consideration. She returned the document to her research folder because it might have some later value. Her objective was not merely to simplify the topic of shared memory, but rather to find a series of thoughtful analogies that could adequately portray the complex issues of distributed resources for a nontechnical audience: her executive team. As with her thesis a decade before, she was convinced there was a better way to portray the role of information technology.

That night, she had resisted the impulse to check her e-mail for almost an hour. She knew well that, once she began reading and attending to her messages, she would never return to her project or get any sleep. Finally, before turning off the lights in the office, she connected to the company's network and scanned her list of unread messages. Among the dozen e-mails about various projects was an urgent one from a major Perkins client.

The client, InsuranceAmerica, was just completing the last phase of a massive SAP migration in North Carolina: four regional banks converting from independent status, custom data stores to one common architecture, and a single global master. The project, completed after 11 months, had cost $12 million and involved 40 Perkins employees, including the construction of an entirely new data center in Raleigh.

She hoped something hadn't gone wrong with their final audit, because Perkins was depending on the same client for additional work in the coming fiscal quarters.

> **From:** Deanna Gladstone [mailto: gladstoned@InsAmerica.com]
> **Sent:** Monday, October 6, 20X4 5:10 PM
> **To:** gmeachum@perkinsglobal.com
> **Subject:** URGENT: Budget cuts

Gillian re-read her client's e-mail subject line and immediately understood the coming storm. Her own financial projections for the next six months were braided with Deanna's plans, and if her budget was being cut, Gillian's numbers for the remainder of the fiscal year would be wrong. She also knew that it was already 2:30 a.m., she was too tired to respond with clarity, and she had an early morning staff meeting. She made an "executive decision" to read Deanna's message when she arrived in her office, with a clearer head and, hopefully, a better sense of her alternatives.

> If the server doesn't hear from a processing client for a certain period of time, possibly because the user has disconnected his system and gone on a business trip, or simply because he's using his system heavily for long periods, it may send the same application package to another idle system.[5]

By the time she climbed into bed beside Jonathan, it was almost 3 a.m., and she was already worried about the following day. She kissed her husband on the top of the head, as she did every night when she came to bed late, and again every morning, when she left the house before he woke.

Their dinner table argument, with all its related complications, would just have to wait.

The Managing Partner of PerkinsUSA headquarters was already waiting when she walked into her office at 8:15 a.m.

"Okay, Ted," she said to him as she unloaded her briefcase. "Tell me the bad news."

Theodore Brankowitz only came to regional offices when something urgent was in the works. He had a reputation throughout the industry for taking the most difficult assignments in their company, and she had heard about him long before she came to Perkins. In fact, her former employer at USA Financial had warned her about him when she was recruited by Perkins two years before. "Call me if you ever get a visit from Brankowitz," he had said to her, "and I'll be glad to give you your old job back."

The man was a dark legend.

"Tell me what you know about InsuranceAmerica," he said in a tone of voice that would give most midlevel managers the shivers. Gillian didn't flinch, although she was surprised that the news had traveled so fast. This meant that word had already come across the morning investment wire. Brankowitz was in her office for damage control.

"Oh, *that*," she said, pretending to be relieved. ". . . I've already drafted a plan to respond to their current situation. Every client claims to have budget problems, at one point or another."

The man did not smile, or even change his facial expression. He tapped his finger on a photocopy of the morning's news, from MSN's financial pages.

3000 Laid Off at Second Largest Insurance House

October 9, Raleigh NC: While the Republican administration continues to laud improvements in job numbers, large companies around the nation are eliminating white-collar jobs in record numbers. The latest is InsuranceAmerica, the country's second largest insurance carrier, which announced this evening, after The Bell, that 3000 positions would be eliminated by the end of the year with the goal of improving operational margins. While cuts will be across the board, a company spokesperson disclosed, the largest portion will be in operational staff, technology, and administration, not in direct customer service.

Gillian didn't need to read any more. She leaned across the table and asked Ted if there was something specific he was seeking from her.

"This is one of our core accounts, Gillian," he said calmly. "Therefore, I presume that you will have very specific actions in your *plan*." He emphasized the word *plan* with harmonic misgivings. "Three areas of concern: first, I need you to verify that they will be able to pay all outstanding invoices. Second, I will need a complete list of your Reduction in Force—90 staff is my estimate, but I will leave the specific number to you."

Gillian held up her hand and counted to herself. Either she had missed one of his stated concerns, or he was intentionally game playing. "And the third, Ted?"

"Pardon me?"

"You said you had three concerns, and I believe you only mentioned two: their invoices, and proposed layoffs."

"Of course," he said, pretending to be amused that she was actually counting. "The third is *your* reduced projections for your year-end numbers. We believe you will need to reduce your overall capital expenditures for the remainder of the year, substantially reduce them, I'm sorry to say. Whether this means shutting down some of our facilities is something you will have to decide. We will want to see your complete revised budget, given the 50% reduction in staffing and CapEx."

He excused himself from the table, pausing at the office door to say, ". . . and yes, tomorrow will be fine."

Gillian was impressed by the man's understated capacity to instill alarm in a matter of moments. Ninety positions eliminated, and $2 million removed from her annual budget. He had done the math and already drawn his conclusions. She also recognized that he had given her less than 90 minutes to come up with an alternative because the topic would surely be raised in that morning's Executive Staff meeting. By telling her she needn't provide her plan until the following day, he was preparing the stage to pose an unanswerable question in the meeting and then offer his conclusions without debate.

8: 15 a.m.

Jonathan was reading Gillian's Good Morning Post-It, stuck to the coffee machine, and already worrying about his father at the new nursing home. At the very moment he was wondering whether he should call to check, Gillian was moving at corporate speed of light.

She adjusted her ad hoc presentation, no longer on the topic of Shared Memory, while simultaneously completing phone calls to Accounting and Human Resources. Then, as she sifted through her research for the best way to explain the unexplainable, she phoned Stefan Bricknell, her old friend and Wall Street mentor with the legendary connections and remarkable insight. He owed her a favor from her intern days, if he still remembered her exceptional work for him. She thumbed again through her research folder, hoping to find an elegant quote to use at the beginning of her presentation, but the sections she had so far outlined were too technical for her executive team.

> Each process repeatedly takes some work from the data structure, performs it, puts back the results into the data structure, and possibly generates some more work. All workers essentially perform the same kind of task, until all work is done. The workers are loosely coupled; they only interact indirectly through the data structure.[6]

A sign on her door told everyone that she was only to be disturbed for matters of Life or Death, and only then if the Death was revenue related. Unfortunately, there wasn't a filter for incoming phone calls. When her phone rang, Gillian assumed it was Accounting and answered it without checking the caller's extension.

"You've got to get me *out of here*, Jonny," the voice said between sobs.

Her father-in-law at the nursing home had been cursing away at the morning nurse while refusing to take his medication and then tearfully demanding to speak to his son. He had dialed Gillian's office phone by mistake.

"Mort, is that *you*?" Gillian asked.

"Who is *this*?"

"You called me at work, Mort," Gillian said, stopping her keystrokes long enough to wish there was a time-machine that could transport her back 30 seconds, to the moment when she took the call. "Mort, did you try Jonathan at home?"

"Get off the goddamn phone, witch, and give me my son!" the old man barked. At least he had stopped crying long enough to insult her.

Gillian was already dialing her husband on her cellphone as his father continued to complain how she always got in the way. Always.

Thankfully, Jonathan picked up their home extension and seemed awake enough to understand the urgent situation. She stayed on the line until he had reached the nursing station before she flipped her cellphone shut. In years past, the old man would have been enraged that she had hung up on him but his Alzheimer's was just advanced enough to ensure that he would forget the incident by the time they visited him on Saturday morning.

Chaos continued for the next 45 minutes: Accounting was not able to verify the contractual viability of Account 1944567. They promised to investigate further, to provide a schedule of payments and receivables.

Gillian's worn-out brown briefcase slumped by her feet like a tired puppy. In a moment of sudden insight, Gillian realized that the document she sought was an online journal, not in her research folder or the briefcase. She turned back to her desktop and searched for the .jpg image she could use for her executive staff.

8:45 a.m.

Gillian added the final slides to her presentation. As she sent the presentation to Sherry's printer, she checked her Palm Pilot and impulsively dialed Stefan Bricknell's direct number in Manhattan. Surprisingly, instead of his voicemail, Stefan answered the phone.

"Gillian Meachum?!!" he exclaimed when she shyly introduced herself, unsure of his recollection. "Of course, I remember you. Remember you? Christ, I still get requests to explain that little concept of yours."

"Thank you, Stefan," she said, "I'm flattered." She looked at her watch, and she knew she did not have time for a lengthy digression through memory lane, although on any other day, this one morsel could have become an entire meal. "Listen, I have a hurried request, and I'm headed into a meeting, so . . ."

"I still owe you that favor," he said quickly. "Tell me what I can do."

Gillian hastily explained her InsuranceAmerica idea, wondering aloud whether he might have any insights into the company or whether he could introduce her to someone who had. She admitted that her proposal was 90% intuition and only 10% statistically viable. In five minutes, she was scheduled to meet with her executive team, and she was just about to suggest a second phone call when Stefan interrupted her.

"Gillian, Gillian, Gillian," he said with a balanced mixture of admonition and respect. "I long ago learned to trust your intuitions. And I can do more than an introduction, I'm glad to say. IA's new Chief Operating Officer is actually a very good friend of mine. I had lunch with him yesterday, just an hour before they made their announcement, so unless there's a conflict of interest, I can help. What did you have in mind?"

Gillian spent the next three minutes explaining her proposal further. Stefan promised to send a return message as soon as possible. She thanked him, apologized for the hurried conversation, and was out the door with minutes to spare, reminding Sherry to forward any messages from Wall Street directly via e-mail to her cellphone.

She began the long walk to the elevators, and the Executive Conference Room on the top floor.

Fourteen blue leather chairs circled the long conference table. Gillian looked at the printed agenda positioned on the table beside her bottle of Crystal Geyser. Her original presentation on "Best Practices in the Distribution of Resources" was Item Four. The room itself was still empty and she glanced from side to side, taking a moment to observe the room's elegance: a Jackson Pollack painting covered one entire wall, directly opposite a row of tinted windows that looked out over the whole city. On the rooftop of an adjacent office building, several floors below, toddlers played on a multicolored playground as two daycare staff blew bubbles, to their obvious delight.

"We're all looking forward to your presentation, Gillian," Ted Brankowitz said when he entered the room. "What's the title?"

Her cellphone vibrated. "You'll have to wait with everyone else, Ted," she said casually as she read the text-based message on the tiny phone screen.

When she closed the phone, Gillian looked out the conference room windows again with a quiet exhilaration, breathless although careful not to appear so, amazed at the sudden turn of events. Thanks to her friend on Wall Street with his truly remarkable connections, she was coming into the Meeting of Meetings with enough ammunition for her return volley to the expected attack.

Sometimes, she even impressed herself, pulling rabbits out of hats, coins from ears, red scarves from thin air. But she crossed her fingers, just in case.

The senior partner and CEO called the meeting to order, and the first 20 minutes were consumed by various issues concerning the opening of their new Pacific Rim offices. She was relieved to hear her boss's voice on the other end of the teleconference phone. They hadn't seen each other for two weeks, and there had been no time to update him on her new proposal.

There was a brief discussion on the status of the new data center in Singapore and additional staffing costs that had been successfully negotiated under budget. As the others reviewed projected costs associated with the new initiative, Gillian quietly looked over the files Sherry had printed for her, moments before the meeting began. She knew that firms such as IBM Global Services and Hewlett-Packard's Technology Consulting teams were poised to benefit from the pending transformation in technology. Perkins Global could benefit also, if they had the courage to leap beyond conservatism and champion her rearchitecture.

"Gillian?" Brankowitz asked.

"Yes, Ted?"

"I believe you have the floor." he said quietly, adding, "I know it isn't your topic, but I was hoping you might have some numbers for us today, given the news about our largest account."

She simply smiled, saying nothing, and connected her laptop to the overhead projector, greeting each of the partners by name as she waited for the desktop image to resolve on the large white screen at one end of the room. Function 7.

Gillian was the only woman in the room. It seemed she was always the only woman in the room.

"Gentlemen, I must apologize," she began. "My original topic, as you can see on the agenda, was to explain briefly Shared Memory and Distributed Resources, based on our experience at InsuranceAmerica, our region's largest client. By now, you have all read their disquieting news, so I thought I might substitute a broader topic and postpone our discussion on architecture for a later meeting."

There was no objection, so she continued. "As you know, that account has been credited with 30% of our revenue for the past three quarters and is currently projected to continue at that rate for the next 24 to 48 months. Obviously, any shift in their financial viability would, at first glance, be a cause of great concern to Perkins."

She looked directly at Brankowitz, who suddenly leaned forward in his chair. "First glance, Gillian?"

Rather than responding to him, she continued with her opening remarks.

"I have been asked to present our revised numbers, and while they aren't formally due until tomorrow, I thought it would be prudent to present them today, in response to this morning's announcement from InsuranceAmerica that they are reducing their operational expenses, including a substantial downsizing of their IT function."

She paused, in part because her next statement was bound to trigger alarm and in part because her throat was thoroughly parched. She always got a case of dry mouth when she spoke publicly, and she sipped from her bottle of water before continuing. A bit of water dripped onto her blouse, but she did not look down.

"I have reviewed our projections, factoring in a worse-case scenario from the client. Here is what I believe: We can actually *increase* our revenues from InsuranceAmerica," she said, pausing to look toward the screen, "upward to 40% in the next quarter, and continuing at that level through the first two quarters of 2006."

Ted Brankowitz lept as if catapulted from his chair and walked to the screen, his silhouette darkening most of the diagram as he pointed to the figure she had chosen only ten minutes before the meeting started. "How can you project *this* level of revenue when they are *cutting* their budget? Surely, this is a joke. Is this a joke, Gillian?"

One of the men nearest to him joked that it was *his* shadow projected across 2006, not the InsuranceAmerica problem.

"If you would take your seat, Ted, I will explain."

"*Please* do," he said, with his familiarly harmonic disbelief. "I'm sure we're all interested in learning some *voodoo* economics from the IT division."

Gillian first explained that they were on the cusp of another transformation in technology, equivalent to the Internet in its impact on how large institutions would solve the paradox of the need for *increased* computing capability and *decreased* cost. The challenge is not new, she said, we are always being asked to do More with Less.

"However, the sophistication of the networks, storage, and commodity server prices are now factors that make this paradox more than an exercise in efficiency. We are not talking about simple productivity improvements," Gillian explained, "but rather a radical departure from rigid and expensive architectures to an environment that will improve the *agility* of the enterprise."

"Agility," the voice said from the phone console. "Good term. Can you explain?"

"Actually, Robert," she said, hoping he would hear the affectionate tone in her voice, "our friends at Credit Suisse were the first to use the term agility in connection with their IT initiatives."[7]

The room was suddenly quiet, as they all began to realize that she was serious about her projections, serious about her willingness to propose an alternative to the Brankowitz model of reducing costs and managing margins.

"We are at a very unusual intersection of two very distinct trends in technology services, gentlemen," she said, stepping away from the table and circling behind the senior partners. "The confluence of these two trends is beyond the capacity of companies such as InsuranceAmerica. Indeed, it's beyond the reach of most of our financial clients, and therefore it offers a significant opportunity for Perkins. The first trend is the New Distributed Computing model. Compute centers around the globe are processing at a much higher rate of speed and reliability—and at a fraction of the cost. As you can see from our modest architectural design, I believe we can increase our compute capacity, perhaps by as much as 500%, without a single dollar in additional capital outlay. This involves the transition to commodity WinTel servers from our current Unix infrastructure and the implementation of Linux clusters in distributed fashion.

"The second trend, which we have previously discussed and which is the central element of our Singapore operation, is the decentralization of human capital. Offshore talent is now abundant, and at a much more palatable cost, than ever before."

Robert interrupted on the phone as if they had scripted their performance. "I agree about the human capital issues, Gillian, but perhaps you could help me understand how this applies to the current problem."

Exhibit 7.2   *Blade Server Success*

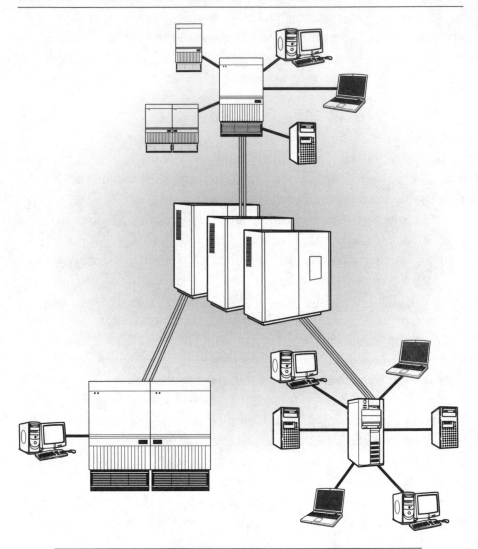

One Financial Institution noted a 980% performance improvement without an increase in their capital budget with the introduction of blade servers.

Source: United Devices, Inc.

Gillian thanked him and continued. "These two trends—diffusion of the infrastructure and diffusion of the sourcing pools—combine to produce a state of decentralization unlike anything we have seen before in the IT industry."

Several partners began to murmur about outsourcing, the loss of American jobs, the dangers, the risk of becoming another wave of investment offshore. Gillian allowed the murmurs to continue while she returned to her laptop, and to her almost empty bottle of water.

"As this slide implies, we simply cannot afford to address our current economic challenges with expensive servers and expensive talent, only to leap backward during an expense management cycle. We simply have to find an alternative strategy that will allow us to reduce our costs while expanding our business. I believe there is an approach that will put us in a position to do so."

Robert's welcome voice crackled again from the Polycom speakerphone in the center of the room. "I believe Gillian is striking the right chord here, guys," her boss said from Singapore. She was relieved to have his support, given that he was completely blind to what she was proposing. They were an excellent team, and she reminded herself to tell him so, next time he was in town.

"The second part of my proposal—and the only way to accomplish the objective of increased compute power without an impact on our own resources—is to immediately begin a transition in our data center from the existing Unix servers, with their projected capital budget in the coming year of over $1 million, to an entirely distributed environment based on Linux and cheap commodity boxes we can order from Hewlett-Packard or Dell *without increasing our budget* in the coming 12 months and yet increasing our compute capacity by 500 times."

"That sounds too good to be true." one of the men said. She knew that someone was going to say it.

> IT must fully embrace business-oriented, bottom-line efficiency-oriented thinking to reduce costs of how it delivers solutions while continuing to decrease risk and providing order of magnitude improvements in service levels and agility. These imperatives combine to create an *economics of agility* that exerts profound self-reinforcing feedback for improvements across areas of cost, risk and quality.[8]

"Oh, it can certainly be done," Gillian said, "the question is simply whether or not we at Perkins Global have the courage to leap in front of events or whether we allow those events to lead us."

Then she sat down amid a growing wave of whispering that at times threatened to drown out her boss on the phone, who summarized the proposal.

"Thanks, Robert. Gentlemen, we are a *provider* of IT services, and we are poised to take excellent advantage of our new Singapore operation by responding in a different manner to InsuranceAmerica's problem. The standard approach would be to simply reduce our costs as the client reduces their pay-out," Gillian said, smiling at Ted Brankowitz.

"It is the traditional professional services response, and it has served the industry well in the past. Yet, according to that strategy, we would eliminate hundreds of IT staff, reduce our projections, and continue with our existing infrastructure in the hope that business gets better, on down the line."

She looked directly at Ted.

"However, with the two trends I have described for you today, we now have an alternative approach. My proposal," she said, moving to the next slide in her presentation, "is to take over the entire IT operation for InsuranceAmerica. In essence, to use the clichéd terminology of the press, I am suggesting that they outsource *their* operations to *us*, moving everything except their core operations to PerkinsGlobal. In this model, as you can see, rather than reducing our headcount by 92 staff—and by the way, we have invested heavily to train and educate these very talented people— I propose that we *absorb* 100 of InsuranceAmerica's staff and perform the work of 200 to 300 others with resources soon to be available in Singapore. By transitioning to a distributed computing model and concurrently taking advantage of the Pacific Rim talent pool, I believe we can actually increase our margins in the next 24 months. I will be able to provide specific numbers by tomorrow, as requested, Ted, but I thought it might be worth discussing today, since we're all in the room."

Gillian waited, an appropriate theatrical pause, before adding her punch line.

Her corporate intuition told her to wait until Brankowitz expressed his disapproval, and in the awkward silence that followed, seconds grinding slowly forward, she wondered if she might have miscalculated. Finally, he spoke.

"My apologies, Gillian, but even if your grandiose architectural projections are correct, we've missed the boat. We've missed the boat. They've already released their staff and the situation is beyond remedy," he blurted out loudly, like gas that could no longer be kept inside.

Their CEO looked at Gillian. He was giving her one more chance to respond.

"Well, since you have asked, I am so very pleased to report that the new COO at InsuranceAmerica, the architect of their restructuring plan, has already indicated he would be very interested in discussing the possibility with us, at our earliest convenience. I received his message just before our meeting began."

The room was so quiet she could hear the hum of her computer's fan.

"As I understand it, Gillian," said her boss over the phone, "perhaps we could begin this effort by identifying three target accounts that would be excellent test cases of this dual strategy: we would first implement new technologies at the client sites that were designed to deliver service-oriented applications across a distributed architecture. Second, we would negotiate the transfer of staffing responsibilities that would, over time, increase Perkins operating margins while allowing our clients to continue their current levels of business at reduced costs."

"Yes," she said, relieved again to be getting such unexpected support across telephone lines. "Remember, Unisys accomplished a very similar transition some time ago, and IBM is already moving in this direction. Perkins risks losing major clients to IBM and others if we do not develop a similar strategy."

Her CEO stood up at exactly this moment, noting the lateness of the meeting. "This isn't just about InsuranceAmerica," he said, "or just about triage of one client account. That is the short-sighted view. It is about becoming a leader in IT services, using InsuranceAmerica as our launching pad. Is that correct?"

She nodded.

The meeting dispersed, with an agreement to take up the issue at a special session on the following day, and Gillian wondered momentarily if their non-decision was a bad sign. However, just as she was closing her laptop, the CEO leaned over the table and quietly said, "This was good, Gillian, *very* good. Tell their COO to call me—and make sure you are on the call, too. By the way, how in the world do you know him?"

"I was an intern for his equity portfolio firm, back in my college days, and his lead investor is a terrific guy," she whispered.

By 10 a.m., Gillian had performed the sleight-of-hand and saved 92 jobs, at least for that day.

On Saturday, at the end of the longest week she could remember, Gillian and Jonathan were on their way to the nursing home. Jonathan was clearly nervous about his father. To keep his mind off the anxiety of finding his father in even worse condition than when he had last seen him, he asked Gillian to talk about her week.

"I'm really sorry I wasn't listening the other night, honey," he said, knowing that the apology was three nights overdue. "But I'm listening right now, and I could really use a . . ."

". . . distraction?" she asked.

"That makes it sound unimportant," he said. "I know what you do is important. I know you saved a lot of people's jobs this week, and that is great. And it *is* more than a distraction," he insisted, "because I actually feel a lot better on these visits to my dad when you and I are together."

Gillian thought about that for a moment and then asked him to elaborate. "When you say you feel a lot better, what does that mean exactly?"

Jonathan described how he was always inclined to keep his worries about his father to himself, that he didn't want to bother her with the daily ups and downs of an old man who was rapidly declining. After all, there was so little anyone could do at this point, it didn't seem worthwhile to spend precious time discussing it, when they had so much else to talk about. But then he explained that, when the problem seemed truly beyond his capacity, the simple act discussing it with her alleviated the pressure. "It's as if I'm taking some of my worry and sharing it with you, and then my own level of distress goes down. Two brains better than one, I suppose."

"You know what, honey? That's *exactly* what I'm working on at Perkins," she said. "Distributed computing, lots of small brains connected together are more capable of solving complex problems than one big brain." As they drove across the bridge on their way to the home, she realized that there is a very human aspect to distributed computing, that there are resources that can be leveraged, and that when the workload is shared, it alleviates the pressure on any single machine, or any single human, and this extends beyond the normal boundaries of a business. She remembered one of her research notes, as they drove.

"Two *are* better than one," she joked. "Four are better than two, et cetera, et cetera. That's what I'm trying to prove at work."

When they arrived at the nursing home and spoke to the night shift nurse who was just getting off work, they learned that the old man had completely forgotten why he was there and was very upset. No one on the staff seemed able to console him.

"It's a horrible feeling," the nurse said quietly, "a bit of hell on earth, I think, to wake up in strange surroundings, not knowing the reasons why you are where you are, trusting no one because you recognize no one."

It was, from the family's perspective, a good facility, clean and well managed, with a capable staff that seemed to be directly involved with the elderly in their care. However, the seniors who lived there had a decidedly different perspective. For them, it was a constant reminder that their families had opted for an institution, instead of inviting them to live in their homes. No amount of consolation would assuage that sense of abandonment.

Jonathan and Gillian spent the entire morning in almost childlike conversations with a man who could no longer remember his own son's name.

They showed him pictures of fishing trips when he was younger, pictures in which the old man looked much like Jonathan did that day, gray hair just beginning to appear at his temples.

They had brunch in the cafeteria, The Commons. They reminded him that he shouldn't be using too much salt and that he was allergic to strawberries. Around them, other families were visiting their mothers or fathers. Most of the table conversations seemed lively, but some were filled with sadness and others with contempt. On their way back to Jonathan's father's room, they passed one of his neighbors and over-heard someone's extreme distress.

"I don't want to see this man!" came the crackling voice from behind the half-open door. "I don't even know who he is!"

Jonathan peeked into the room, waved when he was recognized by someone inside, and rejoined Gillian as they wheeled his father back into his own room, to his own bed.

"Just Linwood," Jonathan said, "visiting his father-in-law."

Gillian sometimes wondered whether Jonathan was jealous of the neighboring resident's son-in-law Linwood, who came to the facility every day to play checkers. The old man complained about the visit in the beginning, but at least there was recognition in the end, at least there was a remnant of a relationship to rely on.

They helped his father into bed, and the old man asked again if it was time to eat.

"We just had brunch, Dad," Jonathan said patiently. "You put too much salt on your eggs, remember?"

The old man looked up blankly, first at Jonathan and then toward Gillian, wondering why two strangers would talk about eggs that he did not remember eating. Jonathan patted his father's shoulder and soothed him with another story about his own childhood—a family vacation to the New York World's Fair, the Unisphere, the talking robot that looked like Abraham Lincoln.

Instead of calling on the old man's memory, they offered their shared reminiscences of his life.

This exercise in shared memory absorbed much of the old man's distress that morning, until he seemed stable, comfortable, and willing finally to take a brief nap. They watched quietly as he leaned back into his pillow without the overwhelming fear that he would wake up again in unfamiliar surroundings, unable even to remember his own name.

NOTES

1. For more information about the profound work carried out at CERN (the European Organization for Nuclear Research) during the 1980s and early 1990s, which eventually resulted in a web-based collaborative suite of applications, see www.kronodoc.fi.
2. Carol Brown, "The Succesful CIO: Integrating Organizational and Individual Perspectives" (Bloomington, IN: Graduate School of Business, Indiana University, 1993.
3. Leon Erlanger, "Distributed Computing—An Introduction," *ExtremeTech*, http://www.findarticles.com/p/articles/mi_zdext/is_200204/ai_ziff25002, April 2002.
4. Henry Bal, Jennifer Steiner, and Andrew Tannenbaum, *ACM Computing Surveys* 21 (September 1989).
5. Ibid.
6. See note 4.
7. *The Economics of Agility*, Executive White Paper, Credit Suisse First Boston, December 2003.
8. Vision, Executive Brief White Paper, Credit Suisse First Boston, June 2003.

CHAPTER 8

FLASH TEAMS

Historian and philosopher Tomas Lucida is credited with being the first to declare that the modern corporate organization "is dead, dying, or in a state of paralysis not unlike late-stages Alzheimer's patients who are unable to move at all."[1] His seminal three-volume work on organizational architecture[2] continues to be "required reading" in most university postgraduate programs in business administration, management, and organizational development.

Lucida, now retired and only occasionally writing for a select few university journals, launched his assault on corporate management in the early 1970s, having learned about the transformations occurring in the workplace from his father, the late Edward Winston Lucida, the corporate counsel for Metro Goldwyn Mayer from 1945 to 1958. It was Edward Lucida who originally proposed the notion of independent film production in Hollywood, as the large studios were on the decline. Tomas Lucida has said that one of his father's notions was inspirational for him. That notion was "magnetic teaming," in which various artisans (producers, directors, actors, film technicians, designers, and so on) would come together on a project-by-project basis, gathering and disbanding to form new groups.

In his autobiography, *Lucida Is Not Just a Camera*, Tomas says that his father's groundbreaking work in Hollywood was the root of his own work and that much of his writing "should be understood as derivative."[3]

Giving proper credit, first to his father, and later in his autobiography to colleagues such as Tom Peters, who first advocated a change in how employees should be considered (1996),[4] Lucida observes that the notion of a changing employment environment is "neither new nor of much interest. What is worthy of our speculation is less when our organizations changed, or who had the initial idea, but rather, when we actually changed our *behavior*."[5]

According to Lucida, one of the most significant examples of what has now become known as the modern "non-organization" is the rarely cited work of Langston Kollinger in 1988. Kollinger is now on the board of Hypothekon, but in 1988 he founded a business incubator chartered to transition academic inventions into products for the marketplace. It was Kollinger's team that created the first detailed study of complex information architectures utilizing the model of the "see-through man" in science textbooks, wherein each layer of the overall structure could be seen as a transparent page above and below other transparent pages.

"Kollinger's contribution," said Lucida in an interview with *Time* magazine, "was the first real evidence that *we can learn about what we do not know* from *what we know*." Furthermore, Lucida claimed that any current organizational or structural dilemma in business can be solved by discovering the appropriate truth in other disciplines and applying it to the organizational construct. "We know everything we need to know," Lucida says, "we just haven't learned how to apply it correctly."[6]

Lucida's most often quoted examples of the transposition of knowledge from one discipline to another involve the many Japanese technical manuals that apply the lessons of gardening, for example, to archery, or to penmanship, or to swordsmanship. In the context of this book, Lucida's most appropriate and timely theory, first proposed in 2004, is that service-oriented *architectures* require service-oriented *employees*.

To become a service-oriented employee, one need only understand the role of a web service in the overall architectural framework (how it interacts with other systems, how users might engage a particular service) and apply those rules to human behaviors: your expertise, for example, should be available throughout the organization that might need your skill set, even for only a few hours. Consequently, your hierarchical relationship becomes less significant than your availability and responsiveness to the entire enterprise.

"We didn't need to learn anything new," Lucida observed, "only how to apply our technical comprehension to more human pursuits. If you hide in your cubicle, if you avoid dialogue with your colleagues, if you are unaware of emerging issues and trends, your value is smaller, and getting smaller every day."[7]

Although additional knowledge may not be necessary, in Lucida's view, the transformation required of corporate employees is no less dramatic than the change being imposed on our technology architectures. "Wholesale reorganizations of corporate structures have been set in motion by the inability of a company to adequately address the political implications of an information-based and service-based economy."[8]

Students of Lucida's work are now applying his principles in thoroughly creative ways throughout the business world, and although many of them are disavowed by Lucida, one of the few who deserve consideration, according to the man whose principles they espouse, is the CEO of Celleration Systems, Dieter Kahn. Kahn credits the recent success of his new company to his application of Lucida's principles, foremost among them being Lucida's notion of Flash Teams.

> I first learned about "flash teams" from a colleague in the financial industry. The prototype project at this person's company went well; however, when they began the enterprise rollout of the new environment, there were political disagreements and struggles over resources that often delayed even the smallest project by days or even weeks. My colleague said that it was only when they began to apply the notion of "flash teams" to their new initiative that any real progress could be made.[9]

In this essay, we intend to examine the most recent models for teamwork in Celeration and other technology organizations, ranging from multinational corporations with immense globalized workforces, with the additional challenge of cultural differences to overcome, to small, high-tech startups in growth mode that add employees more quickly than they can be properly oriented. In the following selected case studies, we hope to identify the thematic principles underlying each of these examples, which, when taken as a whole, can be seen as evidence of Tomas Lucida's propositions. Chief among them is that hierarchical management will no longer be a viable approach by the end of the 21st century.

Finally, we will examine the impact of managerial change on our corporations, their employees, and the larger market in which they function. This change, Lucida states, will transform economies and political balances as dramatically as "early Spanish explorers' realization that their world was not flat."[10]

CASE STUDY 1   *Leviathan Oil and Gas, Incorporated*

Main Industry: Energy Research and Development
Headquarters: Houston, Texas
Number of employees: 22,450
Sample team: New Energy Research Task Force in Houston, Bangalore,
St. Petersburg, and Buenos Aires
By Stanley Dormer, Director of New Markets

In 1992, the budget for research into alternative energy supply was 5% of the total corporate budget at Leviathan. It was doubled in 1993 and has continued to increase at that pace, now occupying 65% of our company's R&D budget for the 2004–2005 fiscal year.

In 1992, our vision of alternative energy was limited to replacements for fossil fuels. As the budget expanded, we also expanded our viewpoint concerning energy supply–from a consumption-oriented model to a conversion-oriented model. By 1998, our experiments had shifted from hydrogen-fueled engines to large photovoltaic cells. In 2003, a new division was launched, based in California, that is investigating photosynthetic conversion by thousands of granular, networked microcomputers. These microcomputers are individually smaller than a grain of sand; however, if applied to a surface (for example, mixed with exterior house paint), their aggregated production levels would create enough energy to fuel a family's needs and, in addition, provide 10 to 15% overage to be rechanneled into a grid-connected power supply for use elsewhere. The challenge, in production, is to reduce the cost of

(continued)

these experimental resources, which remains prohibitive for use on a scale large enough to be consequential.

Leviathan is dedicated to meeting this challenge by the end of the current decade.

From 1990 to 1996, there were numerous project failures that cannot be attributed to faulty technology or design. Our analysis of these failures identified that our ability to manage joint, distributed, multi-year projects was the central breaking point. It was no longer enough to maintain existing revenue streams, nor was it critical for the business to simply increase market share by increments each financial quarter. We learned that, to be competitive in the coming decades, we must change our management approach.

As with most oil and gas ventures, our organizational history until 1997 could be best understood as classically hierarchical. Decisions were made "at the top" and delegated "downward" for implementation. One's influence within the company—defined for the purposes of this case study as an employee's ability to overcome barriers and achieve success for their particular efforts—depended solely on the employee's reporting structure. At Leviathan, until perhaps 2000 or even 2001, your capacity to influence decisions related to where you were in the corporate structure (vice president, director) and whether your supervisor was well known in the company.

That approach served us well in the 1980s and early 1990s. It meant that decision making was in the hands of two or three dozen informed executives who understood the industry, the company, and the challenge before them.

By 1997, the centralized, top-down management style that had been efficient was becoming more and more of a bottleneck. There were too many unique business situations for the small group of executives to comprehend, too many emerging technologies to monitor, too many regulations to be kept in mind. We began to develop "competency centers" but retained central control of those teams, and it was not until the final months of 1997, as we faced several concurrent crises in multiple departments, that we recognized the need to distribute authority (strategic decisions, budgetary considerations, staffing, local policy) to those who best understood the complicated issues involved.

It was not a painless transition.

Many Houston executives, accustomed to their authority and the absence of any collaborative interactions with their colleagues around the country, did not want to release authority, particularly if that authority was being pushed "down the ladder" to teams in their organizations. The political struggle, which unfortunately continued for several years, was driven only by a handful of executives who did not understand or agree with the new policies, yet this small group had a disproportionately large impact on the company. Their resistance provided an unexpected braking mechanism on the forward momentum of the company. Few of those individuals are still employees of Leviathan.

Perhaps it would be useful to explain my role in the company. I was hired in 1995 to manage an R&D team, and I observed our management transition first-hand. In the early years, I was responsible for bringing information about developments in the industry to the R&D team; however, I was not their direct manager. Today I am the director of multiple R&D teams, and we have the benefit of six or seven key business process teams—attended by members of our entire research organization who serve as liaisons for their specific groups.

I do not mean to indicate that we have fully transformed Leviathan into a process-oriented corporation. Indeed, some of our processes are essentially tedious and bureaucratic, and we have not yet learned (there are exceptions, of course) to be as "light on our feet" as some of our newer competitors who have more fully embraced new technologies that encourage collaboration and communication.

I have been told that the move from vertical to horizontal management is as difficult as it is for a smoker to stop smoking cigarettes. Sometimes we fall back into old habits. In the case of Leviathan, the transition is reinforced by the nature of our business—we no longer drill vertically. (Actually, in practice, we continue to do so, but it is considered "old technology.") Instead, we are studying horizontal equations of energy conversion, or in the case of photosynthetic production, massively parallel yet minute, multidimensional systems in which the words "up" and "down" have little meaning.

In the meanwhile, as we stumbled into this unknown land of interconnected and distributed organizational behavior (aided, of course, by

(continued)

CASE STUDY 1   (continued)

a variety of outside Change consultants who specialize in altering the behavior of a large number of people in a small amount of time), we have identified numerous side effects that can only be described as unintentionally beneficial. This has not prevented certain executives from claiming credit for instituting these reforms; however, an objective analysis would suggest that these are byproducts of the effort to repair ourselves in the face of monumental failure:

With unique specialization (of skills, knowledge, experience) now recognized throughout the company, these employees are more readily available to do interdepartmental work. This has alleviated the need for every group to hire its own individual experts and, overall, has reduced the workforce by an average of 10 to 20%, with the single exception of regulatory teams, which continue to increase each year, as the regulations become more complex.

Possible acquisitions, once the province of a small team of secretive negotiators, are suggested from many teams in the company. Companies acquired by Leviathan are involved in the company's framework more quickly, because information, policies, and even anecdotal history are exchanged with the incoming staff more readily, and more accurately. This is also true of new employees, who now become productive with less orientation, as their team absorbs part of the responsibility for incorporating them.

Information technologists, once considered second-class citizens by the more elitest R&D staff, are now clearly recognized to be enabling the business in their support for and delivery of the various compute environments needed for international collaboration, from instant messaging and videoconferencing to accessible data sets and archived knowledge bases.

There are other benefits: the advent of a learning culture, the increasingly collegial atmosphere, the sense of momentum spurred by an absence of barriers. However, our new system is not a panacea. An overemphasis on consensus can cause delays in decision making, the decentralization of innovation spurs the possibility of unnecessary projects, and the risks inherent in a lessening of competitive edge in the marketplace. Time alone will tell whether Leviathan is successful in its transition to nonhierarchical policies and processes.

CASE STUDY 2   *Celeration Systems*

Main Industry: Wireless Security

Headquarters: Palo Alto, California

Number of employees: 370

Sample team: Network Support Services

By Dierdre James-Tolly, Vice President, Corporate Program Management Office

There is a Silicon Valley myth, perhaps based in fact, that Webex Communications' flagship product was, in the company's early days, merely an internal tool used by their professional services staff to communicate with each other, and it was only when the company was on the verge of dissolution, as they were determining their unique assets, that they identified the potential for their conferencing software—just a small piece of custom software, an experiment in a remote corner of the company, unknown to the executives who thought that their company was supposed to be doing something else.

It is not unusual to find fissures within the enterprise into which even the most critical business information can fall, and be lost. And contrary to what many in the software industry have been preaching for the past 20 years, the gaps (perhaps chasms) into which so much value falls are not closed up by the purchase of a new software application or a new repository. E-mail alone can be sufficient if the company's employees communicate thoroughly; however, millions of dollars of servers and software are insufficient if the employees do not talk to each other.

This is the fourth company in which I have been responsible for program management. We are the small group of dedicated individuals solely responsible for ensuring coordination between/among the various functional groups, reinforcing governance procedures when there are disagreements and serving as the communications link between teams that otherwise would never speak to one another.

(continued)

CASE STUDY 2   *(continued)*

The unofficial motto of a previous employer was "Our systems communicate better than our people do," as if this was something to boast about.

Celeration, which is a pioneer in the field of "directory-based situational protocols," is the only company of the four that has given me the authority to be successful. Even with an enlightened management team, and a Chief Executive Officer who is an energetic advocate of what he calls the Flash Matrix, the task is often beyond my team's capacity.

Sometimes it seems that people in our company communicate even less than they did before the creation of the Project Management Office (PMO), because they know that our group is there somewhere, behind the scenes, making certain that information is moved throughout the company, as necessary. Perhaps they simply leave it to us—so they can attend to the more important aspects of their jobs, such as negotiating better prices for long-distance telephone service, or configuring the e-mail servers for redundancy and performance. They would rather pay attention to the systems that provide the ability to communicate than to the actual communication.

It is a miracle that any company is successful, given human nature, which encourages gossip but feels anxious about candor.

On my first day at Celeration, I was pleased to learn that Dieter Kahn, our CEO, was an advocate of Tomas Lucida's management philosophy. I had not read Lucida's work since graduate school, yet I was nonetheless aware of its role in the changing attitudes about what was once called cross-functional, then matrixed, and then networked organizations.

Dieter himself did not always comprehend the importance of collaboration instead of command/control, and of cooperation instead of intense competition.

As he tells the story, the company (founded in 2001, with 38 employees and three customers) was struggling to remain afloat, caught in the curious gray zone in which young companies are forced to say Yes to every customer request and find themselves unable to deliver on the request unless the customer pays them to respond. His days and nights were consumed by financial dialogues with a variety of investors involved in a collapsing market, and with the small circle of very dedicated "angel" investors who had already provided more money than originally planned yet were being asked again. When he was not pressing his investors, he was on the road, preaching the company's gospel at any conference he could attend. Many of his weekends were spent catching up on his e-mail and re-engaging with his management team who, subsequently, were required to work weekends with him if they wanted him to know about their latest efforts.

So much was happening of significance that Dieter's weekly staff meetings had become a two-hour monologue during which he tried to communicate the many important meetings, opportunities, developments, and crises he had navigated since the last meeting.

It was during one of these performances, at a moment when Dieter believed he was heroically trying to communicate as much information as possible to his overworked team, that Margaret—his most trusted colleague, employee 3—made an observation that nearly broke Dieter's heart.

"With all this talk," she said in a clear, crisp voice that broke through his monologue like a pistol shot, "you're not doing much listening."

Almost 12 months (to the day) later, as he was interviewing me for the newly created vice-presidency, Dieter confided that Margaret's statement sent him into a tailspin—fueled by exhaustion, stress, and insomnia (another story). Dieter fell into a depression, which, at its worst, caused him to consider resigning the position of CEO and leaving the company entirely.

"That's when someone gave me the first volume of Lucida's book on the death of the organization," Dieter told me that day. It changed him. "I realized we were going about our business entirely wrong and to correct it, we'd have to start from scratch."

Celeration was reborn.

The PMO was only part of the company's overhaul. Dieter himself quickly assumed an entirely different management style—collaborative instead of fanatical, aware instead of paranoid, inclusive rather than too hurried to invite the right people to a meeting. In the engineering group, we've established a flash team methodology whereby groups are called together to address a single issue in the present tense (in other

(continued)

CASE STUDY 2   *(continued)*

words, today). In the marketing organization, we have learned how to survey select customers and partners in real time when decisions need to be made quickly about our product launch or about a change in the look-and-feel of our web site. We can now do so in less than six hours with 90% confidence in customer satisfaction. Productivity, by itself, provides more than ample return on investment; however, the objectives of this approach are broader than that.

The PMO, no longer the only cross-functional champion in the company, can now focus on extended schedules and complex project mapping, with the proper amount of time to focus on analysis, and risk management scenarios, in short, all the things we were supposed to do but could not, because we were the only communication vehicle in the company.

Will we be successful?

It is too early to tell. Startups can implode for any of a thousand reasons. However, now that we have organized ourselves to behave like the products we are building, the alignment is creating a massively innovative and quick-footed company. It will be an interesting year.

CASE STUDY 3   *GMX Global Funds*

Main Industry: Private Equity Investments

Headquarters: New York City

Number of Employees: 1750

Sample Team: Information Technology and Systems Support

By Delia Bohannon, Managing Director, Worldwide Field Operations

After more than 20 years in the financial industry, I have come to the conclusion that most of my colleagues are simply unable to comprehend alternatives to authoritarian leadership. Like the inhabitants of

17th-century philosopher Edwin Abbot's imaginary Flatland,[11] it is a limitation in their perspective.

Abbot's Flatland was a two-dimensional world, and its inhabitants could only understand two-dimensional concepts. Subsequently, if one were to draw a straight line on the ground in front of a Flatlander, they would not be able to step over it, convinced that they were prevented from doing so by the Straight Line. Abbot, a mathematician and theologian, intended his story to be a critique of Victorian thinking, however, I believe Flatland is a perfect analogy for most corporate behavior which is limited by the narrow perspective of the executives responsible for those corporations. As a Flatlander cannot even imagine a third dimension (space), these executives cannot even imagine the interconnectedness of their company's divisions, or indeed, their business partners and their competitors. They are simply stymied by the absolute truth that the Straight Line is insurmountable.

Our information systems division can be best understood as a technically capable schizophrenic. Almost half of our group—those who support worldwide customer databases and business-specific applications—are residents of Flatland, as are most of the financial executives beyond New York City's border. They do not interact with their business constituents. Their focus is maintaining what they have, rather than experimenting with what they could have. They believe that change, on an institutional as well as architectural level, introduces too much risk.

The remaining members of the information systems group–infrastructure, internetworking, messaging, and program management, as well as a handful of forward thinking managers in our New York offices–have completely shifted to a model which I have recently learned is called "Flash Teams."

In Flash Teams, supported by instant messaging and ubiquitous mobile devices, small groups of experts are called together in real-time (or as close to real time as human beings can respond) to address technology issues as they arise. Security breaches are addressed within minutes. Requests for authorization (the obverse of a security breach) can also be addressed within minutes. Technologists located in any of the 142 branch offices worldwide can be included in the brainstorm-and-

(continued)

implement tactic, forming a true sense-and-respond scenario. While this was initially prototyped in "break/fix" situations, where a mission-critical application was not functioning (for an unknown reason) and needed to be repaired immediately. However, as we learned from our Grid initiatives, it is a model eminently suited for the nature of our technology itself, which is networked, distributed, horizontal in its architecture, and rootless in its taxonomy.

Some readers may question the wisdom of publicly criticizing, in this forum, those in our institution who have not yet embraced a new way of thinking about workspaces, decisions, and innovation. I hope you will not, however, question the sincerity of this case study, which is tied to a basic tenet of Flash Teams (and the neo-organizations that form around them): candor, at all times, in all things.

Candor.

I am not sure if the technology came before the methodology (instant messaging), or the methodology (swarms) came before the technology. Whatever the history, it is now possible to call an immediate meeting, conduct it "virtually" (insofar as attendees do not need to physically attend) and proceed with a decisive set of actions. All of this can now occur within the time it took merely to determine, via everyone's calendar, a day in the coming week when everyone was available.

Meetings, therefore, become the vehicle for discussing strategic issues—on the company or the team level, and even within teams, there are subgroups that will utilize the cellphone-based videoconferencing to hold a 15-minute meeting when a network hub goes down, to first isolate the problem; second, prescribe the cure; and third, assign it appropriately.

Imagine this scenario: Your Executive Vice President, responsible for all strategic customer accounts, is across the country in the office of a disgruntled customer who has just approved a million dollar deal but has questions about the specifics (when will the product be available, how many consultants will be required to install and configure the product, etc.). In the past, such an EVP would note the questions and promise a timely response. Email/voicemail made that period shorter during the past decade. Now, the answers can be provided—along with video clips, training, documentation, and even a direct view into the team's project plan—at the very moment the customer is asking the question.

Finally, and perhaps the most unusual (and, in my opinion, the most interesting) example of Flash Teams at our company (among those who have adopted the approach) is that a manager can be responsible for a theme instead of a team. The theme might be Quality or Regulatory Compliance or Technical Support, and she is now able to call a corporate version of a smart mob[12] to address the issues of the day, disband them when the problem is solved, and re-compose them in different arrangements as a new issue emerges. It is object-oriented management, and we have become the objects.

Managing a corporate theme may require 20 or 30 types of meetings, with a variety of teams composed of individuals with the right expertise for the "agenda," and when we solve the problem of laggards (those Flatland types who simply cannot comprehend this approach), we may see an entirely new kind of organization develop within and beyond our institutions.

Lessons Learned

It is not merely coincidence that the institution most hierarchically defined was Leviathan, in large part because of the history of the company, which grew, over five decades, on the basis of *vertical discovery*. When the mission of an enterprise is entirely focused on a *downward approach* that brings value from below to the surface, it is not surprising that the oil industry—indeed, all of Leviathan's partners and competitors—has remained essentially hierarchical in its management style.

The Houston headquarters has a prescient sculpture in its lobby, a wall-sized construction of compression valves (Poppet, Ring, Plate, and COP[13]) with glistening brass tubes, precision lathed elbow joints, LPG burners, regulators, meters, and vaporizers. It is a physical manifestation of the importance of networks, even in the distribution of natural gas; however, the executives at Leviathan would pass by the sculpture every day without understanding that there must also be horizontal flow, without which vertical discovery would be an improbable experiment in denying the principles of gravity.

The sculpture is now a symbol of how the company hopes to transform itself. It is attempting to do, on a multinational scale, what Dieter Kahn accomplished at Celeration in a matter of months—turn the entire ship around and rebuild the navigation and controls according to an entirely different set of concepts, allowing flash teams to become the dominant operative force. Macro and micro business processes, both undergoing a radical change, both aligning their organizations with the types of business they are doing with and for their customers.

The financial institutions, whether they are GMX, USA Financial, or Providence International, are perhaps the most complex. On the one hand, they have been "early adopters" of technology for the past decade, always seeking a better way to manage their portfolio investments lest their competitors find a way to do so first. On the other hand, many of the financial firms have retained very senior executives (true experts in their industry) who, as Delia Bohannon boldly asserts, simply cannot comprehend a different way of behaving. Like the residents of Flatland, who live in two dimensions and cannot see any three-dimensional objects because their understanding of the world does not include a third dimension, there will be many who will not understand the nature of Flash Teams.

When they watch such a team operate, they will think it is simply a faster way to do what has been done before.

The Flatlanders (using Delia's metaphor) do not understand that Flash Teams, smart mobs, and swarm intelligence create a participatory governance model, one in which we are all involved very directly and immediately in the corporate environment. Their virtual presence allows for increased participation, and their increased participation allows for a different type of governance. Decisions will no longer trickle down, they will spread out.

Eventually, the corporation as we know it will become a relic, and we will move on.

NOTES

1. Tomas Lucida, "The Organization Is Dead, Long Live the Organization," *Journal of Human-Centric Sciences* 2 (19XX): 112–114, 1979.
2. Tomas Lucida, *The Modern Organization* (Paris: Presse Academie, 1979 and New York: Library of Work, 1985).
3. Tomas Lucida and E. Champlain, *Lucida Is Not Just a Camera* (New York: Scrivener's and Sons, 1991), 219.
4. Tom Peters, *San Jose Mercury News*, April 28, 1991.
5. See note 3, p. 311.
6. "A Man in His World: Tomas Lucida's Life," *Time*, July 1999, 77.
7. Tomas Lucida, "Systems are Systems," *American Science Digest*, June 2004, 79.
8. S.A. Robbins, *Turbulence: The System is a Mirror* (Association for Computing Machinery, 1995).
9. Deiter Kahn, interview with the author, March 17, 2005.
10. See note 1.
11. Edward Abbot, *Flatland: A Romance of Many Directions*. Originally published in 1884.
12. Howard Reingold, *Smart Mobs: The Next Social Revolution* (New York: Perseus Books, 2002).
13. COP is a registered trademark of a unique poppet valve design.

Editor's Note: Tomas Lucida, Langston Kollinger, and the individuals in the case studies are fictional characters. No resemblance in personality or theory with a living person is intended.

CHAPTER 9

NETWORK AS NARRATIVE FORM

Inebriated and alert, his fingers were poised above the typewriter in the expectant position that often preceded new work. It was midnight — cold, maudlin, magnificent.

The tradition had begun more than a decade before, on an impulse to spur the students' thinking about relational prose, the Professor distributed 12 prose poems (written quickly, mere examples to be used by the students, although over the years, he'd revised a few of them, enamored with a certain cadence or metaphor that appeared elsewhere in his work), and the students' assignment was to arrange them in a preferred order. He had simply hoped to demonstrate that these distributed objects, each a self-contained entity, could be rapidly recomposed to display entirely different themes.[1] To encourage their creative attentions, amid the wider array of preholiday distractions, he had instructed the first class to imagine that Ted Nelson and Robert Coover would be judging their responses.

During the passing decade, it became known as the Nelson-Coover Experiment, and each year, it provoked wildly unpredictable and innovative efforts: students produced a one-act play using the Professor's prose as dialogue, others used them as lyrics in an operatic comedy, and, most recently, one of the students linked the poems to the university's Labyrinth web portal, sending them directly from his wireless laptop in the lecture hall as Home Page inserts.

That night, the Professor decided to conduct his own imaginary conversation with the eminent colleagues whose work had guided his own thinking for so many years. Part ego, part theatrics, it had become the Professor's way of infusing his own approach to the topic with an energy that was otherwise ebbing in his recent classroom performances. As he grew older, the Professor found himself in need of the same kind of tricks that he generously offered to his students each December, to send them into their vacations with renewed intellectual curiosity.

"Mr. Nelson, perhaps you could compare these 12 boxes of prose arranged in a matrix not unlike a spreadsheet with your recent notion of *zzstructure*. Does your *zig-zag* approach offer a similar evolutionary step to data management?"

The Professor smiled at the impossibility of knowing Ted Nelson's actual response to the question, and imagined this response:

"Actually, Professor, I have many specific theories about New Literature; however, zzstructure is a programming paradigm, not a creative writing methodology. Perhaps it would be more appropriate to consider the function of a zzcell, in the consequent requirement of two-way links."

The Professor had long admired Nelson's vision, so contrary to the corporate Internet that had emerged in the 1990s that emphasized profit derived from software programs constructed for profit, rather than for the benefit that could be gained by using them wisely. It was always enjoyable to allow himself the vicarious act of invoking the Nelson persona in his classes.

"And Mr. Coover, this is certainly familiar ground for you, if not simplistic in comparison with your efforts at Brown. Might you tell us, like the wizened Marine vet speaking to young recruits about to enter the jungle for the first time, what we might expect in that thicket, and what dangers we might want to cautiously avoid?"

It was almost 1 a.m. and the Professor had an 8 a.m. departmental meeting on budget reductions for the next semester, but he couldn't leave the office before composing his colleague's imaginary response.

"I defer to Ted's experience with programming, though I'm sure we both agree that a good piece of code is well written for the same reasons that good prose is well written: standards (grammar), sequence (plot), and language precision (voice). But frankly, I'd recommend using the *students'* prose poems for the exercise, not yours, Professor. The goal is to get them to understand their own work, is it not?"

The Professor was immersed in a creative dilemma: the illusory introduction of his colleagues into the course of the text brought with it the requirement to attend to the relationship, howsoever imagined. Without follow-up, without additional dialogue, the insertions would seem gratuitous. However, these were not minor influences, the two gentlemen had a profound impact on generations of programmers and writers, and the possibility that the Professor's objectives could be altered by their introduction (into the text, into the story) now had to be considered.

For example, imagine a collection of short stories in which the author not only allows such imaginary dialogues, but actually inserts a connection, by means of a dynamically linked URL, to the online work of Ted Nelson. Over the course of time, Ted Nelson's pages will be updated/refreshed/revised, and, therefore, the link would create the possibility that future versions of the linked object might introduce topics that were not in the author's original vision. Thus a responsibility would exist to remain responsive—such is the nature of online text, which allows for continual revision. A printed book (frozen at a point in time) prevents that continuity. The link, therefore, introduces risk.

Any entity linked in such a manner is a two-way correspondence, and systems management provides possible tools to ensure the quality of the links. Such is not the case between people (whose relationships often suffer from inattentiveness on one or both parts) and between partners. However, the end result of the absence of such attentions is clear: a database may be shut down (the data no longer being available in "real time" to the query tool), or a server may be taken offline for maintenance (its resources temporarily transferred to others in the "pool" that may not be optimized for performance). However, organizationally, we often neglect our links, because we have not created the series of monitors (alarms) to notify us that the relationship is at risk. Enormous problems can occur, on down the line, when a fundamental relationship goes awry, at which point the problem may be too large to resolve easily.

Any system of relationships is only as reliable as the most poorly managed in the system, and, therefore, the inadequacy of their technical reflections may be noticed before the sociopsychological issues are known. In other words, a broken hypertext link is easier to test and correct than a soured relationship with a colleague or business partner.

How, therefore, should the Professor continue? Has he inadvertently created a dependency on the real characters of Robert Coover and Ted Nelson, and does he have the obligation to maintain those relationships? If he does not, what does that tell us about the underlying principles he originally intended to convey? Is it just another example of "interesting theory, poorly implemented?" Furthermore, what happens to the experiment and, indeed, to the text of the story, if Mssrs. Coover and Nelson elect to participate directly in the narrative?

Coover interrupts, "So far the project idea's more interesting than the writing. Just bare bones here. Too much abstraction. Are the prose poems any good?"[2]

The Professor considered the question. Of course, the original objective was to help his students understand that the Network can be seen as a Narrative Form involving certain liberties and their consequent responsibilities.

Nelson adds, "Sorry, I don't like homework, never have. I'll look at it while we're talking (at your expense). Will try to schedule soon."[3]

When the idea occurred to him, the Professor was startled that he had not envisioned it before. Even the imaginary interventions of Coover and Nelson provoked a new way of looking at the experiment, proving yet again that collaboration was a state of mind.

The Professor pulled out the university directory, dog-eared, scribbled on, his Bible of connections within the institution.

He knew there were technologies that could serve him better than a stapled stack of photocopied paper, but there was more information in the marginalia than he could ever hope to convert to software—like the New York Public Library's challenge when they finally replaced the card catalogues with online directories, for they too were unable to capture the many years of hand-written intelligence that had accumulated on the actual cards. The Professor scanned the old directory for the name of the university's Studio Forum director. The woman who managed the Studio owed him a favor.

"Can you do it by tomorrow afternoon?" he asked.

"I already have the plexiglass cubes in storage. We used them for an exhibit last spring," the woman said.

The Professor promised that one of his students would meet her at the Studio at lunchtime on the following day, just in time for his 1 p.m. lecture. Then he returned to his desk, shuffling through a stack of papers for a single blank page, on which he sketched his vision of the Coover-Nelson matrix (see Exhibit 9.1).

When his doorbell rang, the sound moved through his cottage like a gunshot, snapping the Professor from his reverie and bringing him back to the reality of missed appointments and nagging obligations, the steady state of unwelcome interruptions that academics suffer.

Who would be at the door in those predawn hours when everyone is supposed to be asleep, or working?

The Professor despised unannounced visitors. The hallway was littered with discarded coats and boots, atop the standard disarray of boxes and books (and boxes of books) that had become his usual en-

EXHIBIT 9.1　*Narrative Networking: The Coover-Nelson Experiment*

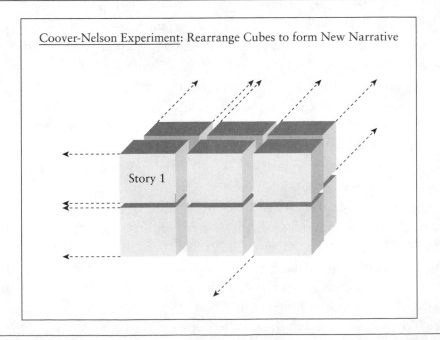

vironment since the divorce. The kitchen sink was filled with at least a week's worth of crusted dishware and half-filled coffee cups, and the whiskey bottle was open on the counter. If he had known who was standing at his front door, he would have taken a moment to put away the whiskey and gargle with Listerine, but at 3 a.m., his intuitions were otherwise occupied, and he opened the door, startled to find his ex-wife.

"Can I come in?" she asked, entering without waiting for an answer.

"Do I have a choice?"

She weaved through the cluttered hallway and sidestepped several boxes as she removed her mittens and scarf and placed them on the radiator, as she had always done during their marriage. She knew that he hated the smell of damp mittens as they sizzled on the radiator, but neither of them debated the point.

"Since you're drinking," she said matter-of-factly, "perhaps you could pour me one."

This was entirely out of character, and the Professor wondered aloud whether he might be dreaming this unusual visit by the one person who had sworn never to enter the cottage again, someone who rarely drank alcohol except at faculty gatherings and on New Year's Eve.

"This isn't a nightmare," she called from the living room in response.

The Professor said that remained to be seen, relieved that there was at least one clean glass in the cupboard. He brought her the drink, and asked why.

"Why am I drinking, or why am I here?" she replied.

The Professor shrugged his shoulders; either would be an interesting answer.

"You're probably working," she said. "Let's see, end of the semester, is it already time for the Coover-Nelson thing? Did I interrupt your conversation with your imaginary friends, dear?"

He nodded. He dared not confess that they had actually responded to him recently and that neither of them had been particularly impressed.

Then he sat down, not beside her on the couch, but on the opposite side of the room, clearing a space on the large upholstered chair they had purchased together when they bought the cottage, ten years before. He remembered every detail about every object in the room—the candlesticks they found at a flea market in Manhattan when she was lecturing at the New School for Social Research, the small glass sculpture in the corner given to him by Jan Zandhuis when he was teaching at Carnegie-Mellon. His memory had served both of them, when they were together, as if his recollections were a mounted file system she accessed when necessary that did not reside in her own remembrance system.

"Well, I saw your lights on," she said, taking a sip and wincing, "although it seems they're always on, and I was driving back from the lab so I thought I'd make a dreaded 'unannounced' visit. Actually, I need a favor."

"From *me*?" he asked, feigning surprise. "*You* need something from *me*?"

She frowned and he lifted a hand, a silent apology. She continued. "I'm doing a book for the University Press—you know, the series on Social Theory and Practice—and Douglas says it would be much easier to market if it had a foreword from you."

The Professor imagined that she dreaded the request, imagined that she had driven by the house for several evenings before finally resigning herself to ask for the favor, and he tried to remember the last time she'd asked him for anything—tax information, old medical records, a keepsake she'd left behind when she moved into the condominium beside the new cinema complex.

"Who's Douglas?" he asked.

"Now, don't get started. Douglas is one of the editors at the Press, that's all, but he knows how well your last book sold, the one that started as an essay for the New Yorker, and he wants to tap into that 'interest zone' for Amazon—you know, if you bought *this* book, then we have *another* you might be interested in purchasing."

"Hmmm."

"I was thinking the foreword could focus on that application of Social Theory to computers, you remember, how a Fundamental Attribution Error in programming is the most difficult problem to solve."

The Professor remembered talking to her about the idea, years before, at the Peet's on Embarcadero. She had mentioned her lecture on bias in statistical analysis and he had drawn a comparison with software programming, how an assumption at the very earliest stage of application development (opting for a Zero instead of a One, for example) would lead to a result that was 180 degrees in the wrong direction. Then standard testing procedures (which go backward from the error to determine the cause) could often consume many weeks of investigation before (if ever) discovering the Fundamental Attribution Error.

"I was thinking it wouldn't be hard for you to toss off five or six pages on the idea," she concluded.

He smiled. She never really understood how much work went into five or six pages, how much pacing back and forth, how much reading in preparation for the writing. Like an engineer's "design phase," the Professor's early work for an essay often required weeks before a single page was actually written. The writing itself was always easy for him.

"The writing is the easy part," he said.

"And I'm sure Douglas would be willing to commit a percentage, 10 or 15%, of the profits. I told him you were never interested in the money, but maybe now..."

"I haven't changed all that much," he said.

"Great," she said, standing as she finished her whiskey. Then she moved to the radiator to retrieve her mittens and scarf.

They eventually returned to the front door, zigzagging between the litter at their feet. In the awkward goodbye pause, she laughed quietly. The Professor asked what she found so funny, and she reminded him of a scene before they were married, when he was looking for a publisher for his first book. It was raining hard in New York that afternoon and he had used the *New York Times* to shield his head as he ran from Grand Central to the Doubleday offices on Madison Avenue.

"Remember," she said with an affectionate grin, "the newsprint left letters across your forehead, and you spent the entire evening with the editor like that?"

The Professor nodded. At least she remembered the funny things.

She deftly turned, pausing in the open door, to say good night.

"Rumor has it that you've been working closely with a grad student in economics," she said, smiling. "I hope she breaks through your loneliness." And as quickly as she had arrived, she was gone, leaving behind a wistful vacuum that often left the Professor with a profound sense of loss.

But on that night, as he closed the door behind her, the image of text printed clearly across his forehead reminded him of his original efforts before she had arrived, and he bolted, breathless, back to his office.

He realized that he could print the prose poems on transparencies, placing a portion of the text on each side of the Plexiglas cubes, so that the rearrangement of the cubes would actually lead to new combinations of the text, clearly discernible for the class to see. Each paragraph, like an independent entity, would appear next to random paragraphs from other prose poems, creating new (unintended) results (see Exhibit 9.2).

Furthermore, the Professor could see that his new idea, a demonstration of wraparound text extending to the aligned cubes/prose, was connected to his ex-wife, her unexpected 3 a.m. proposition, and their long history of alternating requests and refusals, denials and distortions, something he had once called The Law of Coordinated Opposites (one moves while the other remains still[4]) that led ultimately to their separation.

In those days, she often claimed that his work (his "damned muse") was worse than his being with another woman, because it was omnipresent, even in their own home. His work made her feel like she was the odd person out, which eventually she became. Now, it was as if her sudden appearance at his front door, at 3 a.m., had derouted his original idea and inserted variations he could not ignore.

Subsequently, he added a "visitor's cube" to his diagram, to take account of the natural occurrence of outside influences. The intrusion resonates, creating added meaning to preexisting works (see Exhibit 9.3).

EXHIBIT 9.2   *Multidimensional Text*

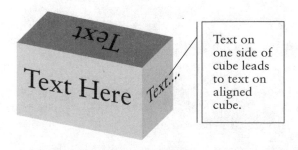

Text on one side of cube leads to text on aligned cube.

EXHIBIT 9.3 *Narrative Network Interrupted*

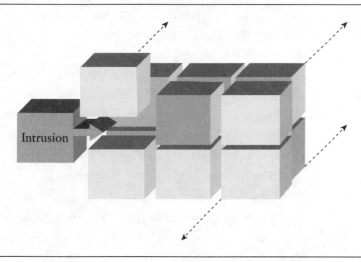

Intrusion

This was the Network as Narrative Form, a pluralistic and more in-clusive approach to text, one that naturally evolves as readers/users interact with the text in ways that can not be imagined by the author/architect but can be enabled, if the architecture affords such interactivity.

In such a grid, any new interaction influences related objects, deem-phasizing some, and in so doing, creates an apparently unique moment defined by a new series of relationships. The number of unique (newly defined) moments is mathematically uncertain, possibly infinite.

Thirty minutes before his Coover-Nelson lecture in the adjoining building, the Professor was hurriedly cutting one dozen prose poems, printed on transparencies, into six blocks of text each, creating a pile of scattered paragraphs that covered the floor of his office. Scissors in one hand, roll of adhesive tape in the other, he had just begun to connect the paragraphs with the Studio's plexiglass cubes when Esther appeared at his door.

"Decidedly high-tech," she said.

"I've always found that my students are more likely to embrace a con-cept if they are given a physical manifestation of it," the Professor said, carefully placing the sixth paragraph onto the first object, and holding it up to the light. In the sun, words intermingled, becoming more complex by their simple arrangement on each side of the plastic cube.

"I don't think you give them enough credit," she said.

"I'm sure that's true," the Professor admitted, adding, "but since you're here, you might as well help. Here," he said, handing her a transparency and pair of scissors. "Cut this into six relatively equal sections, and then tape them on one of the cubes piled over there."

Esther pulled off her icy mittens (the second time in less than 12 hours that a woman had undressed her hands in his presence, something that deserved a line or two of poetry if he was able to remember it) and eagerly joined the Professor in his sculptural preparations. When they were done, the blocks were randomly scattered on the office floor, yet even without intentional order, the impression was clear, compelling, inviting.

"And just how did you intend to get them next door?" she asked, and this was how it came to pass that Esther attended the Professor's tenth annual Coover-Nelson Experiment in Relational Prose, to conclude his semester's course on the Network as Narrative Form.

The Professor carried six blocks, and Esther the remaining six. The two of them carefully walked along the corridor that connected the academic offices with the main lecture hall. Students turned to admire the cubist juggler's parade. One of the Professor's colleagues asked Esther if she was studying for her Arts & Crafts degree. The janitor, a skinny old man with an eerie resemblance to Irving's original sketch of Ichabod Crane, offered to assist their parade, but the two cubist jugglers merely thanked him for his offer and moved down the corridor, intent on their objective: the lecture hall by 1 p.m., without dropping a single cube.

The hall itself was filling with students when they arrived, and Esther noticed that there were as many graduate students from other departments as there were students actually enrolled in the course. She realized this must have been one of the Professor's mythic lectures that students returned to hear each year, not only to recall the first time they heard him draw these comparisons, or to observe what had become a university tradition equal to the freshman bonfire or the graduating senior cap toss, but to witness the Professor's modifications to his original theme.

He never presented the same lecture twice; each one was a transformation of the one delivered the year before.

The entire front row, except for one corner seat, was filled with laptop-enabled students, ready for their chance to participate in the experiment. Esther helped the Professor stack the cubes on the table beside the lectern and then took the last front row seat.

The Professor, slightly winded, and more than a bit washed out from his late-night whiskey interludes, moved to the lectern and noticed that Esther was sitting nearby. He remembered his ex-wife's remarks about loneliness, exhaled a mournful, middle-aged sigh, and welcomed his class to the final lecture of the semester.

"We've been discussing the network as a narrative form since September," the Professor began, "and we've discovered some remarkable similarities and one or two fundamental differences, during this time. Can someone identify a similarity for me?"

Six hands shot into the air, jack-in-the-box fashion, waving eagerly and with an energy the Professor found reassuring. He pointed to the fellow in the back row who, in week two, expressed the classical skepticism (shared by most of the Professor's colleagues) about interdisciplinary principles. After the fellow's well-intentioned minority opinion was expressed, the Professor pointed to the spectacled student next to him.

"The narrative theory is a stretch for me, admittedly. But I've been impressed by the comparisons to Social Network Analysis (SNA) and the Zachman Framework,[5] because there are definitely links between architecture, information, and people." This particular student had joined the class mid-semester as a transfer from Indiana University, yet he'd absorbed everything the Professor had thrown his way. So far.

"I particularly liked the comparison of readers and writers with technologists and system users," a woman said from the front row. Angora sweater. One of Esther's peers from the Sociology department.

The Professor asked her to clarify a bit further. "Stories as distributed objects," she stated.

"And those of you who are studying information systems," the Professor inserted, "what can you tell us about distributed objects that may be pertinent to literary efforts?"

"They exist as autonomous entities," one person called out.

"They may physically reside anywhere on the network," another added.

"If they are designed with standard protocols," a third student remarked, "they can be interchangeably accessed by various applications."

A wave of murmuring rose as several students began to offer observations at the same time, a small cacophony of voices becoming a chorus of indistinguishable lyrics. The Professor moved to the nearby table and stacked the Plexiglas cubes in two rows, three above and three below. Contrary to previous Coover-Nelson experiments, the Professor did not provide his own order to the cubed text but allowed the randomness of convenience to provide the first combination. Yet he could not help but notice that the cube about Hypertext was directly above his recent prose poem in which an unidentified author struggles with the architecture of his prose. In all the various combinations that had been demonstrated during the past ten years, the Professor had not seen this particular bridge between standard (enterprise) architecture and the flexibility that must be incorporated to support hypertextual connectivity.

"Welcome to the famous Coover-Nelson Experiment," the Professor announced, silencing the aisle-by-aisle debates. "For those of you who are new to this lecture, I will explain the basic process, and for those of you who are revisiting from previous years, you will note that I have introduced a three-dimensional element that offers, hopefully, a more thoughtful perspective."

"They look like immense ice cubes begging for a bit of Jack Daniel's," Steven joked from the front row. Steven was this year's class clown, bright red hair in dreadlocks and a swatch of freckles across his nose. Despite the young man's occasional insolence, the Professor enjoyed Steven's willingness to speak "truth to power" in the university.

"Let us not get sidetracked with a discussion of alcohol as a narrative form," the Professor said, and laughter surged up.

"Ah yes, the process," the Professor began. "It begins."

The lecture, brief and highly conceptual, reviewed the basic proposition that all information delivery mechanisms, from Guttenberg and the printing press to the telegraph and Morse Code to the more recent efforts of Google to index entire university libraries, followed certain shared principles and that we can learn about one by studying another.

This had been the Professor's quintessential lesson for his students since first coming to the university with his wife ten years before: the most important truths are those that apply to multiple disciplines and the "interstices" between those disciplines (concepts that apply to more than one field of study) are the places where true education occurs.

Then he introduced his imaginary colleagues, Robert Coover from Brown University, and Ted Nelson, most recently of Oxford University. Many of the students were familiar with the twosome's body of work, yet the Professor always found a detail to add, in this case, the fact that the two men had recently had lunch in Barcelona.

". . . and today, we will play a game of Pretend. Even though my colleagues prefer to think of it as Pretension, they have agreed to judge the outcome of our efforts."

He then invited everyone in the room to imagine what the lunch conversation in Barcelona might have touched on.

"My guess is that they talked about their children and didn't discuss theory at all," Steven blurted out.

"Failure of imagination," the Professor replied, and the oohs and aahs of his peers went out toward the class clown.

The assignment, to be completed in the next 30 minutes, was for groups of five to come to the table and combine the cubes in new arrangements, noting the changes in the narrative as they placed various cubes beside others. Each would note a particular example that the group felt was most illustrative of their innovation and then present the example to the class at the end of the 30 minutes.

"I will play the role of the eminent Mssrs. Coover and Nelson," the Professor said, "offering commentary from their imagined perspectives as you work."

The students clustered into groups of five or six, and several began working before even coming to the table because they were familiar with the Professor's prose poetry, or because they came to the lecture prepared to demonstrate a particular concept, irregardless of the physical experiment at the table. The Professor acted sheepdog to the clusters of students, nipping at their heels and barking instructions; the whole hall became a swarm of activity, like a virtual hive circling around their cubist queen.

Esther, standing along the far wall and observing the effervescent humming of the students as they bounced among the cubes, the Professor, and their notebooks, recognized another layer of the Professor's metaphor: if a video had been produced of the room's activity—various individuals navigating to and fro and alternating among reading the cube-poems, making notes for their presentation, and listening to other group discussions for an overheard piece of wisdom—she thought that a map of their pathways, from each group's hub, would appear not unlike the information maps of Internet searches—people as nodes and cubes as repositories. She admired the Professor for allowing such apparently wild (ungoverned) milling about. It was no wonder most of his colleagues held the Professor's methods in such contempt—they were so entirely contrary to the traditional mode of teaching.

"Do not simply copy someone else's words," the Professor, in Coover-mode, warned one of the students. *"This is most of all an opportunity to insert your own thinking into the process."*

Later, as he watched one of the teams stack the cubes into one tall column and attempt to look through the top cube to observe the merged text throughout the stacked work, the Professor, in Nelson-mode, reminded them that a linear approach is overly simplistic. *"Avoid straight lines,"* the imaginary Nelson instructed, *"think of a zigzag pattern, which will get you farther and faster to something new."*

For the Professor, the 30-minute period flew by like a Paul Goodman snowstorm. He enjoyed the hectic, uncontrolled enthusiasm of his students, their zeal to uncover something previously undiscovered in his other classes. He did not know, in his heart of hearts, deep down where it counts, whether this lecture was a gift to his students or a gift to himself.

Finally, only minutes before the end of the official class period, the Professor asked everyone to take their seats so he could announce the judges' first- and second-place winners. The room fell silent, as if Robert Coover and Ted Nelson were actually in the room and about to speak.

"Second place, and one of two actual examples that have never before been uncovered, is awarded to the group that completed an analysis of terminology shared by each of the cubes and identified their primary theme which is referenced in each of the prose poems, yet is often unnoticed within each independent piece: objects and patterns."

The class applauded, and one of the students in the recognized group stood and gracefully bowed from the waist.

"First place . . . ," the Professor said with an emphatic pause, "is awarded for truly innovative work—to the group that did not engage with the text but instead observed the interactive behavior of everyone in the room. The assertion is that interwoven, very human behaviors—how we navigate, how we interact, and how we leverage each other's discoveries— constitute a fundamental principle at work in the experiment."

The Professor raised his hands and began a slow applause, a cadence that was quickly joined by everyone in the room. The applause was not only for the individuals in the group that made the assertion, but for the assertion itself, that the interactions of the community, in response to structure and text, should not be overlooked but should rather serve as the hidden active element that underscores and clarifies the experiment's essential principles.

Then the Professor wished everyone a healthy and safe holiday, admonishing the students to avoid excess except in generosity to others.

He greeted four or five of the students who came up to the front to thank him for his efforts during the semester. When everyone had filed out, he and Esther decided to have a coffee at the Student Union. They closed the lecture hall doors and shut the lights, leaving 12 cube-poems scattered randomly in the dark.

Perhaps Robert Coover and Ted Nelson were there too, sitting in the back of the room continuing their unknowable Barcelona conversation.

NOTES

1. The operant theory is that hypertext creates a relationship between distinct objects. To manage hypertext endeavors successfully, one must therefore manage the system of relationships that the links represent. As with any relationship, there is a consequent obligation to maintain an attentive consistency, for any relationship (between spouses, between business partners, between dynamically linked objects) may "break" without that attention.

2. From Robert Coover's e-mail to the author, December 29, 2004.
3. From Ted Nelson's e-mail to the author, February 28, 2004.
4. *¶: A Magazine of Paragraphs*, Oak City Press: Holyoke MA, 1987, 37.
5. David Dreyfus and Bala Iyer, "Enterprise Architecture: A Social Network Perspective," Boston University. Proceedings of the 39th Hawaii International Conference on Systems Sciences.

CHAPTER 10

IDENTITY

The true entrepreneur, it is said, has only two fears: the love for a bad product and the love of a good woman—the former for its almost religious loss of objectivity and the latter for its capacity to alter entrepreneurial priorities. To his clients, Avram Rabinowitz appeared essentially fearless, for it seemed he had conquered both dangers. The first is the subject of this tale.

When he was younger, Avram thought there were principles to be adhered to, special rules to be followed. In those days, he believed there were good people and bad people and that his professional role in the world was to protect the good from the bad. His life's work was simpler then. Avram was a Captain in the Israeli Army's cyber security division. Computer jobs in the Army were clearly defined, manageable, and executed with precision and an absence of surprise. Avram helped his government colleagues understand their risks, prioritize the most important among them, and secure them, one by one.

Then Avram moved to the United States and eventually accepted a small consulting assignment for a friend who worked in Silicon Valley. That job led to another, and then another, and Avram soon became a very busy consultant. His current assignment, like the others, was not complicated. Several intrusions, none malicious, had been noted by the system administrators of the company, and their Operations Manager wanted to address the issue before it came to the attention of the executive staff.

"We're a small IT organization," the man said with unusual humility for an American. His name was Yashia, and Avram wondered if his family, too, came from the Middle East. "There's nothing unique about our computing environment, most of which is managed centrally. Our web systems are fairly standard, we have a basic DMZ and firewalls, and there are very few established connections with outside networks, other than Port 80."

The man provided an architectural overview of the company's basic computing systems (see Exhibit 10.1),[1] and Avram asked for a copy of the diagram, noting only that it is often the standard architectures that are the most vulnerable, because they are also the most predictable to those who want to gain entry.

Avram was given a tour of the data center, which was located directly adjacent to the manufacturing floor to take advantage of the cameras and air conditioning. There were several dozen servers, several racks, and two cubicles with terminals that ran the company's logo as a screen saver.

EXHIBIT 10.1   *DMZ Diagram*

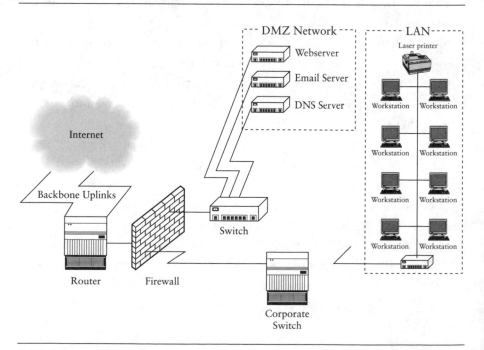

Source: Lockdown Networks

Yashia gave him the administrator password—permissions to the operating systems and application logs, but not any client information—and Avram spent the first morning reviewing the logs and hardening kernels one by one to eliminate any unnecessary access leaps. Then he downloaded some scripts from his own laptop, which took about 30 minutes to execute fully.

"Your intruder left a footprint, like a worm, which leaves runtime executables that launch whenever the host server is rebooted," Avram said later.

The Operations Manager made an unusual confession before asking his next question. "To tell the truth, I've only been managing this team for ten weeks, and I really don't want to escalate this issue if I don't have to. Is everything removed? Are there any further risks?"

Avram sensed that the Ops Manager was a visual learner, not an auditory learner, and with clients such as this, he found pictures were much more useful than even the most articulate and profound explanations. He retrieved a folder from his bag and produced a diagram he had discovered the night before.

"Think of your DMZ approach as Good But Not Sufficient," he said, hoping not to bruise the manager's ego. "We've been using DMZ-like strategies for a decade, and the security risks have become much more complex . . ." Then Avram showed his new diagram, same company, new model (see Exhibit 10.2).

"With cell phones and Blackberries and remote access from anywhere at anytime, you might want to consider a different tactic," Avram suggested.

Avram then acknowledged that he had removed the rogue executables before lunch, but the intrusive code had returned the same afternoon, in the same locations, so he had installed some trace computer scripts that he had written for a previous client, because they had the dual capacity to execute in reverse and operate entirely in a hidden corridor.

"Help me understand what that means." Yashia said. He was very young, still willing to admit his ignorance to strangers.

Avram explained that he had designed a set of shell scripts that would be triggered by the worm-like code. The scripts would record each of the code's steps and then would then trace those steps backward to

EXHIBIT 10.2   *Enforcement Points in a Mobile World*

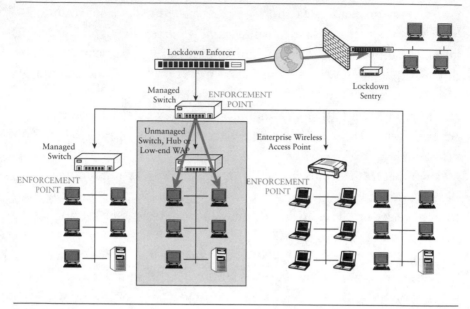

Source: Lockdown Networks, copyright 2006. Diagram provided with permission of Lockdown Networks.

determine the source. The scripts would then establish a secondary access point in a location only he knew, on a dedicated subnet that functioned like a hidden corridor between the outside world and the internal network. (Later, when Avram launched his own company and was asked by the venture capitalists for his product's name, he would say, "Dark Hallway" which also had the capacity to monitor internal traffic, device to device. But that is another story.)

He used his software so that suspicious traffic could first be diverted to the hallway, minimizing further harm, and then traced without an impact on the primary compute environment until the problem was resolved.

Avram's jobs were often finished in weeks instead of months because of his software programs. Subsequently, the excellence of his programming led to shorter and shorter assignments, a source of pride but also a hidden concern, from a purely economic perspective.

This project, however, was different. His personal security programs found no externally inserted malware, and he informed the Operations Manager that he would need another week to investigate the cause of the problem and fully immunize the site. He was given a badge and employee number, he completed all the necessary paperwork (including the background check, which they said would be finished over the weekend, although he knew his Israeli work experience would be difficult to verify). Avram returned home in some distress. He had never before encountered an environment that did not immediately benefit from his approach; usually so many threats were present that he was certain to locate *something* during his assessment.

He realized there were only two alternatives: either his approach was deficient (possible), or there was something unusual going on *inside* the company (probable).

"In my business, there are four quadrants," Avram explained that evening to his roommate, "ranging from intrusion detection to identity management and from virus protection to threat management. Each of these must be addressed for an institution to have confidence in its security infrastructure. No one seems to be doing enough, so there's plenty of room for me to help."

"Which quadrant are you?" She asked, only partially interested, her attention pulled to CNN on the muted TV atop the kitchen counter.

Self-aware networks, autonomic security that gets stronger over time, strengthened by the Dark Hallway approach that minimized risk—these were the objectives of Avram's approach. The principles on which his program was founded were the very principles espoused by the industry's most revered experts. "I'm realizing that every consulting project leads me to write the same software programs for each client," Avram said, slightly exaggerating, "and I'm thinking maybe I should start a company."

"Oh no, not a startup?" the roommate said, mournfully. Her biggest concern, or so it seemed to Avram, was that he would suddenly be unable to pay his portion of their rent.

"Don't worry, Red," he said, using the nickname she preferred. "I will always pay on time; you can be sure of this."

Billy Ignacio's eyesight was so poor that, despite thick glasses, he needed to read his computer screen from inches away. Everyone told him it wasn't healthy, and the Facilities team even offered to get him a magnifier for his monitor, but Billy was stubborn. He didn't take advice well, even if it was good advice.

Yashia had only been Billy's manager for ten weeks, but he had worked side by side with Billy's team for several years, and he was awed by Billy's programming prowess. Billy had often solved software problems when no one else in the engineering department could do so. Yet Yashia was equally aware of Billy's capacity to ignore supervisory requests. Billy was the only one in the entire department who refused to complete status reports and failed to come to team meetings. He socialized only with a few select employees and only in the lunchroom.

Yashia also knew that he needed to update their new boss on the status of all projects before he went home for the evening, and that meant getting Billy to talk.

"Regressions?" Yashia asked.

Billy nodded once without turning.

Yashia watched over Billy's shoulder as lines of software code scrolled by, Billy's head moving from side to side as he read the scrolling text. Software was easier for him to read than poetry or newsprint, with its natural forms and brackets and rules. Even from several feet away, Yashia recognized a good "if-then" statement, and he had a fairly solid understanding of Billy's latest proposal: automated error checking that would accomplish, in minutes, the job of several highly paid engineers who were currently spending hours testing the software, usually making mistakes while doing so. Invariably, something slipped past them, only to be noticed by customers months later.

"If you have a moment, I'd like to go over a few things with you, Billy."

"No moment."

"I was wondering if you could update me on your project," Yashia said quietly.

"Sent mail already."

"Yes, I know, Billy," Yashia said, holding out a few pages of paper. "I have a copy of your diagrams here. They were in the folder given to me when I took the new job." He rustled the pages as evidence. "I was hoping you could tell me the important points in your own words."

As he had moved up in the company, Yashia had learned much from his predecessors, some of whom were good planners but inadequate technologists. Others were skilled team leaders but did not communicate issues to the executives in a timely fashion. Each manager seemed to have a strength and a weakness, and he hoped to model the attributes and learn to avoid the liabilities. Yashia also knew that Billy liked to teach, especially when a manager confessed ignorance in his area of expertise.

"Could you do me a favor, then," Yashia asked, "and simply circle the four or five areas on your diagram that you think would be good places for your automation? That just might help me get our senior management to support the project."

Billy turned in his chair, reached for a red marker on his desk, and leaned very close to the page (see Exhibit 10.3).

"Some others will not like my ideas," Billy finally said.

Yashia asked why.

"Okay . . . so I am working on verification testing automatically, see? I know I can do a better job with code in half the time, better than four or five of the test engineers working in sequence. You know this, too. But to prove it, see, I have to produce verifiable results. You know, measure the resulting quality in comparison with similar tests done by the engineers themselves. Of course, they will know they are being tested and their attention will be better than on a usual day when no one is looking over their shoulder."

"We all work a little harder when we know someone's watching," Yashia agreed.

"Sure, sure. And no one wants to be beaten by a machine."

"So . . ."

"And so, *that* is what I wrote my *e-mails* about! I think we need to do this in secret. If they don't know they're being scanned, it will be more natural. The comparison will be more accurate." Billy was animated now, eagerly engaged. "Don't you see? We could run batch scripts on the servers, you know, in the background, over the next six or eight

EXHIBIT 10.3   *Software Testing Life Cycle*

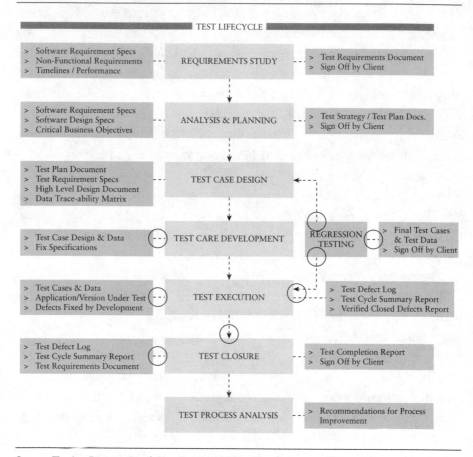

Source: Testing Process, ReadyTestGo.com, 2004.

weeks, and no one would know we're monitoring the test cases. Much more useful simulation."

"Yes," Yashia agreed, "the comparisons will be much more accurate. The only thing that would get in our way would be their right to privacy."

Billy stared at him.

"Think about it, Billy." Yashia said, taking the rare opportunity for a quick policy lesson. "What if I was running tests on you, behind your back, as part of your performance review next month? I might be able to justify a bigger raise for you, but what if I stumbled across something in your private life that you didn't want me to know?"

Silence.

Billy swiveled his chair back to the screen again and leaned forward, nose almost on the glass. The conversation was over.

He was ignoring the management dilemma that Yashia had proposed, and was now ignoring Yashia himself, who left the cubicle quietly. Of course, Billy's proposal was a good one. Very good, particularly in light of the new directions being outlined by their COO as part of the upcoming merger—virtualized data centers, dynamic resource allocation. Some type of automated testing would be absolutely necessary. As he walked down the brightly colored hallway to his new boss's office for his 5 p.m. meeting, Yashia looked over the diagram, the circles in particular; he studied the flow of the shapes and their positions on the printed page.

Linwood Eddy was on the phone and greeted Yashia with a silent friendly wave, gesturing for him to come into the office and close the door behind him. It was clearly a personal call—there was a forced awkwardness in Linwood's voice, a slight distress that made the man seem more interesting, more human.

". . . I *will* go visit him, just like I *always* do, " Linwood was saying on the phone, while Yashia was pretending to read through his paperwork. ". . . because some things are *still* important."

Then he hung up and slowly lifted his eyes toward Yashia in an unspoken apology for the modest indiscretion.

Linwood reached for a yellow folder on his desk and Yashia recognized the Purchase Requisition form, yellow folders indicating Signature Needed. "Before you fill me in on our projects," he said, "can you tell me why we have a new security expert . . . that fellow from Israel . . .?"

"Of course."

Yashia retrieved his literature from the recent conference and showed Linwood the white paper from Sun Microsystems,[2] an examination of security challenges at the corporate level.

"One of the most difficult challenges of moving to the Grid involves the expand-collapse-expand requirement of cross-functional teams," Yashia explained, drawing arrows between various levels (Exhibit 10.4). "Rapidly composed engineering efforts, coming together to solve problems and then disbanding . . . not unlike the composition of our merger transition team. We're using the idea of interfaces for the team: once we

EXHIBIT 10.4   *Identity Grid*

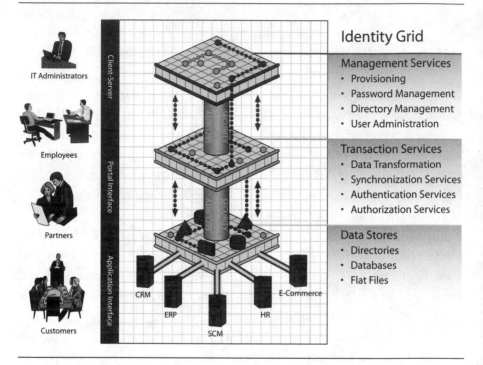

Source: Sun Microsystems

have identified our People APIs (Application Program Interfaces), how do you propose to actually use their network of networks? Who is going to be the traffic controller? Who is going to decide which person in which company should be given permission to access files, before the merger is complete?"

"The fellow from the Israeli Army is a solution to this problem?" asked Linwood, with only a modestly disguised degree of doubt.

"I don't think this is a technical problem. The issue lies in the ability of cross-functional teams to communicate with each other. Provisioning the right people, at the right time, without compromising our corporate assets, is part of the operational challenge, which is one of the reasons why I brought Avram in to review our environment."

Linwood grimaced, and looked at Yashia with an unspoken question.

"Yes, sir?"

Linwood waved his hand and asked Yashia to stop using *sir*. Then he told his new Operations Manager that he'd been an executive long enough to know when an urgent issue was on the lips of someone who was trying to find the right time to raise the subject. "I don't know how your previous supervisors handled bad news, Yashia," Linwood said with his unerring sincerity, "but I'm not the kind who shoots the messenger. Tell me what's going on."

"Sir? I mean, Mr. Eddy . . .?"

"You didn't hire an expensive security consultant to review the notion of Grid computing just to enable our merger team," Linwood observed.

"No sir, I didn't."

With a big sigh of relief that he could be candid, Avram explained that the DMZ safety zone separating the company's internal computers from the Internet had been compromised. Several servers seemed to have been hacked, although no damage had been done. True to his word, Linwood did not overreact, even though he knew this was a critical issue coming during a vulnerable time in the company's strategic position. He also did not belabor the possibility that the security violation was related to the upcoming merger.

Instead, he countersigned the Purchase Requisition in the yellow folder, handed it to Yashia, and instructed him to continue on course.

"I'll trust that you are managing the situation," Linwood said, "and will escalate anything that requires my attention."

Yashia glanced at the clock and realized he had little time to provide an overview of the other operations and engineering projects under way. He quickly explained that none of them seemed to be impacted, as yet, by the creation of the merger transition team. Those involved in the transition were not directly responsible for any short-term deliverables, and therefore most projects seemed to be moving forward according to plan.

"Most."

"Yes, uh," Yashia said, haltingly preventing the word *sir* from leaving his mouth. "There's one last item I'd like to explain." He drew Billy Chan's Test Diagram from his folder and highlighted the primary pros and cons of Billy's proposal.

Linwood Eddy's response was entirely unexpected.

"Yashia," Linwood said, glancing at his watch, "sometimes executives are required to make decisions based on only 10% of the information they need. The good executives are the ones who are right 80% of the time, using that 10% alone."

"Oh," Yashia said.

"I say this because I'm unfortunately in a hurry to get somewhere, but it seems to me, based on very little information, that you might have two overlapping situations."

"Overlapping situations?" Yashia asked.

Linwood Eddy had always been good at pattern recognition. Even in the early days, when computers were immense and their output was a series of sorted punch cards, he had had the remarkable ability to see one that was out of sequence. It was intuitive, but he had come to trust that intuition, trust his relationship with patterns. He offered a suggestion for Yashia to consider.

"It seems to me," Linwood said as he closed his briefcase, "that it would be useful for you to show this Test Diagram to your Israeli fellow, in case there's some similarity between Billy's little red circles and the security issues you want to resolve."

Linwood apologized again, saying he had a personal obligation across town.

"Why don't you walk me to the parking lot?" he said, reaching for his overcoat.

The two men were both new to their roles in the company, a common bond between them that Yashia increasingly appreciated. On their way down the back stairs, Linwood further blurred the boundary between his professional and personal identities, explaining that he was going to visit his father-in-law, as he did every evening after work. His candor further cemented Yashia's budding respect for the new COO, a man who seemed to have retained his personal values amidst his obvious success in corporate endeavors.

"I'll leave you with one final observation," Linwood said as he unlocked his car door and placed his briefcase in the back seat.

Yashia noticed that the car was filled with suitcases and boxes of dinnerware, as if his COO had been living out of his car.

"It's been my experience that 5% of our problems stem from technology issues, and the remaining 95% of our problems are caused by people. If I were you, I'd let your Israeli fellow trace the technology problems, and I'd concentrate on discovering if there is a breach in between the departments. You won't truly solve the problem until you find it."

Avram Rabinowitz returned home and fell asleep at his desk, only to be awakened by the sound of the cottage door slamming shut. In his dream, he had been awake and working at his computer. It seemed that only minutes of sleep had passed. He looked at the red digital glare of the clock and was surprised to see it was 3:30 a.m. He had been asleep for hours, not minutes. He pulled himself away from the desk, rubbed his neck, and plodded in stocking feet to the hallway, peering toward the lighted kitchen.

"You okay, Red?" he asked as she lifted a heavy case onto the kitchenette table. Its weight thudded densely in the otherwise quiet cottage.

"Go back to sleep, Avie," she called out. This meant she did not want to talk. "I'll show you in the morning," she added. She hugged him as if it was a tradition, the intimacy of roommates, and Avram realized that this housemate had many moods, many selves, and that each self possessed a unique greeting gesture.

Avram walked through the house to check the front door, as he did on most evenings after she had retired because she often forgot to lock it. He went to the kitchen for a glass of warm milk and saw the immense, suitcase-sized computer on the table. It was an Osborne 1, decades old.[3] He had never seen one before. It fascinated him. Inside the case, the *User Guide* had a chapter on connecting the TTY link via telephone lines to information sources at a university.

> Unwarranted access via public telephone lines is punishable by a fine and is not recommended. Any use of this computer in association with telephonic connectivity should be attempted only when prior permission is granted.[4]

Twenty years, he thought to himself. The machine was at least 20 years old. In all that time, with all the technical achievements defined as progress, Avram thought to himself, we are still burdened by unwarranted access. Why, as a culture, have we failed to address the challenges of connectivity, of proprietary information and the urge to obtain it without permission?

That thought kept him awake, debating whether to try for sleep or begin his day. Avram's mind wandered to his work: he was faced with the disagreeable task of identifying the source of an inside security breach.

Avram truly disliked this part of his work.

Everyone knew the Gartner statistic—that most security events (80%) are internal, caused by a disgruntled employee, an errant engineer. They are not security issues, but issues of poor management, issues better addressed by corporate counselors than by security professionals. He preferred the truer intrusion, the white hat hackers, the thieves of identities or intellectual property. He imagined that his distaste for internal threats was not unlike that of the city's police units when they are called to resolve a domestic dispute. As peace officers, their duty is to help resolve the conflict, but there are no good guys or bad guys in such cases, only unhappy people in a state of overwhelming discontent whose problems will re-emerge as soon as the squad car drives away.

Avram switched on the overhead halogen lamp Red had loaned him when he moved in and began reviewing his Rogue Element Identification scripts. Of course they could be modified to identify the source of the problem within the company's DMZ; several hours of scripting, an hour to test, and by breakfast, Avram would be ready to identify the source of his client's recent breach. Finding the employee responsible for the rogue software was the simpler of the two tasks ahead. Preventing the situation from reoccurring was beyond his scope of responsibility. He could supply answers, but in those early morning hours, in the grip of his predawn qualms, he wondered whether they were ready to hear what he had to say.

Do they really want to know?

NOTES

1. *Vulnerability Management Best Practices,* white paper from Lockdown Networks, April 2004.
2. *Identity Grid,* a Business White Paper from Sun Microsystems, May 2004.
3. The Osborne 1 had 64 K of memory, a pair of 100-K floppy disk drives, and a 5" screen (24 lines of 52 characters) and weighed 26 pounds. For more information, see http://oldcomputers.net/osborne.html.
4. *User Guide for the Osborne 1,* 1981.

CHAPTER 11

ORGANIZATIONAL ARCHITECTURE

I cannot resist the observation that if ever a book called for blogging, it is this one. Books that initiate lines of thinking complete themselves in the dialogs they engender. As Web 2.0 emerges from Web 1.0, readers have the opportunity—maybe even the obligation—to become writers, to take the story to the next level, to participate in the wisdom of crowds, which exceeds the wisdom of any single individual. I hope you have the kind of experience with this book that warrants blogging, and if you do, I hope you will hop on the Web to get your voice into the act.

—Geoffrey Moore, September 2005

SELECTIONS FROM A CORPORATE BLOG

Entry by the Author, September 20, 2005

In the next room, Isabel and Max are remixing songs on garage.com.

Theirs is a remarkable friendship, filled with significance, but that is a subject for another day. What caught my attention today, no less than other days but worth mention in this blog, is that those two navigate the Internet with the same comfort that I played ball in the street 40 years before. The other evening, Max actually taught me how to search for graphics in Google, something I'd never noticed before. He found penguins, lots of pictures of penguins, and was delighted.

Why I mention it, at this moment, is that it demonstrates for me how the next generation works collaboratively and non-locally, with a casual grace that should be instructive to those of us mired in hierarchical institutions. Corporate structures are not built to nurture an upward trajectory of knowledge. As this generation's engineers graduate college, they come into the workplace with experience and intuition that senior managers cannot yet emulate.

As with the disciplines of technical documentation and quality assurance in previous decades, the field of organizational architecture has long been ignored, although the problems encountered by project teams during endless failures are evidence that the organizational design and decision-making elements in our IT departments require constant attention and skilled, thoughtful review. I am convinced that our teams and corporate structures need to be considered at the beginning of every major initiative and then adjusted—sometimes dramatically—to ensure success.

How we are organized must be dynamic, adaptive, and fine-tuned to the specific needs of every project team.

If we can adjust our organizational architectures to be as flexible as the software architectures we hope to construct, they will allow *the upward trajectory of knowledge* that currently occurs only in the most unusual circumstances, when a gray-haired manager realizes that his webmaster, 25 years his junior, has much to teach him. All he needs to do is listen to her with an uncritical ear.

This is what I strive to do, with Max and Isabel, each and every memorable day. Our employees require *at least* that effort.

Entry by a Ten-Year Employee, Silicon Valley, September 21, 2005

If my grandmother, who was not entirely sane, made a quilt that reflected her Byzantine personality (though she despised artisans of any sort), that quilt would be more coherent and systematic than our company on its finest day. It is a patchwork of acquisitions, divestitures, realignments, and legacy systems that were launched so long ago that no one in the company can remember the rationale for their existence.

Our company, in comparison, makes my cross-stitched childhood in grandmother's care seem like precision craftsmanship.

Some have said that my dysfunctional home environment well prepared me for success in our company—that youthful boot camp of confusion was training me for the dissonance that our executive team seems unable to correct, as if the contradictions and cross-purpose objectives of each division in the company are driven by our corporate DNA and cannot be altered, only slightly moderated, as if leadership in our company is best understood as systemic compensation for the inherent handicap of our unending lack of balance.

Some claim to remember a time in our company's history when everyone—staff and management alike—was faithfully aligned and focused on making the company an industry hallmark.

I don't remember such a time. I have been employed here for what seems like an eternity. My teen-aged son was a first grader when I was hired as the project lead for our first hypertext initiative. In 13 years, I do not recall a single fiscal quarter that was orderly.

In those early days of the company, before the mergers made management almost impossible to achieve, the lack of coordination could be ascribed to the zeal associated with any young company in a period of rapid growth. Everyone seemed to be doing two or three jobs simultaneously. If we were asked, each one of us would articulate entirely distinct Number One goals for that quarter. In those days, it seemed exhilarating in the way a traveling carnival can be exhilarating to the children who ride the roller coasters and shoot at moving yellow ducks—but somewhere in the past 13 years, that electric atmosphere petrified, our zeal lost in the face of too many changes in direction.

Entry by an Organizational Psychologist, Boston MA, September 22, 2005

It seems quite evident to me. No further research is required.

One need only read Ray Kurzweil's notions of logarithmic progressions with regard to technology, and Kevin Kelly's observations about the hive mind, to recognize that we are at the cusp of a massive transformation in how we organize our work efforts, how we come together (swarm) to achieve the objectives of the group, and what we may become as a result of those efforts.

Simply put, the momentum of network-based technologies plus the ubiquity of network-enabled devices, fueled by the dual mechanisms of global economies (corporate) and social evolution (individual) are leading us toward a monumental shift—away from centralized authority (top-down management) toward the emergent activity of swarms, clusters, communities. If this trend proceeds without the unwitting hindrance of middle management, which simply does not comprehend how the next generation of workers (who have been using Internet gaming and instant messaging since they were in grade school) should be managed, the corporation will be transformed into niche hives (each with its own type of honey) in which the "law of increasing returns"[1] will fuel itself.

This transformation of The Firm will lead to what might be called The TransFirm—an institution with a heightened sensibility and productivity, in which frenzied innovation produces almost unpredictable results, unhindered by managers who have stopped "giving orders" and shifted to a more participatory engagement in the efforts of their hive counterparts.

The TransFirm will be recognizable for the absence of boundaries, its business generated in a grid-like interaction with multiple alliance partners and service providers, a network of similarly architected institutions succeeding in cooperative rather than competitive engagements. This, in turn, will create a trans-market operating on two sets of principles— retaining a framework of the existing corporate "make-market-sell-invest" mechanism while immersing itself in the less rigid, even playful chaos of information-based product multiplicities. They will come from the edge and move inward, rather than being created in the center (old process) and being distributed outward.

We should not need doctorates in Economics to understand the process, as the changes have already become evident in our personal lives and we simply have not observed them. We are not paid real money, nor do we keep our monies in our homes. Our employers transfer it electronically to the banks that manage our money for us. We do not gather our own fuel or harvest our own food, relying instead on specialized teams to do this on our behalf. We have long ago stopped fixing our own plumbing or owning our telephone lines—we have outsourced this to specialized groups called upon when they are needed. Indeed, we have been living with a technological and skill-based exoskeleton for years, until it has become so commonplace that even the remarkable view from Google Earth of our own neighborhoods, from satellites hundreds of miles above seems just one more mildly interesting Internet entertainment, perhaps a tool to find a local Japanese restaurant.

Our technology prowess has far outpaced our social ineptitudes and awkward relationships. We might land a satellite within yards of its intended target, yet a child starves every three minutes and we haven't yet figured out a way to get some food from our filled pantries to another location on our very own planet.

It is not emergent or disruptive technology that will enable our success.

It will be the TransFirm that will address those inequities, countless businesses, large and small, that have transformed their competitive energies (eat what you kill and hide the leftovers) into a moderated cooperative process that reinvests the billions of dollars now (mis)spent on "beating the competition" into a joint effort to improve the overall business environment of the planet so that success can be maintained over time, simultaneously, by multiple parties with common objectives.

Entry by a Temporary Secretary, September 22, 2005

I'll be honest. I didn't know much about this—about blogging—until I was hired to be the secretary for our VP of Facilities. He is responsible for all the company's buildings, utilities, cubicles, and new construction, and his administrative assistant is on maternity leave. Before she left, she gave me the password to the group's web site so I could keep the meeting minutes updated. Before I came to this company, my knowledge about Internet stuff could be held in a thimble. Not literally, of course, because knowledge doesn't have size, so actually, a thimble might be able to hold a great deal of knowledge. Perhaps that wasn't a good comparison.

The legal department takes blogging very seriously, and on every employee's first day of orientation, someone from the corporate counsel's office explains the various ways an employee could cause trouble for the corporation—that's how he said it, the corporation—and therefore, we all had a responsibility to take extra care with our written comments. Even a personal journal entry like this one could become a threat, for instance, if I casually included some information about an executive who had recently left the company because of improprieties. I would never talk about something like that in my blog, but I suppose there are those who enjoy the gossip and want everyone to know how much they know that no one else knows.

Of course, there are some things that secretaries are told in confidence—the reasons why a manager suddenly takes a leave of absence and comes back 30 days later, having graduated The Program. Or perhaps there are things in the departmental budget, you know, the little places where a few extra dollars are hidden for expenses like the candy that fills the big bowl on my desk every morning. I suppose everyone in the company has something special in their job that they should probably not put in print, but I'm just a temp worker, so the way I look at it, if they're telling me about something, everyone else already knows about it, and it isn't confidential anymore.

Entry by Anonymous Sales Support Engineer, September 24, 2005

I never understood the need for anonymous blogging; after all, we have a suggestion box in the lobby, but I am now the only staff remaining in our office tonight (we are the European division, located in the United Kingdom), and there is a crisis in the United States that our senior partner has decided to ignore. Were she to discover that I was, even without names, discussing her decision to allow the crisis to continue, I would be fired immediately, so I am posting this entry with the knowledge that there are three possible outcomes:

No one reads this posting, and everything proceeds in crisis mode on the assumption that no one could have prevented the crisis.

The wrong people read this posting, and I am identified, blamed for being the cause of a problem, and am terminated.

The right people read this posting—someone honest in our corporate counsel's office, for example, or one of our key shareholders, perhaps because they read everything, and when they investigate this issue, they will learn that the crisis could have been averted, were it not for the actions of a very small group of people who are more concerned about their commissions than they are about the welfare of the company.

Why would anyone allow the company to undergo a dramatically negative day in the markets? After all, even their own stock options will lose most of their value, correct?

To understand their reasoning, one must understand that there is actually a synchronicity of events unfolding—poor performance on the part of the U.K. team (something they wish would not be discovered) and a massive e-mail outage. The outage is being blamed for the bad quarter, but in reality, it is more akin to a murder inside a building that later burnt to the ground, the secondary event coincidentally masking the facts of the first event, at least long enough for the guilty parties to arrange the appropriately complicated excuses.

I am saying it here, and someone should respond. We missed our numbers. It is not the fault of our American e-mail administrators.

Entry by Experienced Hi-Tech Manager, September 26, 2005

Organizational Change is constant, as with any entity in nature: a colony of ants, a flock of birds, a tribe of aborigines.

Life and death, order and entropy, blossom and decay—no entities remain still except those that have not survived. Subsequently, the charter of our team is less about causing change than it is about guiding its boundlessness in some artful direction, guiding that change and informing everyone in our team of our three states of being: our history (how we came to this moment in time), our present circumstance (the reality that surrounds and challenges us), and our possible futures (including the potential to improve ourselves amidst this ongoing flux).

I am reminded of the story of Babek the Sculptor, who, according to the myth, was the creator of the first gargoyle. Babek lived in the dark ages, when anything unexplainable was quickly cast out from society, and so he lived most of his life far away from the castled villages and Magna Carta rules. Babek's theory was that all material contains an essence, a potential for being, and that a sculptor's duty was not to impose his or her own imagined form upon the rock, but rather to carefully remove the layers and liberate the embedded spirit from its rock encasements. Subsequently, his sculptures were often considered grotesque and alarming, but it is said that, when Babek was finished, the essence that had been inside the granite was enabled to move about the earth, free.

I mention this mythical tale, first retold in a college sculpture class many years ago when I believed corporations were evil and to be avoided (if not openly battled), because it seems to me that each corporation has its own embedded and essential character, and that the duty of its executive leadership is to carefully remove the unnecessary and irrelevant outer bindings so that the corporation's essential character can move among other characters in the marketplace with the distinct compassion that comes from having been liberated, a compassion that allows that corporation to engage cooperatively in manners that benefit itself and all the other liberated characters who bring energy to the marketplace, their world.

The ultimate challenge, then, for our team of Organizational Change managers, and for our executives who must approach the task with Babek-like sincerity, is to take the current hardened, unremarkable, and awkward, undifferentiated mass and locate its rightful boundaries, finding the enlivened edges of the corpus of the Firm so that it may become the transformed and open-minded entity, the TransFirm—as the previous entry suggests, a modern business for our network world, freed from its century-long imprisonment in a shape someone else has imposed, becoming the lively, ever-changing, and cooperative being that we, the employees, so hope that it can be.

Entry by a Senior Financial Analyst, September 27, 2005

We have been told that we no longer fit the mold of "A Company," as defined by tax codes and city charters, and they have asked our legal team to provide a newer vocabulary to, succinctly please, define our institution's reason for being, hoping that we might be able to use the familiar terms they have come to understand: service provider, manufacturing X to be purchased by Y, or perhaps an aggregator of what others have manufactured, a type of 21st century bazaar, with all manner of wondrous treasures brought (not without some danger to the crew) to our lands for our use and for our appreciation.

Our corporate counsel's office responded with the most recent published document, the 10Q, which, as everyone knows, describes our business in the consistent format we struggled long to agree upon. Included in that format were the requisite statistics that define our financial health and well-being, and accompanying those statistics, in the manner prescribed by the courts, were the appropriate disclaimers and disavowals that are in no way to be construed as forward-thinking guidance during this very delicate cycle in our industry.

We returned the counsel's document, completed and signed by those who are specifically issued D&O (Director and Officer) insurance. We didn't need to wait more than ten minutes—hardly enough time for them to validate its authenticity and transport the document to the correct midlevel authority who first made the request, hardly enough time for that round-bellied and bushy-eyebrowed fellow to burst through the front doors of his office building and race—if race can be used to describe the pace of the limp-step-and-pause-to-breathe fellow, who, upon arrival, announced that he was the County Auditor for All New Businesses, as legislated two weeks previous in the Omnibus State and County Regulatory Reform and Distribution Act of 2005 (OSCRRDA-2005). He looked directly at Sheri, who is called the company's receptionist (whereas I see her as our first line of defense in the effort to prevent any elements of real life from seeping under our doors, slurping past her desk, and then into the elevator where they can wreak havoc on the innocent bystanders who are simply doing their jobs).

"This form is not complete," the round man whose name was McGuffin exclaimed. "Surely a question as easy as this one . . . well, perhaps it was simply overlooked in your haste."

And this is how I came to the sudden pinnacle of my career, having identified one among the many company business processes that actually reflected the company, somehow provided the type of carnival caricature that looks too good to be honestly improvised. So I explained it this way:

> In our company, key customers enter their own information and requests for our products and identify which of our many warehouses has the correct number of the required item. Then they contract with our transport partner to deliver the items on the requested day, finally completing the purchase requisitions, which are automatically approved for key customers, who then initiate a funding transfer

that is completed in less than two minutes because both companies use the same banking institution for eCommerce. When the transfers are complete, the customer notifies our warehouse (which is actually leased from one of the customer's competitors) to schedule delivery. With the single exception of the actual transport, which has been sourced to UPS, every other step/event in the sale and delivery of their requested items is performed by the customers themselves. We find they pay more attention to the details and make far fewer mistakes. The cooperative nature of the interaction is further reinforced by current regulatory practices suggesting that "appropriate levels of monitoring" are provided for each company by the other.

Entry by a Company Consultant, September 30, 2005

I've reread what others have written and feel compelled to participate, if only to note that we have not been talking about organizational architecture, we have simply been complaining. They are not the same.

If we were truly interested in learning about architectural alternatives, we would be looking to the field of biosystems, to understand how our bodies—our *corpus*, a highly sophisticated interaction of networked systems—function, at the cellular level. We would be looking to the field of organic chemistry, to understand how molecular groups can recombine dynamically to address new environmental or elementary change.

When a virus attacks the human system, as occurs so many times each day, it is most often repelled through a series of autonomic counterbalance measures, with the immune systems and the blood working to immediately address the virus. Yet, when a virus attacks our information systems, we blame the inadequacy of firewalls, the lethargy of bureaucratic security committees, the paucity of funds, the disgruntlement of fellow workers.

It is not difficult to find information about "federated systems—teams of semiautonomous value-producing entities bound together for a higher purpose . . ."[2] What I find constantly surprising is that, instead of considering alternative structures (of which we know a great deal), we continue to repeat the antique (feudal and futile) work structures inside of which our fathers and grandfathers and their grandfathers ground away.

I imagine Mr. Vanderbilt standing in his ornate bedroom with three-clasp locks to prevent any intruders, gazing down on his acreage, and the hundreds of enslaved workers managed by their field hands who were managed by their bosses who reported to the men having dinner in the elegant dining room, lined with tapestries and velvet-flocked wallpapers.

It is the same parent-child organization (previously called master-slave) that represented our computer systems in technical documentation. Every company is the same, every company has the same complaints, and no one seems to notice a similarity among them, which, if it was an illness, would have teams at the National Institutes of Health seeking cures.

Federated systems with loosely coupled functional clusters, orbiting around an intellectual commons, combined and recombined in rapid response to current conditions: We know how to document them, we know how to diagram them, and we know the complexities they are best suited to address. Change in our institutional hierarchies, based on those learnings, is long overdue.

"This just sounds like another complaint," you might say.

Now that I have raised the issue, let me identify one example that actually addresses this complaint.

For several years, research and development teams have identified the various architectural requirements of a service-oriented architecture in technology. Many of those requirements include a virtual resource market[3] enabled to quickly field requests and assign the appropriate resource (application service) in response.

They are now learning that the very same architectural framework can be used at the human level to organize available resources rapidly (human-centric services) in a cost-efficient and highly successful manner.

If we gave even 33% of the attention paid to our products to our organizations, the improvements would be immense. It is long overdue.

NOTES

1. Kevin Kelly, *Out of Control: The New Biology of Machines, Social Science, and the Humanities* (New York: Basic Books, 2004), 62.
2. Jay S. Byrne, "Automation and Control in Grid-Connected Federations," Proceedings of the IEEE 3rd Annual EIT2003Conference, June 2003.
3. *Service Oriented Development*, Presentation by Steve Yatko, Credit Suisse First Boston, 2005.

CHAPTER 12

(THEORY OF) RESONANT USABILITY

H e was not the tallest or the smartest or even the best looking member of his very large family, but Bobby knew he was, by far, the happiest professional among them.

Others might be wealthier (being in real estate and banking) or perhaps more fulfilled (being schoolteachers), although they all complained a lot, but none of them had the daily joy of coming to the ballpark with its magnificent green grass and perfectly shaped diamond, none of them heard the sweet sound of a wooden bat meeting a 90-mile-an-hour fastball, and none of them had the pleasure of working with other adults who truly enjoyed what they were doing, reaching for that bat, touching their skin to the skin of that wood.

With the single exception of Eddie, the Unix systems administrator who had worked for two startups before joining the technology team of the St. Louis Cardinals' organization, everyone loved their work. They were the epitome of IT professionals who were completely integrated with the business. They completely understood the game, were enamored with even the most arcane statistics, believed that something unique could happen every day at the ballpark, and often provided innovative technical approaches that were quickly adopted by the organization because those innovations solved a real business problem.

Bob didn't like Eddie, partly because of the natural conflict between the "iron and wire" infrastructure guys and those who focus on the "user experience," which was Bob's area of expertise. They simply didn't appreciate each other. Another reason for Bob's contempt was that Eddie was an asshole.

"My name's Bob Roberts," he'd said, sticking out his hand, when Eddie came to the park for his first day as the IT group's Unix administrator. "You're going to love this job."

Eddie didn't bother to return the handshake. "Your parents actually named you Robert Roberts? How depressing is *that*?"

So Bob stayed away from Eddie. Even his boss, their CIO for the Cardinals' organization, had seen that Eddie would be a challenge for the rest of their IT team. However, they really needed someone of his caliber to plan their migration from Unix to Linux, and Eddie's skills were highly recommended. The way Bob looked at it, if his biggest complaint about his work environment was that he was working with a group of nine terrific technologists and one talented asshole, then things were pretty damned good compared to everyone else who was at the family picnic on that Sunday morning.

"When do you go to work, Bobby?" Uncle Tim had a missing finger from his shipbuilding days during the Korean War. As a young boy, Bob used to be fascinated with Tim's missing digit, how it felt when he touched the stub.

"Not till noon, Unc," Bob said, pulling a Pepsi from the cooler. "We did most of the prep work last night for the game."

"Still love it?"

Bob nodded, but before he had an opportunity to explain why the convergence of his favorite hobby with his chosen profession had been such a charmed event in his life, Bob's fiancé inserted herself with a bit of characteristic hyperbole.

"He invented software that *Tony LaRussa* said was *genius*," she said, practically singing LaRussa's name. "Let me show you the picture."

Before Bob could stop her, Sophia had retrieved the article from *Popular Mechanics* that showed an earlier version of what Bob had recently invented for the team (see Exhibit 12.1).

The crowd that gathered behind Uncle Tim ooh'd and aah'd. Bob glanced at his watch, hoping for a timely exit, but it was too early to leave for the stadium and he was forced to explain himself.

It was not, as Sophia believed, a lack of pride in his accomplishments, for Bob was pleased with his accomplishments since coming to the team 12 months before. Rather, it seemed that he was always explaining technology to nontechnologists, making technology more appealing to the techno-phobic ballplayers, many of whom would rather lift weights than look at themselves on a video screen. His adjustments to the software currently in use by the team made the various reports and views infinitely more interesting to an athlete, and if it was more interesting, it would actually be used.

EXHIBIT 12.1   *Business Intelligence: A Baseball Manager's View*

Source: Photo by Chris Lee/*St. Louis Post-Dispatch*, insets by Inside Edge Scouting Services, as printed in the article by Jim Kaat, *Popular Mechanics*, May 11, 2004.

However, at home with his family, he tried to avoid situations in which he was asked to explain computers. He was a graphic artist, not a poet, and his family needed metaphors, not descriptions of advanced user interfaces with heuristic display engines automatically adjusting in real time the display of information based on previous uses by other team members.

"Did you make those?" one of his cousins asked. She was a realtor, and she recognized a good report printout when she saw one.

"Oh, goodness, no," Bob said, "that's what they were using when I came to the team. My work makes that information more . . . well, useful to the players."

"That's why Mr. LaRussa called it *genius*," Sophia sang again.

Bob scowled whenever she used the G-word, partly because he did not consider his developments to be either elegant or groundbreaking. From his point of view, his contribution—a new software engine that resided on the web server and pulled data from various networked databases containing all the personnel information for each of the players—had been to apply the theory of heuristic search technology to the presentation layer, to the user interface. It was Bob's belief that every time a ballplayer used the system to review his pitches or hitting from the previous game, he individually adjusted the display to look at the data just as he wanted it. What Bob's engine provided was a method for aggregating information about the various individual choices that the ballplayers made each time they accessed the system. His method delivered a slightly modified display, based on everyone's use of the system. Each time, the information was improved.

Therefore, if a rookie had just been promoted from Triple A and given a Cardinal hand-held device, he would see information in ways that the more experienced players viewed it, conveying some of that experience to a new user.

A heuristic user interface, for baseball players.

An essay published in the *Modern Technology Review* (July 2004), presented a new perspective on operating systems and programming languages. When Bob read the essay, he recognized there might be a higher level of interconnectedness between disciplines than he had realized.

If language is a system, and computers are systems, then it may be proposed that information enlivens both systems as if it were blood and they were bodies. So complete is the analogy that one can begin to consider what we know about language itself as a guideline for what we do not yet know about computer systems. With this in mind, let us consider the following syllogism.

Reuse, of any matter or mechanism, will not occur until there is Use. Therefore, any attention to the Ease of Reuse should not occur until Ease of Use has been duly attended to.

From this theory, we may deduce that Ease of Use, or what has, in other circles, been called Usability (of the computer-human interface), must be duly considered before the engineering of modules that are designed to be used more than once. Now, this presents us with a serious problem, as most software development organizations have long considered these two aspects of computer engineering distinct and separate enterprises. This composition, an improbable essay on the contradictions of technology organizations, aimed to dismantle the standard assumptions first, in order to discover a Different Way of Doing Things.[1]

Bob paused to consider the work he was doing for the team. It seemed to be part of a larger trend. Then he continued reading . . .

Subsequently, we will assume, for the purposes of this essay, that *Reuse* has been handicapped because it has been severed from its predecessor, *Use*. We will set the record straight by establishing the principle of Resonant Usability: usefulness of any system is an aggregation of the usefulness of all parts of the system, a corollary of which states that User Interface Design cannot be detached from the foundation architecture on which it rests.

According to the Theory of Resonant Usability, standard interfaces and exchanges (protocols, markup languages, data maps) have been burdened by awkward frameworks that occur underneath. They have been used, until now, as a means of redress, which is to say, two contradictory foundations are made to look the same by means of XML standards, EDI, or electronic data charts that translate one term as another so that an exchange can be made.

With Resonant Usability throughout the architecture, the power of synchronized user interfaces can be unleashed. Global knowledge sharing (multilingual, multicultural, multifaceted) can occur in real time.[2]

The author then diagrammed the history of computing, not using the traditional upward curve (based on Moore's law), which begins with mainframes and swings upward through Client-Server and Internet toward Grid Computing, but in the shape of what the author called a "gyre," with the thinnest part of the hourglass always being the Present Tense (see Exhibit 12.2).

Bob understood that the industry had long overlooked the "computer-human interface." In his previous jobs he had struggled simply to convince the rest of his own team that user interface issues were important. This article said that progress in the lower portions of the gyre had now led the industry to a fundamental moment when the computer-human interface must finally be addressed, lest the industry become stagnant. From this perspective, concerns about the commodification of technology could be understood as a real danger if the next stage (computer-human interface) was not sufficiently addressed.

EXHIBIT 12.2 *Era of the User Interface: Number 1*

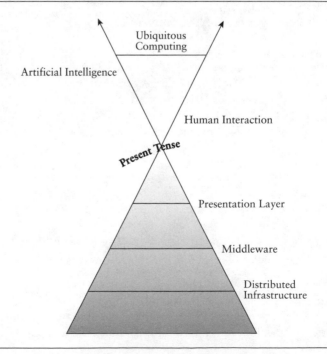

In other words, if we continue to avoid usability issues, the steady march of progress will indeed become frozen. The technology will become a simple commodity and never reach its true potential.

The conference on Ubiquitous Computing was attended by the entire St. Louis Cardinals' IT staff, part of their CIO's effort to keep his employees up to date on current technology trends, and one of the many conferences they attended when the Cardinals were "on the road." Like emergency room doctors and firefighters, their work schedule was not the standard five-day, eight-hour routine.

Bob opted for the panel discussion on User Interface Design and Architecture, which was described as a "provocative dialogue." Just before the session began, he saw Eddie coming into the auditorium. Bob slumped in his seat so he wouldn't be seen. The panel moderator, an amusing fellow with a bowtie, was a Dean at Florida State University. He introduced the session by briefly describing his notion (based on the work of many others, he admitted) that an individual's "mental models"[3] influence the person's ability to absorb new ideas. He then introduced the two panelists, a woman who worked at Oracle as a "User Experience Designer" and a System Architect from a company that provided "virtual machine" operating system software for Linux clusters.

> Moderator: The two of you are an apple and an orange, it seems to me. I can't imagine what you have in common, except to an academic like me, who sees you both as fruit, you know, both high-tech geeks.
>
> UI Designer: I consider it a compliment, so I must be a geek.
>
> Architect: I've been a geek since I was born, but I was in the closet for a long time.
>
> Moderator: But really, if the two of you worked in the same company, would you spend any time at all trying to get to know the other's work? I've seen your products, and, frankly, it doesn't appear that the people who work on the user interfaces ever speak to the people who are responsible for the architecture.

UI Designer: My experience at Oracle, and before that, at People-Soft, was that our architects were the ones who were constantly telling us we couldn't do this or we couldn't do that, because the products weren't built to allow the kind of flexibility we need.

Architect: She's right, of course. The only interactions I have with our "look and feel" teams are tedious meetings at the end of a long development cycle when I try and explain to them the reasons why a change to the core libraries would require endless testing, just to make the modest changes they are asking us to make.

Moderator: So neither of you sees the other group as cooperative, you know, partners working toward the same goal.

UI Designer: I don't think we have the same goals, do you?

Architect: Nope, different goals.

Moderator: C'mon, folks, the audience came for a provocative dialogue, not monosyllabic grunting.

Architect: Well, here's my thought. Architecture is primarily focused on consistency, stability, like the foundation of your house. You wouldn't want to redo the foundation every time you wanted to paint the kitchen a different color.

UI Designer: He's right, as far as it goes. But it seems to me that we're talking about the quality of life in that metaphorical house, not just a new coat of paint. If the electrical outlets are so far away from the appliances that extension cords are needed, or if the doors are opening the wrong way because they were framed incorrectly, the house isn't livable. It might survive an earthquake, but who would want to live there?

Moderator: God, I hated it when we remodeled our kitchen. The contractors kept explaining why they couldn't put the refrigerator where we wanted it, or why they had to remove an entire wall just to change the position of the sink. Of course, we had to redo the foundation, and of course, it cost a lot more than we expected.

UI Designer: Exactly. But if the house had been designed with those kind of changes in mind, in fact, if those kind of changes (we call it Personalization) had been enabled at the beginning, it would be much easier to remodel any room in the house.

Architect: Right, but consider the community. There are regulations for drainage, for support walls, for electrical distribution. We have an almost unending series of requirements, just to make the domain comply with all the civil regulations. And here we have the interior designers, begging us to make the whole thing like Legos, where you can put anything anywhere.

Apparently, Eddie had heard enough. He excused himself, to one person after another, going down the aisle and toward the exit. Bob watched him force his way past the people seated to his left, in full view of the panelists.

Moderator: Uh oh, folks, we're beginning to lose the audience. You, sir, the one heading for the door. Can I ask you a question?

Eddie looked up, embarrassed by the attention and emphatically shook his head no. Then, in a sudden demonstration that he had known Bob was in the room, Eddie pointed instead to the middle of the row.

"Ask *him* a question," Eddie said, pointing in Bob's direction, and with that, he left the small auditorium amidst laughter from the rest of the audience.

Moderator: Okay, I will. You, sir, lucky person identified by the man who just left our awe-inspiring presence, are the Designated Driver of our Q&A. Can you come to one of the microphones in the center aisle and pose a question for the panelists?

Bob was once again annoyed by Eddie's poor behavior, yet he was more than happy to ask a question. Now it was his turn to excuse himself down the aisle, bumping into knees, until he reached the microphone, which was not working. One of the tech support team for the conference trotted down the aisle, switched it on, tapped it twice like a drumbeat, and waved to the applause of the audience.

Moderator: What's your name, company, give us all the etceteras.
Bob: My name is Bob Roberts, and I'm a member of the IT team supporting the St. Louis Cardinals.
Moderator: Thanks, Mr. Robert Roberts, for being such a good sport. Toss us a question. Go ahead, stump the experts, if you can.

Bob: OK, here it is. I've been reading some recent essays about the Theory of Resonant Usability. It's the notion that usability needs to be considered at the very beginning of a technology initiative, rather than at the end. I'm wondering if the two panelists have any thoughts on how that might influence their own work.

Moderator: OK, experts. Any comments on Robert Robert's question about the Theory of Resonant Usability?

The two panelists huddled for a minute, becoming more of an entity than two separate objects. They both seemed to agree about something before the Architect responded.

Architect: I'm responding first because I happen to know Gerry Sun at Tuscaloosa, who first proposed the theory. Gerry's a bit of an oddity in our industry, kind of a loose cannon—I'm sure he'd agree with that characterization—and he often turns our behaviors upside down to provoke debate. In this case, I think he has an interesting point. We are shifting away from frozen infrastructures toward a more flexible and definitely more distributed architecture. It's bound to have an impact, down the line.

UI Designer: We huddled for a moment because we both read the essay, though I don't know the author personally. I actually think he's pointed to a dramatic change in how we will be building and releasing technology in the coming years, so yes, I think it's right on point. I also like his gyre design, which forces us to focus on the Present Tense of a user's experience.

Bob glanced to his left and right and then turned to view the audience sitting behind him. No one seemed anxious to ask a question, so he turned back to the bow-tied moderator and asked if he might pose a second question.

Bob: Some of the work we've done for the Cardinals organization aims to take the massive amount of statistical data we have compiled, for each player against every possible pitcher, each pitcher at different times of day, and find a way to present it so the baseball players would be lured into using the system. From my point of view, it seems that the only part of the system that connects

with the ballplayers is the user interface, so we've discovered
ways to attract even the most computer illiterate on the team.

Moderator: So, that's why the Cardinals did so well last year. I
knew Boston was a techie team, now we find that both league
champions depend on their IT staff a great deal. So tell me,
Mr. Robert Roberts, what's the trick? How do we get people
who hate computers to use their computers?

Bob was glad that Eddie had left the room, because he wouldn't have
tolerated their focus on the user interface instead of the back-end systems. He briefly explained the strategy of the heuristic user interface engine, based on many of the concepts already discussed in the session. He
explained that there were many products focusing on baseball players,
umpires, tennis pros, and others. All of them have produced remarkable
results, but none of them have solved the problem of those who do not
want to use the system.

"By constantly improving the interface, based on how other ballplayers are using it, even our novice users are finding the system useful."

"And if it is useful," the moderator nodded, "they will come."

The moderator noted that the time allotted to them had passed, and
another session was coming in. He thanked the panelists, thanked Bob,
for the shared insights, and adjourned the session. Several people in
Bob's row nodded their acknowledgment as they passed him on the
way to the door, and one woman patted him on the shoulder and told
him to keep up the good work. Then a well-dressed gentleman in a pin-
striped suit with a bold necktie approached him, holding out a business
card.

"I'm Ted Lattimore," the man said. "Our venture firm is very interested in this area, the user interface, and I'm wondering if you would be
willing to join me for lunch?"

Bob nodded yes, and that is when his trouble began.

"What do you mean, *millions* of dollars?" Sophia asked as Bob related
his brief conversation with Lattimore. She found the man's use of
hyperbole fascinating.

"He said that a software engine like the one I built for the Cards could become a major product in a new market," Bob said, "and he said this was how technologists could make millions of dollars, *with* the right investors, *and* the right executives."

"So, you're going to do it, right? I mean, going to the ballpark every day is nice, Bobby, don't get me wrong . . ." Sophia suddenly envisioned herself living a very different life as a married woman. "But *think* what you could *do*, just *think*."

Bob didn't like her sudden enthrallment. It was as if Sophia was a prism that had been slightly turned to show a flawed surface he had never seen before. They'd always imagined a modest life together, kids growing up in neighborhoods known for their diversity, friends inviting them on rustic camping trips or weekends at the beach for the cost of the gasoline to get there. In a moment, and with a slight, almost unnoticeable adjustment of her tone, Sophia had illumined a different set of values. "Let's change the subject, eh, Soph?"

Nonetheless, Bob secretly observed a similar shift in himself, as if his own prism had turned by two degrees to reflect an angle of his face he'd not seen in quite the same way. Ted Lattimore's enthusiastic vision of the entrepreneurial life, the Everest-like challenge to create something tangible, a company, from thin air, the potential to offer the entire industry a new way of designing software—with the users foremost in mind—all this was more than intriguing. Bob found himself distracted by the fantasy, more than he would have supposed, and even as they climbed into bed and pulled the immense quilt underneath their chins, he was imagining what it would feel like to be the Chief Technology Officer and Founder of a company listed in Fast Company's 100 Most Promising Startups.

The next morning, after Sophia had gone back to her apartment, and before he was supposed to leave for the ballpark, Bob retrieved Ted Lattimore's business card from his wallet and called the cell phone number scribbled on the back.

Ted answered on the second ring, and Bob could hear children laughing in the background.

"This is Bob Roberts," he said, "we met yesterday at . . ."

"Hello *Bob*," Ted exclaimed with the bountiful generosity of tone one reserves for child prodigies, first loves, and perhaps potential investment opportunities. "I was hoping you'd call. I know I'm abrupt, I'm with my kids. Would you like to meet the woman whom I think would be a marvelous co-founder? We could have sandwiches in my office."

"Well," Bob hedged, "I don't want to set up the wrong expectations ..."

"Good, good," Ted said, "an aloof and disinterested quality is the perfect negotiating strategy, makes us think we need you more than you need us. Lunch on Monday?"

"Can't do Monday, Ted, the Cardinals are playing the Reds and it's Bat Day," Bob explained, "lots to do. But then they leave for Pittsburgh. Tuesday afternoon is OK."

"Tuesday, it's set. I'll send an e-mail confirmation with directions," Ted said, adding a hasty goodbye before he clicked off.

Bob was startled by the intense duality of his response to the call. On one level, he felt a sense of disloyalty to his CIO and the Cardinals' organization, as if he was already married and had just arranged an interlude with another woman. On another level, beneath the anxiety and a growing sense of alarm, Bob was also oddly elated at the prospect of the Tuesday meeting, as if he'd just inhaled some nitrous oxide in the dentist's office and was looking forward to the drill.

On the morning before he was scheduled to meet Ted Lattimore, Bob went to the ballpark as part of the production systems test team. During road trips, the stadium-based IT group split into three teams to ensure that any technology system needed before, during, or after games was put through a documented test sequence. The systems included the 24-monitor Sony Trinitron system that broadcast the game throughout the stadium and in the luxury boxes, the wireless network that allowed fans to access e-mail any time, day or night, the Sportsmaster Pro hand-held devices from Recreational Technlogies, and the Umpire Information System (UIS) that tracked every baseball from when it left the pitcher's hand to when it crossed home plate and that was originally designed for the U.S. military to track missiles.[4] Any anomalies were addressed long before the first player arrived to begin his routine, whether it was reviewing their previous day's performance on a video coaching system developed by Panasonic that uses six rewritable DVD drives and can archive more than 400 hours of pitcher-batter matchups, or simply icing bad elbows and knees.

On that day, however, Bob's supervisor pulled him from testing duty and asked him to give a tour to a new writer from the *St. Louis Post-Dispatch* who was doing a Sunday magazine feature on the Cardinals organization.

"A tour?" Bob complained. No one liked to give an operational tour, because they inevitably were asked for souvenirs or autographs or secret stories about members of the team.

"You'll like this one," his CIO said, waving him over to the business office.

Bob walked through the door and was introduced to one of the most beautiful women he had ever seen in his life. Later, long after the article was published, when Bob had suspended his engagement with Sophia, many months after this first meeting, he would still recall that moment in the business office, remember the odd red-lined boots and purple socks, her firm grip, the way she asked questions that made the responder want to talk all day.

"I'm Katie LaTourelle," she said quickly, extending her hand. "I understand you've got the unfortunate duty today."

As they walked through the operations facilities and into the tunnel that ultimately led to the field, because everyone knew to start a tour at field level for the impression it made on newcomers, Katie explained that she wanted to do the article from the employee's point of view, not a starry-eyed glimpse of famous people or a submerged marketing story to sell more advertising. She wanted to explain the daily routines of the people behind the scenes.

Off the record, to break the awkwardness, she asked him to tell his favorite baseball story.

"Well, I could tell you about the time my grandfather met Babe Ruth," Bob said, putting up his forefinger, "or the time I met Roberto Clemente," lifting his second finger.

"Tell me the Clemente story," she said. She showed him that the tape recorder was *not* on.

They came out of the tunnel into the blinding sunlight, and both of them shielded their eyes for a minute. They began the long walk around the outer edge of the field, heading toward the right field wall and moving toward center field.

". . . and my grandparents lived in Pittsburgh. Their neighbor was old Doc Feingold, the Pirates trainer. This was just after the 1960 World Series, and I was only seven years old, just awed with baseball. Doc Feingold took my grandfather, father, and me down to the Pittsburgh locker room so I could get autographs—this was back in the days when autographs weren't sold, just collected like keepsakes. I walked around the benches, amazed by the size of these men, Clendenon, Stargell, men that seemed twice as tall as my father, and while everyone signed my book, most of them did it quickly and went back to what they were doing. Everyone except Clemente. He was the only player who talked to me, right to me. He knelt down so he could look me in the eye, and he wrote a brief note 'Dear Bobby, Best Wishes to our Greatest Fan, Roberto Clemente.'"

"Do you still have it?"

"The autograph book?"

Bob sighed, and explained that it was lost in the various moves his family made, leading to their eventual home in California, where his grandfather had lived as a child. To this day, he hoped to discover it suddenly in an old box of family things somewhere in storage.

They passed third base and headed for the opposing team's dugout, where, Bob explained, the Cardinals provided no technology. It was a major league rule that both dugouts were to be technology free, which was why Tony LaRussa printed out the reports he used during the game.

"Are you saying that the Cardinals don't have *any* technical edge in the park?" she asked.

"Oh, I didn't say the locker rooms and team lounge were technology free," Bob said. "Any player can come back down the tunnel and access their last at-bat against this pitcher, or their last stolen base . . . just not in the dugouts. Against MLB rules."

Katie nodded, and followed Bob as he took several passageways back into the corridors where their data center was located, explaining that they also had offsite server farms at two different locations in the St. Louis area for business continuity. He talked about troubleshooting database problems, resolving information issues when two players ask the same question of the system and get two different answers.

"There's one more thing I'd like to show you," Bob said, leading her to the IT team's cluster of cubicles between the data center and the business offices. It was cluttered with hundreds of blue cables stretched like arteries along the ceiling, and most of the cubicles contained half a dozen laptops or handhelds that were in varying degrees of disrepair. There, on the long wall above the cubicles, was a picture of a baseball in a wind tunnel (see Exhibit 12.3).

In 1959, renowned scientist Lyman Briggs, who served as director of the National Institute of Standards and Technology, used a wind tunnel previously created to study aviation aerodynamics to prove that a thrown ball can actually curve. At the time, the revelation that the ball's spin and not

EXHIBIT 12.3   *Baseball's Do Curve*

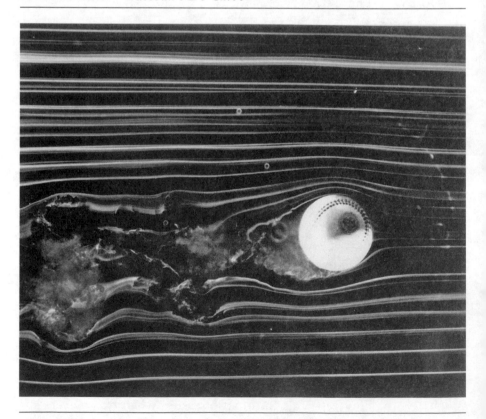

Source: NIST.

its speed was the reason for its curve became a national debate, and the results of his work were published in the *American Journal of Physics*.[5]

"That's worth noting," Katie smiled.

As they returned to the business office, he briefly explained his heuristic user interface engine that had successfully lured almost 30% of the team to begin to use the technology.

"That's worth noting, too" she said, tapping a few words into her Palm Pilot.

Bob reminded himself to mention the Sunday article to Ted Lattimore, who would be pleased with the publicity. Then his mind slipped back into thinking about the afternoon meeting and the decision he would have to make.

"You were just distracted by something," Katie said intuitively, "is everything all right?"

Bob said that things were fine, he just had a lot on his mind, and she looked relieved.

"That's good, because I was going to ask if you'd be interested in doing a guest column for our online magazine," she said, "you know, a bird's eye view of baseball . . . you have such great stories, and such a great perspective on the game."

Bob told her he'd have to think about it. He was interested, but privately he wasn't sure he could commit himself, given the other pressures in his life. She gave him her business card and asked him to give her a call if he changed his mind. They parted at the same place they met, in the team's business office beside the water cooler. Later, Bob would even remember the sound of the water cooler gurgling as she turned away.

Traffic around the Arch was bottlenecked from construction in the middle lanes, and Bob wondered why the Highway Department chose the middle of the afternoon to perform maintenance rather than after dark: as IT teams around the country had long since learned, it is far more expensive to impact the productivity of the workers around you than to pay the incremental cost of overtime when the infrastructure requires maintenance. The Cardinals' IT team performed all maintenance and upgrades during road trips, a schedule determined far in advance and rigorously adhered to. In the entire time Bob had been there, they had not once impacted the organization negatively.

It was a source of professional pride to everyone on the tech team.

The downtown offices of the venture firm were decorated with expensive and tasteful furniture. Steelcase had been one of their early investments, and their flexible design pieces were evident throughout the suite. Framing the furnishings, or rather serving as an artful backdrop to the business being conducted behind closed doors, was a 15th story panoramic view of the St. Louis skyline. While the receptionist announced his presence to Mr. Lattimore, Bob scanned the view for his two favorite landmarks: Grand South Grand with its 19th century architecture (the equivalent of legacy systems in IT terminology) and St. Louis Station, almost 200 years old and still a gem in the necklace of the city.

"They'll see you in the Boardwalk conference room," she said. It seemed that all the conference rooms were place names in Monopoly.

Bob thanked her, agreed to a bottle of water, and continued staring at the skyline until Tim Lattimore arrived, flanked by a sturdy, impeccably dressed woman, probably 50. She stepped in front of Tim to introduce herself, conveying an extreme degree of self-confidence.

"Mr. Roberts, my name is Lucy Stuart, and I am the Entrepreneur-in-Residence for the firm." She realized that Bob did not understand the title, adding, "What this means is that I have previously directed successful companies and am now helping the partners identify potential investment opportunities—with the agreement that I could be inscrted as the CEO, if the company or product is particularly compelling."

Bob nodded and sat in a seat directly across from Lattimore and Lucy Stuart, close enough to the flipchart to diagram something if it was needed, yet far enough away from the front of the room to avoid the expectation of a formal presentation.

"I understand you've designed and implemented a groundbreaking system, if I am accurate—please excuse me if I am not."

"I suppose that's accurate," Bob said, and he realized they were the first words he had spoken since they had entered the room.

'Let me tell you about our approach at Arch Ventures," Ted Lattimore said.

Though their tones were personal and direct, they both sounded rehearsed. They had probably held many such meetings with the people who represented prospective investment opportunities. They had probably performed from very similar scripts. Bob also noticed a slight but nonetheless defined veneer to their speech, somewhat religious, somewhat zealous in their convictions. From their point of view, they were single-handedly heralding the technology revolution. Around the walls, the many framed stock certificates of initial offerings stood as evidence of their success.

From Bob's perspective, the room seemed filled with hubris.

"From many sources and directions, we identify two or, at the most, three products that deserve a second level of investigation. Of those two or three candidates, perhaps only one is substantially funded by Arch, though we have been secondary investors in a broad array of new companies." Lattimore paused to glance in Lucy's direction, and she nodded as if she was approving that he move the conversation forward.

"We don't invite technologists into our offices very often, and we do so with the utmost seriousness," the man said.

It was an obvious effort to make Bob feel special, one of the anointed. Throughout the meeting he would observe four or five other anointment moments, when the ego of the prospective founder is subtly manipulated. Bob was annoyed by the obvious ploys, but there was also a part of him, deep down where it counts, that enjoyed the special treatment. It was refreshing to be the center of attention.

Lucy stood away from the perfectly polished conference room table and walked to the flipchart, quite close to Bob's seat. She was so close that she seemed to be whispering a confidence as she talked.

"My interest, as you must know by now, is in the dramatic shift upward toward the presentation layer that is happening in our industry. Our globalized workforce and our networked software, such as Salesforce.com, have spread our infrastructure outward *to the edge*. Few things are left for any company to claim as its own real estate, its own branded space, and that is the presentation layer—how they present themselves to the world, how they interact and communicate, how they respond, and, as your software proves, how customers can customize their network experience for maximum impact."

She paused for a sip of tea from the cup she had brought into the conference room, and continued.

". . . whether it's IBM's On Demand approach, or Oracle's Utility Computing, we are seeing a dramatic movement away from centralized infrastructure, until a point in the not-too-distant future where I believe everything in the standard IT 'stack' will exist outside the predefined boundaries of the corporation—networks, databases, voice and video applications, spreadsheets. Only the user interface will remain in our domain, in our control."

Bob drank some water and looked at the diagram Lucy had sketched on the flipboard. At one time it may have been doodled, but it had since become a very explicit and defined image (see Exhibit 12.4).

"As you can see from this diagram," Ted inserted, "we believe that the next opportunity for true innovation and market differentiation lies in the uppermost triangle, which is now occupied almost exclusively by Adobe/Macromedia and Microsoft."

Bob inserted, "You forgot Google."

"Oh my gosh," Lucy said. She seemed chagrined that this had not been made explicit.

"The dominant companies at the presentation layer are immense. They have a footprint on 99% of the desktops in use around the world

EXHIBIT 12.4 *Era of the User Interface: Number 2*

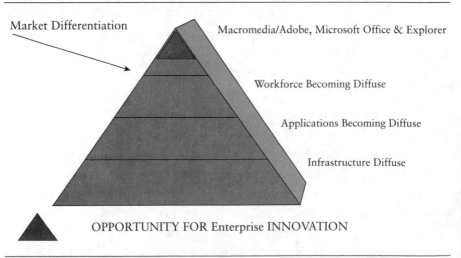

today. Why would *any* small business want to compete with them?" she asked rhetorically.

Bob was ready to answer the question, not only with candor but because he could display a current understanding of the market's terminology. He was glad he'd read Geoffrey Moore's *Crossing the Chasm*[6] on vacation two years ago. The concepts had stayed with him, and this seemed like a good moment to demonstrate it. He then glanced, so casually that he didn't think either of them noticed the move of his arm and the oh-so-slight tug on a blue sleeve cuff, at his watch. They had been talking to him for 30 minutes and had not yet said what they wanted.

"It's *exactly* where our marketing consultants want our new company to begin," Lattimore answered with uncharacteristic enthusiasm, his scripted moment to participate.

This was the underlying element that most intrigued Bob—the pure zealotry of their beliefs. But he had yet to understand Lucy's specific role. Was it sincere and focused solely on his heuristic user interface engine? Or was it part of the charm toolbox that any startup CEO must have, ready and well oiled, to be deployed at any time?

"Ted's right, Bob," Lucy chimed in. This told Bob she had something further to say with regard to the diagram; otherwise she would have resumed her seat on the other side of the table.

". . . like the wind resistance that the Number Two racer enjoys behind the Yellow Shirt in the Tour de France, incredibly synchronized bicyclists with whole teams hunched forward, in the pocket directly behind the frontrunner, who is absorbing everyone's wind resistance himself." Lucy stopped for a moment. She saw Bob's (very intentional) absence of emotion and was trying to understand it. Then she added, "there is a very real opportunity to fall in line behind the larger vendors, ready to make our move as *they* educate our customers. We think your new product could begin at this point as an unknown competitor and take full advantage of the wind pocket."

A silence descended, awkward and empty. All three of them were waiting for someone else to propose Next Steps.

"Let me suggest a modest next step, Bob," Ted inserted finally.

"Okay."

Ted suggested that Bob first investigate his rights to the software he had written for the Cardinals, as a starting point for discussions. Bob's intuition told him that the unique code he'd written for the web server was not easily installable as a product and would more than likely have to be completely recoded, but he didn't tell Ted or Lucy about that. In any event, it was his belief that they wanted to buy the rights to the concept, not the actual code Bob had written, which was really only a prototype, a proof-of-concept that the idea can actually work.

"Then we can, perhaps over dinner, discuss what *you* want to do with your career and whether the time is right for you to make a dramatic move." Ted stood away from the table, Bob said goodbye to Lucy, and he was gone.

That evening, at sunset, Bob found himself pacing back and forth in Lafayette Square Park. He was straddling two immensely powerful potentialities, and his imagination stretched to absorb them properly. He began to mumble to himself as he alternated between Lucy's promise of possible wealth, extreme wealth, and Katie's invitation to write a column, with all that it implied.

Scylla, Charybdis. Scylla, Charybdis. Money, passion. Risk, reward. Cross the chasm, fall into it.

Bob needed a mentor. He needed someone who could explore these issues with him objectively. His boss at the ballpark was experienced and helpful, but Bob didn't want to expose the possibility of leaving the Cardinals organization, not just yet. Uncle Tim, a kind-hearted and country-wise fellow who always had Bob's interests at heart, wasn't familiar with either the practice or the business of technology and would only ask him, "What do *you* want to do?" Sophia? Sophia was not an option: her own desires were all too clear, and he feared they would affect any advice she might offer.

Was it only two days ago that his two biggest problems were Sophia's insistence on bragging about his accomplishments to his family and Eddie's irascible grumpiness at work?

At that precise moment, as Bob was circling the fountain in the middle of the square for perhaps the seventh time and mumbling to himself about his Scyllas and their opposites and the absence of anyone (whom he respected) who could be called on for guidance—at that precise moment Bob realized he knew someone who both understood the technology and had experience with startups, a person who would deliver his opinion with unadorned candor.

It would require the consumption of several humble pies for Bob, who hated the man and made extra efforts to avoid him at lunch or in the hallways, to ask Eddie for some advice.

Eddie, of all people.

The Cardinals were returning for an 11-game homestand, beginning with a night game against three American League teams. Bob was still unaccustomed to interleague play. On most matters, he was a baseball purist who despised the designated hitter option (though it had extended the careers of some remarkable men who otherwise would have retired). He liked interleague play, however, liked the chance to see other teams and other players without leaving St. Louis—though an IT support person was always assigned to travel with the team, something Bob had not yet volunteered to do. That night, they were going to play the Royals. When he walked through the employee entrance, the air was already electric with the rivalry.

The server test team was understaffed that week because Emily and Zeke were on vacation, so his boss moved Bob from the video team. Bob rarely had the need to go into the server room—air chilled to keep the machines cool, racks filled with Cisco, Sun, and Netscaler hardware, walls lined with the orderly groups of blue cables, like spaghetti drying on a backyard clothesline.

"Hey, Eddie," Bob said when they'd completed each step of the test plan and double-checked the failover UPS system. "Could I talk to you for a minute?"

Eddie looked up from the computer terminal where he was logging out of the Tivoli portal.

"It will cost you," the man replied.

"Not about the systems," Bob said, ignoring Eddie's ability to be repulsive even in brief conversations. "I have a personal problem and could use your advice."

Surprise registered on Eddie's face like that of a cartoon character with arched eyebrows and an exclamation point (!) in the white bubble over his head. He pretended to clean his ear out with his little finger, and asked Bob to repeat himself.

"I need some advice."

This was already a longer conversation than they'd had in the three months since Eddie came on board. In a moment of insight, Bob realized Eddie's problem was his user interface. Maybe, if you could overcome the difficulty of engaging with him, Eddie could be a sincere listener, and more, a decent colleague. As Bob outlined the venture firm's interest in the heuristic user interface engine, he could see Eddie's mind absorbing the input, compiling in real time. By the time Bob had finished asking his question, Eddie was prepared to give a thoughtful reply.

"I think you'd be an *idiot* to even consider a startup," Eddie said, with very evident emotion behind the statement.

"OK, Eddie," Bob said, "Don't hold back, don't sugarcoat it."

Eddie laughed. He pulled a rolling chair beneath him and straddled it backward, so he could lean his criss-crossed arms across the back of the chair.

"Look, Bob, I only know one thing about you, the rest of your life is a mystery. But the one thing I know is enough to tell me you're getting seduced by the VCs (venture capitalists) to ignore this fact."

"What's the one thing you know about me?" Bob asked doubtfully, ready to defend himself.

"*Jesus Christ*, man," Eddie said, arms suddenly waving like nestling wings. "You *love* baseball, everything about it, you adore being part of this team. Hell, you could be our poster boy. You adore technology and baseball, and you're doing both right now, so why in the world would you entertain thoughts of walking away?"

Bob stayed quiet, and motionless.

Eddie rolled the chair back to its cubicle, locked the gear cabinet, and broke the silence with an agitated elaboration.

"OK, you'll work terrible hours for little or no money. And forget a social life. Seven days a week, seemingly forever, with a group of people similarly burdened, and none of them really trustworthy. Even with founder's stock, it's highly likely you'll never get paid back for the sacrifice. Someone else will profit, if anyone does."

"Some people have become wealthy," Bob said, unsure suddenly who those people were.

"No different from the rest of the economy, pal," Eddie shrugged. "One percent reap outrageous rewards, and the other ninety-nine percent are overworked and underappreciated. Most startups fail. They fail because of people. Hell, your code might be the best thing since TCP/IP, but the other managers and directors will do one of two things with it. If you're successful, they will edge you out of your profits, and if you're failing, they'll run in the opposite direction and leave you on your own."

"Sounds like you had some bad experiences," Bob suggested.

"No, I actually enjoyed both of my gigs, except for the bad salary thing. I worked with some bright folks who were passionate about the company and relentless in their pursuit of a dream. But I've got dozens of friends with much more miserable histories, lost homes, broken marriages, and not one who says they would do it again."

"Would you do it again?"

Eddie stared at the ground for a moment. He seemed to be truly considering his answer. Finally, he said, "No. I wouldn't."

They signed off the test plans and put the clipboards back on the heavy screen partitions that surrounded the servers like caged animals, stepped out of the computer room, and double-locked the doors, which also had an electronic mechanism requiring a passcode and the right ID card.

"So what's this bit of counseling going to cost me?" Bob joked as they headed back to the business office. Two players passed them in the hallway and waved, both unshaven, both laughing to themselves as if they'd just shared an adolescent dirty joke, which they probably had.

"Omerta," Eddie said. "Code of silence. Don't tell anyone I can be a friendly guy. It'll destroy my rep with the rest of the team."

That night's game was a sellout, and the team had a record number of personalized messages to display on the immense screen in center field, which meant that Bob had a record number of insertions to be keyed in. The software was primarily the same, with variables to be edited for the names of individuals (Happy Birthday, *XXX* from *XXX*), dates of particular events (July 23rd is Bobblehead night), and corporate logos (. . . brought to you by your friendly Geek Squad at Best Buy).

Bob didn't get home until midnight, in part because the video replay units were nearly at DVD capacity, and he needed to compress some of the files to keep all the new Kansas City games on one disc. Sophia was already asleep when he slid quietly into bed. He had made his decision, actually a series of interconnected decisions, as if one choice was linked to another like an endless chain[7] that was his life; and if you touched one end, the other quivered.

The next morning, he had a long and somber discussion with Sophia who was still crying when she left Bob's apartment.

Then he phoned Ted Lattimore. Finally, he had an entertaining and very flirtatious conversation by phone with Katie, followed by another conversation with Katie's editor, about a biweekly column called "Under the Stadium."

The next day, his first column began as follows:

> I am not the tallest or the smartest or even the best looking member of my very large family, but I am by far the happiest professional among them.
>
> Others might be wealthier (being in real estate or banking) or perhaps more fulfilled (being schoolteachers), although they all complain a lot.
>
> But none of them has the daily joy of coming to the ballpark with its magnificent green grass and perfectly shaped diamond, none of them hears the sweet sound as a wooden bat meets a 90-mile-an-hour fastball.
>
> None of them has the pleasure of working with other adults that truly enjoy what they are doing, reaching for that bat, touching their skin to the skin of that wood.

NOTES

1. G. Sun, "Resonant Usability," *Modern Technology Review*, June 2004, 300–310.
2. Ibid., 302.
3. Thornton May, World Bank ISN Conference, June 2004.
4. QuesTec's UIS, as discussed by James Foglio in the IEEE portal, "Technology a Hit in Baseball," July 2001.
5. Lyman Briggs, "NIST Proves It: The Ball Does Curve," National Institute of Standards and Technology, http://www.100.nist.gove/baseball.htm.
6. Geoffrey Moore, *Crossing the Chasm* (New York: HarperCollins, 1991).
7. With due respect for Anton Chekhov: ". . . and when he touched one end of the chain, the other quivered . . . ." From his story, *The Student*.

CHAPTER 13

TURBULENCE

The transformation began the moment Alden Mackenzie stepped into the building and introduced himself.

The story of his appearance at Chimera Design that morning, like so many of his other management consulting assignments, was not unique: first, there is a problem. The company tries the usual approaches, but the problem gets worse. Eventually outside help is called in. It always seemed to Alden that he could have solved the problem easily if engaged when the symptoms first appeared. But the passage of time and the confusion caused by unexpected events often made the challenge much more complex, and by the time he was actually engaged, the difficulties were frequently multifaceted, interconnected, and resistant to most of the standard consulting vaccines. As such, his remedies were dramatic and inventive—and the unfolding of each mystery kept an element of intrigue in his life, an intrigue that Alden Mackenzie found compelling.

Alden's wife, however, despised his work.

At least once a week, at the dinner table or over breakfast, and routinely when they paid their bills on the 15th and 30th of each month, Melissa would complain about the erratic nature of a consultant's life, the long periods between projects, the sudden surges of too many simultaneous clients, and the unpredictability of their finances from month to month. She knew that any of the companies he advised would be happy to hire him for an executive position, and she wished he would simply take a job, secure a steady income with benefits and a 401(k) plan, and help her assuage the ongoing anxiety about growing old.

But Alden enjoyed consulting; he appreciated the ability to work with a variety of smart people on a wide-ranging list of projects. Sometimes he used similar interventions, but the details of each engagement were unique, and he never grew bored, unlike so many of his colleagues, who simply repeated the same processes, year after year. Alden Mackenzie was faced with a various and fascinating set of professional challenges, each one rewarding, each one challenging him to identify the root cause of the problem quickly and put processes into place that would ensure the solution remained viable over time.

"Boredom isn't such a bad thing," Melissa would say when Alden explained the constant challenges of his consulting career.

"Boredom is a death knell," Alden always responded. "Who else do we know who can become the CEO of a company in the middle of dinner?"

The night before his arrival at Chimera Design, as Melissa and Alden were sitting down to a rare dinner alone (their twins had been invited to a Valentine's Day party across the street), their family lawyer had phoned with apologies for interrupting the family's Sunday meal. Melissa didn't want him to take the call, but Alden always took calls, a habit he had developed when his mother was dying of cancer and continued long after she had passed away. The man on the phone explained that one of his firm's corporate clients was days away from an SEC investigation, the Board had just fired the CEO and CFO of the company for malfeasance, and the law firm had been assigned to locate a transitional executive who could be trusted—someone who understood technology, someone who was capable of managing during a crisis and who was available immediately.

"Now you're a *CEO*?" Melissa said incredulously. It was not that she didn't respect Alden's talents, she simply preferred that he find a more stable way of using them now that double college tuitions, higher mortgage rates, and middle age were staring them in the face. "They just asked you to be a *CEO*?"

Alden didn't mention that it would be for his standard fee, not for a CEO-level salary.

Chimera Design was located in the heart of Silicon Valley. In the difficult economic times that most other companies had faced in the years after the burst of "the bubble," Chimera had experienced a meteoric rise. The company had been exceptionally profitable throughout the downturn; its product was an award-winning technology that *Technology Daily* called "the first of its kind, heralding a new generation of software that will transform our lives."[1] Chimera Design embodied the success story that every entrepreneur dreamed about. The company had grown from 10 employees to 500 in two years, providing a family of products that actually worked as promised. It was a story that proved what a good idea and hard work could produce in a free market economy. On the heels of Google's impressive public offering and amidst a wave of consolidation by companies such as Oracle, PeopleSoft, Symantec, and Veritas, Chimera Design's future seemed as certain as the seasons. Its integration products offered a much easier method of accumulating data from many sources, and its customers were passionate about the company, so much so that IBM and Hewlett-Packard (HP) were actively competing for a multibillion dollar acquisition—one that would make the founders, and the employees, very wealthy indeed.

Then something went wrong, very wrong.

IBM suddenly pulled its "due diligence" team without notice or explanation, and the HP team elected to do the same one day later. Within hours of HP's announcement, a press release from the Board of Directors stated that they had fired the founders and suspended any further product releases. According to the article in the *New York Times* Business Section on the morning that Alden walked into their lobby, "No one was answering any questions, nor addressing the rumors that there had been massive fraud, a financial cover-up, and that IBM's decision to suspend their engagement with the company was based upon the discovery of stolen code, and the very real possibility of two sets of accounting ledgers."[2]

Alden introduced himself to the receptionist and removed his drenched overcoat as rain beat rhythms on the plate-glass windows behind her.

"Do you have an appointment with someone, Mr. Mackenzie?" she asked. Then she excused herself for the third time in as many minutes, answering the switchboard, which was blinking like a Times Square sign.

"Lots of inquiries about the *New York Times* article, I expect," Alden said, and the woman nodded as she kept transferring the reporters' calls to the Marketing Department.

He explained that he was also a result of the article's subject and asked politely if he could be shown to the office of the CEO, where he would be working. The woman's eyes widened; she had inadvertently asked her new employer to wait while she took calls. She walked him personally up two flights of sculpted stairs to the executive offices on the second floor, and he told her not to worry, she was doing the right thing.

"Follow your instincts, Carol," he said soothingly when they arrived at the offices. "Just do the best job you can, and we'll be fine."

He learned later that it was the first time in more than two years an executive had spoken personally to her.

The large cubicle outside the CEO's impressive office, traditionally reserved for an executive secretary, was also empty. Alden later learned that the administrative assistant for the CEO and CFO had been placed on leave and was under scrutiny for complicity by federal investigators, who now occupied two conference rooms nearby. The rooms, which were visible to anyone passing by on the way to the photocopiers or mailroom, were swarming with accountants frenetically assembling their newly situated hive of laptops, binders, and transcribed interviews, with the profound drive of the swarm that knows what it has to do, and has set about its complex tasks.

Alden unpacked his briefcase, like a traveling salesperson who knew this hotel room was going to be home for a long time.

It would be many months before Alden Mackenzie fully understood the sequence of events that had brought him to Chimera Design. The next weeks were tumultuous, with none of the usual routine predictability of corporate endeavors, everyone knowing their function and busy at their work. There were many eruptions, triggered by news reports, discoveries by the audit teams, unexpected confessions by ex-employees, and the regular schedule of analyst speculations that followed each spectacular event. Alden's work was done before he learned fully what had happened. In this case, knowledge came after intuition. Only after he had completed his six-month CEO stint did he understand his first day on the job.

If this were a novel, it would be appropriate (and perhaps strategic) to lay out each significant cause and its effect. The whole cast of characters would be portrayed in detail, with their passions, their innovations, and their distractions, a very human story of one company's struggle with adolescence, in competition with the very adult corporations that are landmarks on Highways 101 and 280. For our purposes, which involve the elucidation of principles that fit neatly into this schematic design, only two elements will be highlighted, two early tremors left unchecked that produced immense resonant vibrations.[3]

Three years before, in March 2002, the company had received an additional infusion of capital (called a bridge loan) from their primary investors in order to a) bring their product to market and b) sign their first referenceable customer accounts. The investors' requirement was unequivocal: there must be three legitimate technology contracts by the end of that year. This was the prime objective, the only goal of significance by which the executive team would be judged.

It was not, by anyone's account, an unrealistic objective. The product was fully designed, and three "beta" tests were under way: one at the supercomputing center in San Diego, one at Cisco's Minnesota facility, and a third at the Accenture labs in Palo Alto. Initial results were positive, with only one or two important problems left to be resolved, and the announcement of the bridge financing was a cause for celebration.

The CEO hired Cirque de Soleil, which had just completed a three-week tour of the San Francisco area, for a day-long performance in a massive, two-ring white tent put up in the company parking lot. Clowns, jugglers, acrobats, a giant, and several talented small people kept the audience at the edges of their seats. A performer trampolined on his bed in his pajamas, another in her white nightgown balanced on one-foot as she watched upside-down bicyclists crossing the high-wire above. There were prizes, special T-shirts, a petting zoo for the children; throughout the day, speakers from each of the company's departments gave rousing status reports. Morale was high. The employees were thrilled to be employed by a young company with a bright future, when so many of their friends were being laid off or were staying in a stale job at a struggling company because it was better than no job at all. Whenever a task needed to be done at Chimera, it was easy for the corporate recruiters to find exceptionally talented people to complete it.

Most of the company's employees enjoyed the festivities in the tent, gawking at the performers, or simply watching their children enjoying their day with Mommy or Daddy "at work."

Inside Building Two, however, a small team of programmers was working hard to address an issue that had been raised by the Cisco team in Minnesota. The problem seemed to be performance (memory leakage), but as they investigated further, they found an inconsistent (difficult to identify because difficult to replicate) data transfer error. On certain operating systems, for unknown reasons, small amounts of information were being lost in the exchange from one resource (through the company's core product) to another resource.

Lazlo Sirkus, the lead programmer, was the chief engineer for the company, the man who was singly responsible for their first patent, and one of only three technologists in the company who understood completely how their product could index, map, and transfer structured and unstructured data with such impressive speed and accuracy. While most of his colleagues celebrated outside, Lazlo was learning that the problem noted at Cisco was central to their core and would eventually be discovered by the teams in San Diego and Palo Alto. It was critical that he resolve the issue before the other teams noticed it; he was working on it day and night.

"Maybe we need more people," one of the other programmers suggested. "There's only so much code that you can write in one week, Lazlo."

But Lazlo was a prolific programmer, capable of writing hundreds of new lines of code in one evening, and he knew it would slow them down to hire and train new engineers up to the appropriate levels. In fact, he felt that even his own team was getting in his way. If only he had complete freedom (without interruption)—then he could find the correct algorithm that would serve as a bridge between the layers and the transfer could be accomplished without data loss.

He asked for, and received, permission from his manager to work on this particular "bug" by himself, assigning the rest of the core team to complete the other tasks requested by their beta partners. Chimera paid for a secure T-1 link to his home and transferred several servers and network routers, which the IT team set up in his extra bedroom. Lazlo began to work ceaselessly on the solution. His goal was to write "black box" code, a compact section of undocumented programming (undocumented because it takes longer to document each step). As long as the input and output were correct, and the checksums could be validated by the customers, he could solve the problem and worry later about the documentation (design flows, test plans, comments inserted in the software itself).

No one would ever know exactly when the trouble began. Lazlo was not communicating with anyone at the company on a regular basis, and later, his family said he'd always been a bit melancholy when he was working hard. Sometime during the weeks that followed the tent celebrations, Lazlo Sirkus experienced his first bout of what the literary community calls "writer's block." He simply could not write code. Even the simplest c-shell scripts were a problem, and over the course of the next few days, he could not even rewrite existing sections of code. He froze, hands poised above the keyboard, unable to put into language what he knew in his mind should be written.

Many books have been written on the subject of writer's block, and a variety of therapies, pharmaceutical and psychoanalytical, have been used to treat this kind of linguistic paralysis. But Lazlo was unprepared to face his predicament. He had graduated from his university in Moscow, continued his graduate work at MIT, and programmed for the company for two years without a single problem or block, nor did he have a confidante within his small social circle of fellow programmers and family.

He was unable to tell a soul—and became more and more isolated within his melancholia and his growing desperation.

Lazlo felt that the entire company's future revolved around his ability to solve this fundamental problem in the core product. He had heroically volunteered to deliver the solution by himself. The mere thought that he was unable to solve the problem was an additional burden, fueling his anxiety and blocking him further. As the days turned into weeks, he began to deliver falsely optimistic status reports to his team. Lazlo felt trapped in a maze with no exits, with sheer walls too tall for him to scale, and an immense hourglass suspended above him, with the sound of the sand rushing through his ears. It was the sound of time passing.

He was not sleeping. His diet consisted of NoDoz tablets and coffee, with an occasional burrito from the nearby 7-11. He was losing weight. He stopped going to his sister's house for the Sunday dinner that had become a tradition since he came to San Jose three years before. His arms ached from holding them above the keyboard.

It seemed odd to him that he could write e-mail, navigate the Internet freely, and even maintain an online weblog. (He didn't know that this is not uncommon.) On the weblog, with the angst of a teen-ager stricken by unrequited love, he articulated the emotions that overcame him whenever he tried to write code.

He kept rereading his engineering textbooks. He knew what had to be done to correct the problem, but he simply could not program the fix.

Lazlo didn't know how many novelists had described writer's block over the centuries, and his isolation reinforced the feeling that he was the only person ever to suffer from this condition. Worst of all, he had become convinced he would never again write a line of software code.

E-mail from the team continued to report on the company's phenomenal growth, and his manager sent reminders that his section of code was due in three weeks, then two weeks, then one week.

On the night before his module was scheduled to be released to their internal QA team for testing, Lazlo made a decision that would haunt him in the days ahead. Using his familiarity with university and open source resources available throughout the Internet, Lazlo downloaded a public version of data processing software—a common program used in second-year programming classes at many universities—and embedded it in the company's product. He knew it would correct the discrepancy and meet Cisco's requirements, although it was not optimized (meaning it worked more slowly than they had promised). He also knew that the GNU license allowed for reuse only without financial gain and that embedding the software inside his company's code, without declaration, was against the law.

To disguise the use of public domain software, he located several of the Java "wrappers" that are often used by hackers to obscure a Trojan horse in seemingly innocuous redirect viruses. By the time of deadline, Lazlo was able to deliver his "black box" solution to the engineering team with apologies for the lack of documentation. (He dared not provide references to the source of the borrowed code.) His e-mail simply read:

> It works, and it eliminates the data loss. We can optimize performance in other modules, thereby avoiding the slow-down noted with the original product. I'd prefer that we sidestep any line-by-line design reviews until I come back to work—it should be enough to send them a bug fix that addresses their issue. Mark the bug "closed" and send it to Cisco's prototype team, and send similar instructions via FTP to the Accenture team in San Diego.

That he had utilized public domain software inside the company's "unique intellectual property" was disconcerting enough. In his last e-mail to the team before he was supposed to rejoin the company, he wrote:

> Let's postpone any design reviews until they pass the acceptance tests at the beta site., Just make them happy that it works, and we'll catch up with documentation at a later date. I've written some regression tests that QA should use. Let's get this behind us.

The next day his own QA team told him by e-mail that the bug was fixed. His code worked fine, and the project with Cisco was moving forward. From the company's perspective, he had written excellent black box programming that would confound analysis. Everyone believed Lazlo was simply being Lazlo, and his request to put off design review was enforced.

The crisis in engineering had passed, and the company immediately signed its first three customers to initial contracts. From Chimera's perspective, Lazlo had solved a critical problem and deserved a bonus, a rare and reassuring gesture from management. Hearing about the bonus made Lazlo feel even worse about his lost skills. Deep down, Lazlo knew he had undermined the value of the product and perhaps the company itself.

Lazlo was scheduled to return to work in two days. His manager quipped over the phone, "I know you like to work in your pajamas, but we'd really like to see you soon." The IT team came to dismantle and take back the hardware. (He was flattered that they sent their best desktop team.) When the team was gone, Lazlo walked slowly to his Toyota hybrid (which was underwritten by the company for anyone with a commute). He wished he had e-mailed his sister and apologized for not coming to dinner.

"I cannot do what I do, anymore," he said, exhausted as at no other time in his life.

He turned on the quiet ignition, checked his rear view mirrors, and drove at the exact speed limit to the beach in Alameda, the island community near Oakland where he had always wanted to live. Lazlo aimed his Toyota directly into the waves.

As the car sank slowly into the murky waters overlooking the Bay Bridge, he had no second thoughts. He knew he should have told the legal department that use of public software must be explicitly stated in a company disclaimer. He simply could not face the humiliation when Chimera found out. He was employee 11 in a company that was now the size of a small Kansas farming town, and he could not admit his plagiarism.

"Maybe no one will ever know," he thought to himself as the waters rose past the windshield. Surfboarders and nannies with small children began screaming and pointing to the place where the car was quickly submerged.

As the car sank slowly to the bottom of the bay, Lazlo struggled a bit to keep his breath regular—until he stopped breathing at all. It was surprisingly easy.

Alden Mackenzie's charter, as described in his one-page agreement with Chimera Design's Board of Directors, was to stabilize the company and "keep the train running" during the course of several investigations that promised to uncover more issues than the initial problems that had caused the removal of the CEO and CFO from their posts. Such was the nature of corporate investigations. Every archived e-mail and filed document was scrutinized, and even the mildest oddity had the potential to become the "crisis of the day."

Everyone, from departmental secretaries to senior directors, was consumed by the unfolding events, both real and imagined. Rumors spread like common colds.

TO: All Permanent Employees

FROM: Angelina Ward, Legal Counsel

In accordance with our responsibilities related to copyright infringement claims filed in court this week, you are hereby requested to forward all documentation concerning all matters related to our use of GNU software to our offices. This includes e-mails, presentations, technical documents, specifications, and/or any handwritten notes that exist as of this date.

Alden knew that the employees needed leadership from him, and a new sense of purpose. To create such an environment, amidst the agitation of daily CNN broadcasts and audit team discoveries, the company required a transformation, at every level of the organization, a transformation so complete that everyone would be engaged in the act of renewal. It must also be easy to understand and articulate—massive change, clearly articulated—and it needed to begin quickly, to avoid the very likely exodus of the company's key contributors. He needed to make sure that Chimera Design did not lose "the good people" in the first few weeks of his assignment, yet he did not have time to determine who those good people might be.

Just beneath the surface of the chaos was a secondary layer of turbulence. Human nature was instilling a sense of self-defense in each of the managers. No one wanted to be blamed for someone else's transgressions, and a chilling fog of mistrust filled the main office complex like a noxious gas being pumped through the air conditioning system. No one was immune.

"I am not here to fire anyone," he announced at his first executive staff meeting.

No one in the room believed him.

Each of the remaining executives assumed that Alden had been planted by the Board of Directors to learn as much as possible about the company's problems and to remove anyone associated with the two primary criminal acts that had surfaced: illegal use of public domain software for profit and misrepresentation of company finances. In their first interactions with him, none of the executives were willing to expose anything that might be used against them. It was self-protection (CYA) time, whether or not they had something to hide. Afterward, Alden met with each of the executives privately. Not one of them changed their posture; they were obeying the same code of silence that police officers are known to follow when Internal Affairs is investigating one of the brotherhood.

His second executive staff meeting, three days later, began with his announcement that he had negotiated significant bonuses ($5,000 a month, for the duration of his performance as CEO) for everyone in the room who was willing to remain in their roles, and participate in the transformation of the company.

"You can't buy loyalty," Chimera's VP of Worldwide Operations said.

"How do we know you'll follow through?" another asked. "We know nothing about you, and we've just been fooled by some of our closest friends. Money can't repair that," she added.

Alden waved through the conference room window to Annie, the temporary secretary he had hired, who came in with envelopes for everyone. (Annie, a woman he had known for many years, had been transferred from the law firm that had first contacted him.)

"I don't expect you to trust me," he said. "But I've been asked to turn the company around during this emergency, and I can't do it by myself. I'm good, but I'm not that good."

Elaine Rojas, the VP of Marketing, opened her envelope and whispered to the person beside her that the amount was more than the $5,000 he had promised: it was $5,000 *after* taxes. "This was thoughtful of you, Mr. Mackenzie," she said finally, "but we're going to need more than money to get this company back on its feet."

"Of course," he said. "I'm instituting several programs, which we'll discuss in a minute. I just wanted to begin the meeting with a gesture of good will, because you will all be working very hard in the weeks ahead. Use the money to buy a gift for your spouse, use it for whatever you like. Some of you may be interviewing for other positions," he added, "and I wouldn't blame you. The money is yours, regardless."

One woman, at the far end of the table, had not opened her envelope. She had been quiet amidst the whispered doubts. Alden noticed the unopened envelope and asked if she had something to say.

"I'm going to give this bonus to my team," she said quietly. "They need a gesture of good will, too."

No one said a word. Finally, Elaine broke the silence and asked Alden to spell out his new programs. He distributed two documents and explained that he wanted everyone to share them with their employees. The first document described the creation of a Crisis Response Team that would be based in the meeting room adjacent to his office. The purpose of the team was to respond to any and all rumors, serve as the voice of the company for the press, and interact directly with the auditors.

"I want to take all the eruptions that are filling the company and give them a place to go," Alden explained. "We'll build an anonymous web portal on the corporate intranet so that any employee can submit a concern."

"A war room," one of them said.

"That's right," Alden responded. "Then the executive staff can focus on our regular business—we have a company to run, and we cannot afford to be distracted every time a new discovery is announced on CNN." His goal was to compartmentalize the crisis, move it aside—not ignore it, simply redirect the emergency away from the daily governance of the company. "Elaine will be our liaison with the Crisis Response Team, and she and I will be meeting daily to review any new issues that emerge. The rest of you will be concentrating on my second program."

The second document was Alden's plan for transforming the company. As he handed it out, he noticed that the staff was beginning to pay attention to him, as if, in one grand motion, they had already gathered their distress and set it aside, so they could pay attention to his proposal.

"My initial observation is that Chimera Design is highly dependent on engineering," he confided, "so much so that one technology problem has put the company into crisis."

Alden looked around the room and then interrupted himself. ". . . by the way, is anyone here from Engineering?"

Bob Epifani, the VP of Human Resources, explained that Engineering never attended the executive staff meetings. They had always been exempt.

"Not any more," Alden said, "but let's work that issue offline. They are a department, just like all your departments. We can't improve communications if the significant parties aren't in the room."

Elaine asked Alden to explain the second document. On page one, there was a diagram of the company as it had been organized during the tenure of the previous CEO—the traditional hierarchy, reporting lines clearly delineated, a classically vertical organizational chart (Exhibit 13.1).

"This could be Any Company, Incorporated," Alden said. Several of the executives laughed, a good sign.

"I have always believed that a company should be organized in alignment with the solutions that it provides," Alden explained. "In our case, we integrate data horizontally, yet we are organized vertically. It is an inherent contradiction and is probably one cause for our current troubles."

"Are you saying that we're all going to reorganize?" Ted asked, explaining that his Customer Support team was composed of very young people who need a quite specific "hands-on" management style.

"You are all remaining as the head of each of your departments, and no one is being moved," Alden said.

"What will change will be how we interact with one another and how we organize new initiatives."

The second diagram demonstrated the "new" Chimera Design approach. It was an exercise in constant organizational design (Exhibit 13.2).

EXHIBIT 13.1 *Standard Organization Managed by Functional Area*

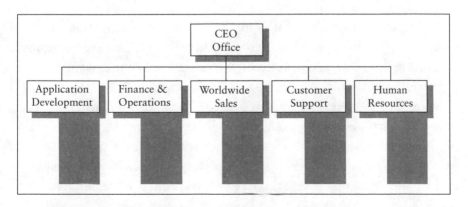

EXHIBIT 13.2   *Organization Driven by Process Teams*

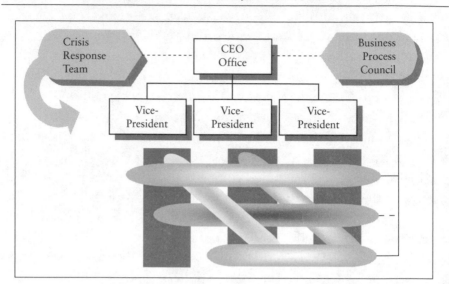

"As you can see," Alden explained, "I am adjusting the management strategy to focus on business processes, rather than functional areas. Each of you will retain your direct responsibilities for your organizations. You will continue to supervise new hires, manage departmental budgets, and coordinate tasks. However, each of you will also be responsible for a primary business process, which will operate horizontally by means of cross-functional teams."

"Process Teams," Bob read out loud.

"Correct," Alden said. "It is my belief that, by converting the company to an inclusive process-oriented structure, in which every employee is working on matrixed initiatives, we can correct some of the communications issues while we jump start a new identity."

Several of the executives were discussing the idea in clusters, making notes, suggestions, listing possible candidates for various process teams. No one was resisting the change. It was as if they had been starved for leadership and were willing to absorb any practical suggestion that he had to offer, a complete reversal from the resistance of the initial meeting.

"I want you to begin thinking *Horizontal* whenever we discuss initiatives, whether large or small. Everything will be managed horizontally. Subsequently, our first task," Alden said, "and I want to engage the entire company in the discussion, is to identify our key business processes and determine who the proper teams are, for each of them. Take this back to your departments, get your people's suggestions, and we'll pull the various ideas together at our next meeting."

He adjourned the meeting, somewhat confident that the executive team had turned a corner and was capable of adjusting to his new approach. In fact, they had embraced the idea whole-heartedly, fanatically, as a starved man embraces one slice of bread.

Alden knew the Engineering situation had not yet been addressed, and he knew what his next task needed to be.

"Annie, find out who manages the Engineering schedule, and get me on their VP's calendar for tomorrow morning," Alden said. Then he leaned over and whispered, so no one else could hear, "Do whatever you have to do to get him to the meeting, even if it means telling him his job is on the line. I want him in my office tomorrow morning, no excuses."

"What if he has sick children and needs to be with them?" Annie asked, smiling.

"OK," Alden said, "*one* good excuse, but no others."

When he returned to his office, Bob Epifani was waiting for him. The two men spent a few minutes discussing employee morale, which was Bob's primary concern. He told Alden he thought an All Hands meeting was in order—all the employees in one place at one time—where Alden could introduce himself and chart the new course. Then Bob handed over his envelope.

"I make a fair salary, and I think this could go to better use elsewhere."

"Then contribute it to a favorite charity, Bob."

"My favorite charity is Chimera Design," Bob said quickly. "Really, Alden, I'd rather not accept it. Please don't misinterpret this as a lack of support. I think you ran a great meeting just now. It's been a long time since that group of people has behaved like a team. It's just . . ."

Alden put up his hand and the man was silenced by the abrupt gesture. "Bob, our operational funds are frozen, and this is the only discretionary money the Board is going to allow, for the time being. Surely you can think of some . . ."

Alden had a sudden idea—and the VP of Human Resources was the perfect partner for his scheme. He wrote a few words on a Post-It and handed it to Bob, telling him to order T-shirts for everyone in the company with that motto on the front, to be distributed at the company meeting. "We'll schedule that meeting as soon as the shirts are ready. How's that sound?" They shook hands vigorously, and Bob left the office with his envelope and a sincere feeling of partnership that would serve both men well in the coming weeks.

"I haven't attended an executive staff meeting since the company was launched *four years ago*," the man said, "and I *don't* intend to start now."

Alden stared at the man sitting in front of him, startled by the hubris that would cause him to greet the new Chief Executive with such bold resistance. Mid-thirties, white shirt neatly pressed, Blackberry in hand, which he used constantly, even as he was speaking. E-mails to his staff, or so Alden assumed. The man's rudeness was palpable.

"Engineering has enjoyed a fairly broad charter in the past," Alden said. "Do you really think the results of your efforts have been that spectacular?"

"You can't believe that I'm responsible for the intellectual property dispute," the man erupted. "I can't review every line of code."

Resistance and denial, two of the greatest risks to the transformation of any organization, particularly one in the midst of a major crisis. Alden was amazed at the man's transparence.

"I didn't suggest blame, Sergei. Honestly, I don't believe the IP issue is our biggest problem and I'm certainly not here to point fingers. And I *absolutely* wouldn't have expected you to review every bug fix submitted for beta customers," Alden continued. "But frankly, I believe Engineering has been much too isolated from the rest of the company. That isolation will need to shift, in the same way all of the departments will be changing in the weeks and months ahead. No one is *that* important."

Sergei Lowenstein was the first engineer/manager hired by the founders when the company was formed. With the loss of Lazlo, Sergei had become the only technologist in the company who completely understood their products, and he was convinced that he was irreplaceable. Alden retrieved a manila folder from his briefcase and handed over a copy of a memorandum that had been signed the evening before by the President of the Board of Directors.

"What is this?"

"That," Alden explained, "is a side-letter to my contract with the company. As you can see, it gives me the authority to make any changes in management that I deem necessary."

Sergei laughed and stood up, signaling what he believed was an end to their meeting. "I'm leaving now. Fire me if you want, but I'll take half the engineering team with me. This company can't survive without me, whether you like it or not. It would be a shame if you learned that after our exit."

Alden followed Sergei into the hallway and, with a subtle request to check his mailbox for an imaginary package, whisked Annie away from her desk. He didn't want her to hear the open conflict.

"Sergei, here's what we're going to do," he said quietly and sternly. "I want you to take the remainder of the week off, beginning immediately." Alden's tone of voice commanded the engineer's attention. "During the next few days, I want you to decide whether you really want to stay with the company and help us turn it around. Alternatively, you can resign, in which case I am sure we can negotiate a fair package. But please believe me when I say that I don't want *anyone* in the company who is not completely dedicated to making it successful again."

Alden paused, and then added, "Frankly, I'm not overly concerned about losing you or the engineering team. I'm sure we can find other, very talented people. But if you stay, you *will* attend all executive staff meetings and fulfill any the assignments agreed on at those meetings. Are we clear?"

Sergei Lowenstein nodded and sullenly walked away.

Alden believed it would be the last time he would ever see the man, and he immediately began thinking of the appropriate "risk management scenario" to compensate for the loss. The second step was to minimize the damage, in the event that Sergei became a security risk. Alden phoned the company's Chief Information Officer (who also thanked him for an excellent senior staff meeting) and asked that a "history" trace file (recording all system interactions) be arranged for one of their employees.

"Usually, the request comes from Human Resources, Alden," the man said, explaining their company policy. Alden told him to verify this with Bob Epifani and that the need was immediate.

When the CIO asked for the name of the employee, Alden said "Sergei Lowenstein." From the sudden silence on the phone, he knew he had just broken one of the company's fundamental taboos.

Think: HORIZONTAL

The words were emblazoned on a 20-foot banner that stretched across the cafeteria wall, behind the stand-alone microphone that was connected by a long blue cable to the speaker system usually reserved for lunchtime music. In the short week since Alden has announced his plan at the executive staff meeting, the slogan on the banner had become the watchwords of the company.

The All Hands meeting was held in the company's cafeteria because there was no other room in the building large enough to hold everyone. As Alden had learned that morning, it was the first company-wide meeting for many of the employees who had been hired in the past six or seven months. Apparently, as the company became consumed by customer acquisition, the previous executives had stopped attending to the needs of the employees, yet another symptom that told him the transformation he envisioned for Chimera Design needed to be comprehensive: every single employee, from the mail room to the shipping dock to the Help Desk to the executive suite, should be able to articulate how his changes would impact their particular job.

As Alden took the microphone, a swift hush, like a warm wind from the hills that preceded a firestorm, swept through the cafeteria. Complete stillness.

"I'd like to begin by explaining that I am not a cheerleader," Alden said candidly. "What you can expect from me, in the coming months, are two things: complete honesty about our current state of affairs and a dedication to returning Chimera Design to a healthy and prosperous state."

Already, an interruption—from a man in the front row.

"How long before we have yet another CEO?" Several around him laughed nervously.

"A good question, and the most accurate assessment I can make is that I will be here as long as it takes to get the company back on track. That won't be measured in time, but it will be measured, and I'll make sure everyone is informed as quickly as possible, as we make progress."

Alden looked across the room, quickly assessing if there were any other questions, and then he continued.

"I won't bore you with my professional biography, though I can assure you that I have helped many companies survive a crisis. I would like to share one story, to give you a perspective on my beliefs. It dates back to when I was in junior high school, attending an overnight camp, the usual mix of cookouts and river rafting and one-match campfires. I had a counselor who explained to us that whenever we left a campsite in the woods, we had a responsibility to do more than clean up our own mess. He thought we should always leave the campsite in better condition than we found it, and he always left a + sign of two whittled sticks in the firepit, to show we had added something to that tiny piece of the natural environment.

"I've always liked that metaphor, and I've always tried to do just that in each of the companies that have engaged my services. So, please understand that I'm not here just to babysit the business until the Board of Directors hires your new CEO and CFO. I want to make a *substantial* difference while I am here. I fully intend to leave two whittled sticks as a + sign for the next person who moves into the executive offices . . . and to do so, I need the assistance of each and every one of you in this room."

Alden studied the faces of more than 500 employees, most of whom were intently listening to every word he said. He did not see Sergei Lowenstein anywhere in the crowd.

"As you know by now . . . and by the way, if any of you have not yet heard of these two initiatives, I want you to complain to your management aggressively, because the most critical aspect of our transformation will be the ability of every department to communicate new decisions quickly. For those of you in Finance and Engineering, I will be meeting with you soon, to ensure that the communications are also consistent throughout your departments.

"The first initiative was the creation of our Crisis Response Team (CRT), located in the Park Place conference room directly beside my office. Given that the CRT has already received more than 50 e-mail messages, I know that at least some of you have been told about the team's role, which is this: I want each of you to be able to focus upon your jobs, the responsibilities you were hired to perform, without the distractions that so easily grab our attentions—newspaper articles, CNN broadcasts, rumors about what our auditors have found. Now we have a dedicated team responsible for addressing these issues full time, so you don't need to be involved, but also so you can trust that the problem is being addressed. Err on the side of too much communication— I would rather three of you send a message about the same issue, than no one sending it because you presumed someone else would notify the CRT of the latest rumors."

Bob Epifani raised his hand, and Alden nodded in his direction from the podium.

"Alden, to encourage everyone to take advantage of the CRT, we've purchased 20 Amazon gift certificates and will be awarding 5 each week to individuals who have contacted the CRT about the most pressing issues of that week."

Alden replied jokingly, "I could use an Amazon gift certificate. I'll have to remember to send one when I get back to the office."

"No fair using Blackberry devices during this meeting," someone called out from the middle of the room, and everyone laughed.

Alden liked how the temperament of the meeting was moving quickly from cynicism to camaraderie.

"The second, and more fundamental, initiative that the executive team is putting into action is echoed by the words behind me. Now, I'm not a 'process fanatic' and I don't believe in bureaucracy for its own sake, but it seems to me that a company dedicated to managing the horizontal flow of information between countless repositories needs to reflect that behavior everywhere. I've always believed that you cannot manage a horizontal effort, such as hypertext or network messaging, with vertical organizations. It simply doesn't work. Therefore, in the days ahead, we will be announcing the creation of a series of Business Process Teams that will begin the task of coordinating our major efforts in a matrixed manner. Everyone in this room will be on at least one process team outside your own direct organization. Some of you may be asked to serve on more than one. Our Information Systems group will be involved in many of them, as they will be building team portals to assist in the collaboration."

"So you're saying we should do our current job and add another job on top of it?" a woman from the back of the room called out. Alden was impressed by the clarion call of her voice, bold without being strident.

"Another good question," Alden said. "In the beginning, it will feel that way, and frankly, I don't expect anyone to spend more time in the office than I do. I am convinced that the efficiencies of this approach will eventually make your core jobs more productive—and it will certainly prevent the eruption of unexpected problems that could detour us. Imagine if we had known the current crisis was coming and could have planned our response." He stopped, quickly gauging the faces of the front row employees and recognizing he needed a concrete example.

"Let's imagine for a moment that we are a software company . . ." Laughter echoed throughout the brightly-lit room.

". . . and let's imagine that, for various reasons, we are burdened by 12 different licensing schemes. The right thing to do is standardize upon one, but in the initial phases, it will seem like we've created a thirteenth scheme—at least until we can, one by one, migrate each product to the new one. Or think of how IT might implement Oracle financials—our finance staff would not stop using their old Excel templates, and for a while, they might be required to be using both systems. But the goal is to move toward one."

"That is the goal of our Horizontal project. We might each be challenged with some additional tasks at the outset, but in the long run, we will be eliminating duplicate effort and communicating more consistently between departments. Over time, that will make things easier in many areas."

"Can I ask a question?" a voice called from the back of the room. It was Sergei Lowenstein, and more than a few in the room gasped their surprise to see him attending a company meeting. Alden was also surprised, and he wondered what the mercurial fellow was going to say.

"Good to see you today, Sergei," Alden said.

For one brief moment, Alden and the rest of the executive team held their collective breaths, expecting Sergei to undermine the new approach. His question surprised everyone.

"You said something about the way in which our technology works, yet our company is organized in another way," he said thoughtfully. "Could you explain a bit more about that? I think it's an interesting idea."

Alden recognized the perfect moment and waved for Bob Epifani to begin distributing the new company shirts.

"Sergei is asking about the link between the behavior of organizations and the behavior of the products made by those organizations," Alden summarized. "There is actually a great deal of research on this topic, dating back to the work of Gregory Bateson at Stanford, but rather than boring everyone with a long discussion of second-generation cybernetics, I'd invite anyone who wants to know more about it to come to my office. For now, I'll summarize it quite simply. As you will see on the shirts that the HR staff is distributing, the fundamental principle on each shirt is this: *The systems will not talk to each other if the people are not talking to each other.* It seems to me that, to fix one, you have to fix the other as well, and that is what we're going to be doing in the days ahead."

". . . and Sergei," Alden added, "I'd be happy to discuss Bateson's work with you. I think we'd both benefit from that conversation."

The meeting was adjourned. Alden noticed that many employees lingered, talking among themselves, some pulling the T-shirts over their regular clothes. There was a subtle music in the air, as if a period of mourning or fear was passing.

Then, his work became difficult.

NOTES

1. "A Company to Watch," *Technology Daily*, December 17, 2004
2. "The Chimera Mystery," *New York Times*, February 13, 2004.
3. The function of Resonant Vibrations is best noted in the Structural Engineering domain. In the construction of a suspension bridge, even the smallest vibration on one side of the structure will be reproduced two-fold at the other side, which in turn reverberates two-fold again. The cost of adjusting for the small (initial) vibration is quite modest; the cost of addressing the resulting problem later could be immense, if not catastrophic.

CHAPTER 14

LIBRARIES

The old man is blind and quite frail. Every Tuesday, his reader visits him in the home he has lived in since childhood. She reads to him, mostly his favorites: Stevenson, Cervantes, and occasionally a modernist, perhaps Pynchon for the humor. He knows each chapter and paragraph by heart, and his lips move as she reads out loud. On Tuesdays.

"The library is a sphere whose consummate center is any hexagon, and whose circumference is inaccessible."[1]

"I know the name of *that* writer," the old man said when the woman paused from her reading to sip tea from her hand-painted cup.

"Of course you do," she said.

The author despises deadlines, or timelines of any kind. He prefers the liberty of an open-minded and unbounded canvas. No, canvas is not the right word. He sits back in his chair and reads what he has written, so far.

The author has agreed to write a series of prose pieces about the common principles found in the mechanism of language and the grammar of technology.

The author believes that every written page is an arbitrary combination of objects (words) and that infinite numbers of combinations are possible, more than can be comprehended.

The author also knows, for he continued to study long after his retirement as chief librarian, that the many books and pages on the language network are also arbitrary combinations of

Then she read about the infinite and incomprehensible library of libraries in which all known and unknown books can be found. She found herself reading silently ahead, so she could glance up quickly to watch the old man's lips forming the next sentence. So well did he know the work that the two of them said "Everything is there" at the very same moment.

The old man knew what she was doing. He had sensed her watching him on several previous visits. He wanted to maintain the appearance that he did not know, however, so she might continue to enjoy the synchronicity of their readings (one from text and one from memory). Maybe she would remain interested in his situation and stay with him as his reader and confidante, at least longer than those that came before.

"I repeat: it is enough that a book be possible for it to exist. Only the impossible is excluded. For example: no book is also a stairway, though doubtless there are books that discuss and deny and demonstrate this possibility and others whose structure corresponds to that of a stairway."[2]

They continued in this manner, as always, until dusk. The old man offered her a light dinner, and, as always, she demurely refused. Today she offered her Thesis as an excuse.

objects, and, as is the case with words themselves, the various arrangements of objects on the network are limited only by our subjective role as audience/reader.

If we cannot imagine it, we will not see it, even amidst the many objects we recognize.

Naming the object, therefore, brings it into our awareness, and therefore, to life.

Looking at the object through different windows enlivens our understanding.

Presenting the object from different perspectives allows us to communicate Meaning to others.

The author worried that the story would merely restate what other, more eloquent and thoughtful essayists had already written. It would

"I still have far too much research to be done to accept social invitations," she said politely, "even from you."

He was grateful for her afterthought. She had the wisdom, or perhaps it was simply well-articulated compassion, to refuse his invitation and at the same time convey the sense that he was unique in her life. For that, he was grateful; moments in his life composed of such deft considerations were rare.

"Perhaps I might assist with your research," the old man suggested subtly. "I once taught at your university, and though I've lost my sight, I've not lost my vision or understanding of graduate affairs."

The woman paused for a moment, a very brief moment, as she considered the old man's offer. It was true that an outside perspective would be useful, and she was hardly in any danger.

"There is one section of my thesis that is still a conundrum," she said, with a smile, lovely and small, he could not see.

not be enough to repeat their keen observations artfully, nor would it be enough simply to provide an impressive latticework that would mirror the theme.

He wanted to add to the dialogue, to honor those who had laid the groundwork for this story, in quantum theory and second-generation systems theory. Our network has become grander and more complete than we have the minds to comprehend. Therefore, to expand the network, we must expand the boundaries of our thinking about it.

He reread what he had written so far and felt he had adequately portrayed not one but two sympathetic characters of some intellect. Now he must shepherd this minimal flock of words toward the farther horizon, his theme, rather than allowing the two characters to improvise. They always preferred to improvise.

He briefly considered an unexpected intrusion, a third character who would serve as a thematic device, but he did not want to lose the intimacy of his two characters' connection and decided to remain with the old man and the young woman, hoping the characters would cooperate.

The old man tapped his fingers lightly across the tabletop, coming to rest beside her teacup. He picked up her cup and stood. He said he would make more tea while they talked. Before he had passed the far end of the table she had gently lifted her cup from his hand and offered to make the tea so he could focus on their talk without the distractions of a whistling kettle or navigating his hallway while talking.

Again, the old man was grateful for her ever-present ability to adjust his expectations with a thoughtful comment. Not gratitude alone. He began to observe that she was capable of pursuing her own directions while observing, and even nurturing, relationships, as if the relationship between them was an entity to be cultivated in itself.

"My first name is Esther," she said.

"Then you must call me Doc," he laughed.

It had been many years since someone had been so informal with him. His wife had passed away long ago, and his few friends had also

The intrusion, then, must be in a topical form, the insertion of a new subject that by its very nature would appear to be an elaboration.

To do this successfully, in a manner that would also expand on the personal atmosphere, would require more than dialogue about networked information; it would also call for some new individual information. The author believed that this combination—a new conceptual direction plus expanded data about the characters—could hold the reader's attention.

On further consideration, he realized that the interwoven elements, data and personality, could also reflect the nature of the network itself, which can be immense and personal at the same time.

Names, some background information, then the shift to a grander theme. The author knew it was contrived, but he hoped to refine his characters' conversation, that is, if his editors allowed him the time for revision.

He recognized that the Turn must be more than paradoxical; it must be consilient.

It is a "jumping together" of disparate facts, evoking a larger (unified) view.[3]

gone, except for one who could no longer remember anything of any consequence. It had also been many years since he had laughed, or so it seemed to him, time being one of the numerous aspects of his life that was less definable, without shape or construct.

"What did you teach at the university, Doctor . . . I mean Doc," she asked, correcting herself.

The old man had not answered this question in many years, and the fields of study had shifted since then. Unable to recall his more articulate responses, ones that in other days would themselves have posed an intellectual challenge, he was resigned to more mundane terms.

"The History of Mathematics," he said, with a sigh.

Then, as if the machinery of his voice had a momentum of its own and sought more familiar territory, he unintentionally qualified his answer. It was "procedural memory," as he remembered it, in which one proceeds with learned behavior by evoking the beginning of the process, which then continues of its own accord. ". . . and my particular interest was the relationship between arithmetic and language, the

He reached the concept for the intrusion as one might traverse a hypertext link placed between one's own work and the referential work of another, in part an extension, in part a forking path. He realized that he needed two windows open to the reader's attentions, two browsers, two sessions.

The author sought to invoke John Allen Paulos's notion that all scientists rely on stories, that storytelling gives meaning to statistics.

The author sought to invoke Kevin Kelly's notion of vivi-systems, a complex merging of bio- and mechanical systems, a grand meshwork, "the network being the least structured organization that can be said to have any structure at all."

The author sought to invoke the reader's new understanding that the recent access to all human (written) thought by countless and inexpensive mobile devices anywhere in the world is changing our structure as profoundly as the printing press, hundreds of years before.

However, the broader concept of similarities between the connectivity of countless devices and sources of information and the social structures moment in our evolution when our ability to write led us to a higher level of mathematics . . . and our higher mathematical abilities led us, then . . ."

He sat down in the kitchen chair, exhausted, unable to continue his train of thought.

Esther brought the old man a fresh cup of chamomile tea and then poured hers into the same hand-painted cup she used on every visit. The two of them sat in silence for a few awkward moments before the old man gathered the energy to complete his sentence.

". . . led us to higher forms of communication, each discipline leapfrogging on the progress of the other, with technology providing footholds in the stone, every step of the way."

Esther waited to introduce her thesis until the old man seemed refreshed from his tea. Their silence was comfortable, with the rare air of compatibility. As coincidence would have it, her thesis sought to prove that human innovation—purely creative output, for its own sake—increases as the more mundane tasks of our lives are automated.

of those who use the devices seemed father away from the author and his characters than it did at the beginning of the story, as if by personalizing the narration with "real" characters, the timeline from one proposition to the next is immediately elongated.

The author wondered if our understanding of history itself was evidence of this idea.

The author also wondered about the capacity of a particular reader to recognize his or her own, howsoever minor, role in this vast blossoming network. Perhaps our limited frames of reference protect us from recognizing the long road still ahead.

As he reread his first pages, the author knew that he was not in control of the story's momentum, that sometime after the woman finished reading, and sometime before they shared a second cup of tea, the story had gone in a different direction than originally intended.

The author had three choices:

1. He could continue the story as it was unfolding, with the hope that it would eventually loop back onto its path. With this

"It seems to me," she said, "if I understand your mathematical analogy correctly, that each discipline clears a path for the others to expand . . . that there is a collaborative underpinning to even the most precise statistical models. Each equation . . ."

". . . tells us something about ourselves," the old man said, nodding his head slowly as one might reverently acknowledge the Lord's name in a synagogue prayer or the presence of a sensei in a monastery where no Americans have ever set foot.

"But I haven't found the bridge," she said quietly.

"There is no bridge, my dear," the old man said, as one might speak to a student, or a granddaughter. "It is a matter of probabilities."

Esther was attentive, focused, seemingly absorbed by every sentence he uttered. She was not, of course, as absorbed as she seemed, and he was grateful for her effort. Enough interest, he thought, to go on.

"When you return to the university library," the old man said, in the tone he had used to give assignments to his students, an authority

approach, he would continue writing until the natural sequence of words revealed a bridge homeward.

2. He could delete all passages after the supper invitation and, instead, allow the woman to leave the old man's home, at which point, an entirely different plot sequence could easily be integrated into the existing text.

3. He could abandon the "two window approach" entirely and return to a more traditional format to explain his theory that human systems and computer systems mirror each other in libraries, too.

The author was unwilling to reject the entire story categorically because of a flaw in its execution. Although he was recognized and widely published (witness the very deadline he is seeking to meet), it could be said with exceptional accuracy that he was frequently more enamored with his prose than any editor or reader could be.

Deleting his writing, however inelegant, was only a theoretical option.

he had not previously displayed, ". . . go to the Philosophy section on the 3rd floor and find a copy of *Mathematical Minds,* by Serrano. Hers is the most articulate description of Bayesian analysis."

Because Esther had been transformed from Reader for the Blind to Student of a Professor Emeritus, she opened her notebook to record the book's title and author.

"Actually, my dear," the old man said. "We only find what we are looking for, so, you should not be concerned with Serrano—she will lead you in a different direction—but with Bayes. Actually, any discussion of his theorem will suffice for your purposes."

"And what are my purposes, kind sir?"

She was now reassuring the old man on yet another level, as if he were much younger, as if he might respond to a mild flirtation. He was grateful that she had introduced the possibility of a more youthful interaction.

"The Bayes Theorem essentially concerns the adjustment of our viewpoint due to the introduction of new information. Your notion that process

---

The author elected to adjust the direction of the story by blending techniques: first, by re-visioning his work, he was quite capable of returning later to a previous rendering, and second, by introducing new information, the story would naturally adjust its course as any dynamic object will be inclined to do.

The author was aware of Zeno's Paradox. An arrow in flight, at any specific moment in its trajectory, can be said to be motionless and thus both stationary and in motion. This legendary rule is reflected in more recent research establishing (to the level at which anything can be established) that a particle may also be a wave, and the Quantum Zeno effect, when all occurrences may seem simultaneous, answers coming even before the riddle is posed.

The story, at any specific moment in its unfolding, can be said to concern relationships, or loneliness, or the Laws of Probability.

The author was aware that one subcurrent of the story, his characters' changing relationship, was the greatest gravitational threat to his nurtures innovation, with the introduction of new methods for automating some of our behaviors, gives us the opportunity for—perhaps requires of us—an adjusted understanding of our relationship with the world. Isn't innovation, really, just a new response to existing boundaries?"

Esther's pleasure in a substantive discussion with someone of equal intellect was exceeded only by her anxiety about the hour. She had a long walk back to her dormitory and it was quite dark.

"It's getting late," she said apologetically.

"A more gallant lad would offer to accompany you to your residence," the old man said, not unhappily.

"You have been very gracious," Esther said, returning her notebook to her satchel and taking the teacups to the sink before saying good night.

"Perhaps you might do me this favor?" he said.

"Of course," she said.

"Perhaps you will call me, when you arrive home," he said with unfeigned hopefulness, remembering younger days of exchanged favors, confidences, shared preoccupations.

original theme. That subcurrent could, of its own momentum, pull the trajectory into a different orbit.

Or it could be viewed as an analogue of "frame dragging," otherwise known as the Lense-Thirring effect, in which the gravito-magnetic influence of an object bends light.

Although the old man in the story would know of "frame dragging," and it could be introduced into the text without disruption, the author preferred to reserve that metaphor for his chapter on Leadership, and therefore he sought another way to influence the direction of the story, away from the Cheeveresque interplay between a young woman and an old man, and back toward the subject of libraries—the physical libraries of our childhoods and the Dynamic Libraries (written in C) that can be linked into software programming, allowing for any number of useful effects enhanced by the network.

He also wanted to portray the immensity of our electronic access—even the Library of Congress can be searched—and how this creates a

"Call you?"

"Yes," he explained, ". . . so I know you're safe."

When Esther had left his lighted doorway for the darkness beyond, the old man noticed the radiant side effects of her visit; even his painful joints were less bothersome that evening as he waited for her call. He began to imagine conversations they might have on the phone, like new lovers, like long-lost friends recently reunited, like a young woman and an old man who appreciated her attentions and yearned for the chance to return, in some manner, the consideration she had afforded him.

He waited for a long time before descending into an anxious sleep filled with vaguely confused dreams.

Esther didn't like the aura of the campus after dark. It became a forest of shadows and hushed voices, instead of the energetic movement of hundreds of students rushing between classes or chasing Frisbees or

Grid Library (all libraries conjoined to form a larger entity, the new Alexandria of Brewster Kahle's imagination).

The author still believed that Esther's understanding of dynamic systems could be an adequate channel for his own observations and that perhaps her story could encompass multiple themes, if it was allowed to proceed.

If a wave can be a particle and an arrow can be both in motion and motionless, he believed that his story could have opposites in a similar manner.

The author understood that his story required an almost mythic quality to contain the immensity of his theme.

He also understood, as he led the woman away from the safety of the old man's home and into the unknowable future, that he must move forward cautiously, avoiding his lifelong inclination to overwrite, this habit of prolixity.

What he wanted to portray, at this stage of the story, is the seemingly infinite edges to our greatest libraries. As children, when we thumbed through card catalogues or as we now search the indexes for simply standing in line at the Starbuck's in the basement of the Student Union. Any woman would be cautious in such surroundings, and Esther had greater reason to feel an imminent threat. But she did not want to focus on an ugly past; instead, she concentrated on what the old man had suggested as they said good night.

"You also might want to read about Xanadu," he said, hoping to extend their conversation.

"Ted Nelson's Project Xanadu?" she asked.

The old man nodded.

"Not for his views on hypertext or his latest attempts to resolve our arcane notions of intellectual property, but for his thoughts about *construct*. If I remember correctly, he has some pertinent things to say about how our current manner of thinking limits our ability to move to the next level and that to transform our systems, we must transform our conceptual construct."

She didn't continue their conversation, not because of disinterest; on the contrary, the old man's suggestions were refreshing. Her anxiety

a certain book, it feels as if there are no walls, that the building continues upward and outward, containing the limitless volumes of our imagined book-world. The finest libraries in our lives have no real boundaries, for their content extends beyond the physical space they occupy.

Networked libraries, in turn, have no edges whatsoever.

Networked libraries have crossed the physical barriers to simulate our expanse of knowledge more adequately, as the early cartographers were led to a broader and more circular concept of the Earth when the various landmasses were envisioned together.

It was not that the world has changed. The physical edges of each continent remained exactly as they were. It was the removal of artificial barriers that was altered, and as we accepted the broader view, we comprehended the world around us more accurately.

The author hoped, in the remaining pages, somehow to capture that breadth, that open-ended expanse of knowledge, that exhilarating extension symbolized by linking one library to another. It did not add to about the long walk home, the darkness, the nightmarish landscape she had learned to avoid—these thoughts led her away and into the night, waving a shy goodbye to the old man, who stood at the door for some time, listening to her departure in the same way that parents watch the plane take off the first time their children travel without them.

Esther knew there was a connection between the innovative surge that is made possible by a standardized and reliable infrastructure and the shift in consciousness that is required for new ideas to emerge.

"Pardon me, ma'am," a voice erupted from the darkness behind her.

Esther didn't turn or respond to the homeless man who was hoping for a dollar. She didn't stop to gauge her exact location, the proximity of friends, the lighted porches glimmering on either side of the street. She only knew she must run, on the very lip of panic. She ran until a familiar building appeared in the distance, and she didn't stop until she had arrived at the marble steps guarded by two concrete lions on either side of the entrance. She was embarrassed as she realized no one was behind her.

human knowledge, it simply removed barriers that we had constructed, because we did not yet have the perspective that allowed us to understand the round world, that map of maps.

The author stepped back, to observe the real story's location, and he recognized that he, himself, had gone astray. He knew he must pull himself away from the gravity of such theories, away from the darkness, and into a brighter place.

His struggle for clarity pushed him out of his self-conscious narrative, reversing the consilience and going back into the first window, back into the woman's plight.

The old man was left behind, and the author tried to imagine the life of a story that occurs in the margins.

While the woman is running away from her past, what is the old man doing in his home, and how can it be conveyed?

Perhaps the old man dreams of his youth, of his relationship to libraries as social exchange, dreams of meeting his wife in such literate surroundings.

The university library was composed of two modern buildings, the Humanities building and a second, now dedicated to the Sciences, where Esther stood, trying to catch her breath, escaping the darkness and finding shelter in the grand archway.

A circular stairway led to the second floor, home to countless volumes on Architecture, Mathematics, and the Physical Sciences. In the central hallway into which all paths converged, literary exhibits were available to the public in an open gallery. She saw several references to Bayes' Theorem and lingered for a moment beside the exhibition entitled "Human Navigation of Knowledge," which included an homage to card catalogs.

She remembered going to her local library as a child, mesmerized by the beckoning stacks of books large and small, but intimidated by her assignment to find three specific titles among them. It was on that day that the librarian, typically white haired and wise, taught her the Dewey Decimal System, with its numeric extensions, and showed her the wonderfully hand-worn cards contained in each tiny drawer.

Perhaps, instead, the author can focus on the old man as he sleeps, dreaming of an essay entitled "Libraries." The essay, author unknown (from our vantage point within the old man's dream, we cannot read the title or the name of its writer), concerns the significant transformation from Carnegie's notion of public libraries (ego, despite its limitations, providing historic access to information for all classes) to the digital world, where the challenge is to navigate among the available information without becoming lost. The essay might be formatted in a manner that simulates having two windows open at the same time on one's computer, two different views that we absorb simultaneously. We can now reach across nation-states to read another's work, and multiple works concurrently, though we may not yet have permission to copy or distribute it.

According to the unknown author, there are new challenges before us: may we build a link between "our" page and "your" page without your permission?

May we, with all due respect, embed a statement from your thoughtful work into ours? Or does the law that is meant to protect you in fact limit the impact of your ideas?

In the center of the exhibit was a display of oak card catalogs from around the world—saved by historians as the libraries converted to computerized indexing. She was particularly drawn to the massive wooden (now seemingly antique) cabinets from the New York Public Library.

"We can index the titles and authors," declared a placard above them, "but how can we capture the purely human marginalia scribbled on so many of these cards, knowledge that will be lost as we convert them to the digital world?"

NOTES

1. Jorge Luis Borges, "The Library of Babel," *Ficciones* (New York: Grove Press, 1962), 80.
2. Ibid., 85.
3. Stephen Jay Gould, *The Hedgehog, The Fox, and The Magister's Pox: Mending the Gap between Science and the Humanities* (New York: Three Rivers Press, 2004), 210.

As an academic, the old man had fought his battles, the university claiming to own the work he had written, the publishers claiming the right to distribute or not distribute his work.

In his entire career, no one had asked him what he wanted, as if the university lawyers and New York editors knew better than he what was best for him.

The author understood that a chapter directly challenging the publishing community to release its grip on intellectual property—as if the word "property" actually applies to thought—was inopportune in a collection of stories addressed to the business community. Even the format itself presented a challenge to the traditional notion of sequence, one page leading to the next.

Yet he hoped, as the old man dreamt and the young woman paused for reflection, that they might see themselves in the dual mirrors of this text, understanding that we have entered a new world, a world of multiple perspectives, a world without boundaries, and that we have a choice of windows. Our selection of that window will define what we observe, and to expand our choices, we need only open another.

CHAPTER 15

ABSTRACTION

The woman could not get out of her parked Lexus SUV—a routine task—and knock on the piano teacher's door to pick up her daughter, without complications.

First she removed a small bottle of lotion from her immense purse and rubbed a small amount across her bare arms. Then she rubbed the rest of it aggressively into her hands. She returned the bottle to the purse and, from a zipped area reserved for cosmetics, pulled out a thin silver tube of lipstick, which she proceeded to apply carefully to her upper lip, pursing her mouth twice and checking her reflection in the rear view mirror before capping the lipstick and replacing it into the correct area of her purse. Then she combed her hair—a few quick strokes through the back and two strokes through her permed bangs—before opening her wallet and thumbing through many crisp green bills. She pulled three from the pile, folded the rest of them carefully, and returned the others to her wallet, which went into her purse, which then went into the back seat.

Reaching across to a small leather bag beside the purse, she retrieved a long, silver-studded belt that she put around her waist, writhing into the correct position on the front seat. She pushed the belt down by a degree, tightened it one additional notch, and checked herself again in the mirror stepping out of her SUV and beeping the locks before walking with a hurried step to the Sorriano's front porch.

She looked at her watch.

10 a.m. exactly on time, as she was every week at the end of her daughter's piano lesson.

246

Inside the house, Lilly Sorriano's attention was divided between the tedium of listening to piano scales and thinking about when she could do the laundry and the grocery shopping. She was also anxiously awaiting the next student. Tuesday brought the one student who made teaching piano worthwhile.

After finishing her Ph.D in Music Theory in 1997, she had stayed on at Stanford as a teaching assistant. Then she had played with the San Jose Symphony for three years before the Symphony suffered serious financial problems and suspended operations. It was the beginning of the downward slide for everyone in Silicon Valley: Lily's decision to return to teaching was one result of this miserable downturn. Her husband had been forced to dissolve his technology startup. Most of their friends had been impacted by the burst of the Internet bubble. Many were on the verge of divorce, triggered by financial instability and the ripple effects in their relationships. For almost a year, it had seemed as if Lilly did not know a married couple that wasn't in serious trouble.

The Sorriano family found themselves in a constant state of distress. They had an immense mortgage on their three-bedroom ranch house in Palo Alto, and both of them had been forced to work at jobs that were too boring to be fulfilling: Frank was back in the corporate world, managing a Help Desk team, and Lilly was giving piano lessons in their basement music room to teenagers whose only grasp of Music Theory came from the lyrics of Green Day or Weezer.

Her 9:30 student said nothing during their lesson. She would remain mute until the moment when her mother arrived 30 minutes later with cash in hand. Vinny was taking piano lessons at her parents' insistence. They were convinced she was a prodigy, but in 11 months of lessons the girl had not once demonstrated the slightest capacity to do anything more than mimic Lilly's movements.

"Let's hear 'Für Elise' one more time before your Mom comes, Vinny," Lilly said, "First, with the music. Then I'd like to hear it once without looking at the music."

Vinny mechanically complied with the request, playing the piece flawlessly with the music. She was capable of perfect (or nearly perfect—

her hands were still too small to position themselves for the broader chords) execution, with or without reading the music, but it was a rote repetition. She closed the music book and was ready to begin again when Lilly interrupted.

"Vinny, can I ask you something?" Lilly said. The young girl nodded wordlessly.

"Is there something we can do to make this more fun for you?" Lilly asked.

The girl shrugged.

"What I meant was, is there a special song, maybe something popular that you've heard on the radio or in a movie? I'd be glad to work on something with you that isn't Bach or Mozart."

Vinny looked down at the keyboard and then out the window. She said nothing.

Lilly listened to the piece again, without the music, and then suggested some alternate positions for Vinny's left hand. She watched the girl's emotionless face as the notes came through in the right order with the right cadence but without any feeling. She could just as easily have been knitting or washing dishes. Lilly made some notes on the pages for Vinny to remember, and when the front doorbell rang, the two walked silently up the carpeted stairs and through the living room again.

"Don't forget about the recital in two weeks," Lilly said as the woman perfunctorily paid her $60 and turned back to the car with her daughter. As Vinny stepped away from the porch, Rachel, the 10 a.m. student, stepped inside. The two of them, Rachel and Lilly, watched as Vinny climbed into the back seat of her mother's Lexus.

Lilly welcomed Rachel and then turned to the end table beside the door, where Frank kept his keys, bills to be mailed, and other daily fundamentals. She opened the small drawer, tucked the $60 into a leather checkbook, and closed it again, thinking about the very different lives she and her husband had planned.

"Not one of your happiest students, is she?" Rachel joked as she walked inside and headed for the kitchen. "I was watching her mother in the car. She doesn't seem very happy either."

They always had a cup of coffee before beginning their lesson. In some ways, college students were more demanding, but in this case, Lilly loved

Rachel's visits to the house. Only a decade apart in age, they were more like peers, and they enjoyed their coffee conversations as much as the lively lessons afterward.

"She's a very different type of student than you," Lilly admitted, "so the teaching experience is different."

"Explain that," Rachel said sincerely, sipping the coffee that was nearly too hot to the touch of her tongue.

"It's the difference between thinking only about the notes or the placement of your fingers on the keyboard or when you depress a pedal and when you do not . . ." Lilly said, describing Vinny's approach, ". . . and understanding the entire piece of music, comprehending the motifs and themes at a higher level."

Rachel said she had always thought it was a matter of experience.

"For many people, that may be true," Lilly said. "But you've been taking lessons for only six months, and already you're thinking about what Tyner was trying to *express* in his work. Our young student earlier has been taking lessons for three years—but perhaps she isn't a good example."

"I think that girl's mother has a lot to do with what her daughter is becoming," Rachel observed.

The two descended the steep carpeted stairs to the basement, where Lilly sat behind Rachel as she began to play her latest assignment. Not all the chords were correct, and rather than stopping, and then starting at the beginning, she improvised one or two melodic chords that simulated the progression until she found her way back to the actual notes on the page. Lilly loved listening to Rachel play. She was courageous and inventive, although some pieces were less proficiently played than others. Rachel approached the music from a different perspective. It was much easier to teach the details to someone who grasped the broader meaning of the work than it was to lead someone from the purely tactical placement of hands on keyboard to a more comprehensive view.

"Play the piece again, Rachel," Lilly suggested, "but this time, I want you to play all the way to the end . . ."

Rachel protested mildly, explaining that she had only been working on the last two pages for a week. When she finally began to play, however, she was able to leap from what she knew to what she imagined was true, with some solid licks and exceptional grace notes. It was awkward, but it seemed closer to what McCoy Tyner had written than Rachel herself understood.

"It's a very complex piece of music," Rachel said, relieved that the experiment was over.

"But somehow you removed the complexity," Lilly said, "and remained with the important themes."

"I needed to simplify some phrasing," Rachel observed.

"*Abstraction*," Lilly explained. "You lifted your attention up a level, from detail to theme."

Rachel turned on her piano stool and told Lilly about one of the teams at Stanford that was working on digital languages for music, specifically, a standard called 4ML that would ultimately allow net-based collaboration on songs utilizing the Internet as the medium of composition, rather than a nightclub or a recording studio.[1]

"So—they're working on an abstraction of the abstraction," Lilly observed, and Rachel agreed, confessing that it was easier to understand abstraction in computers (graphical user interfaces creating an abstraction of complex code so that it is unapparent to the user who need not understand or wrestle with the details) than it is to understand abstraction in music.

"However," Rachel said as she gathered her belongings, "keyboards are keyboards . . ." and they both laughed at the joke.

When the timer rang and their 30-minute lesson was over, Lilly groaned. She was always disappointed when Rachel's half-hour lessons were finished and the young woman was waving goodbye from her unkempt Mustang parked in front of the house.

It was as if an important part of herself was leaving and was not expected to return for an whole week.

For Rachel Eddy, the only distressing aspect of her Tuesday piano lessons was the hurried commute across town for her afternoon seminar on Urban Planning, followed by yet another trek to reach her programming seminar.

Urban Planning was her least favorite class, but it fulfilled her mathematics requirement, for reasons that were never quite clear to her but that she dared not question. It was the only class in her entire course load that offered her nothing stimulating: she simply needed to attend the lectures, complete the "take home" examination at the end of the semester, and not worry about any other math courses for the rest of her academic career. It had seemed a fine idea when she registered, but as she navigated the clogged arteries of midtown traffic after each piano lesson, she frequently reclassified the "fine idea" to the category of Serious Annoyance that Must Be Survived.

The graduate student who usually taught her seminar often explained that he had spent his childhood in Pittsburgh during the infamous urban renewal programs of the 1960s that had transformed what had been a three-river coal town to a jewel of modern architecture. Every seminar included at least one more set of photographs, Then and Now, from his childhood. She often struggled to remain awake long enough to sign the attendance list at the end of each session.

This particular Tuesday, however, was unusual in two respects.

The Pittsburgh-born teaching assistant was not available, giving his humbler teaching assistant an opportunity to present her opinions about metropolitan design. The woman was incredibly bright and very excited about the chance to present her thesis to a group of younger students.

What she had to say was, indeed, a remarkable perspective, so much so that, by the end of the class, Rachel had a new appreciation for Urban Planning. The woman's thesis was this: how humans organized themselves (in their kitchens, their neighborhoods, their cities, and their lives) was predictable, thematic, and quantifiable. Furthermore, the same themes could be seen elsewhere, encouraging everyone, including Rachel, to expand their view of the world around them.

The first PowerPoint slide, displayed on the only empty wall of the classroom they borrowed each Tuesday for the seminar, was an aerial photo of a neighborhood (Exhibit 15.1).

The teaching assistant simply waited for the class to respond.

The second slide was a portion of an integrated circuit. As soon as the woman displayed the circuit board on the wall, everyone gasped at the clear similarities (Exhibit 15.2).[2]

EXHIBIT 15.1   *Vancouver Neighborhood*

Source: www.cityfarmer.org/aerialVancouver.html.

EXHIBIT 15.2   *Portion of Circuit Board*

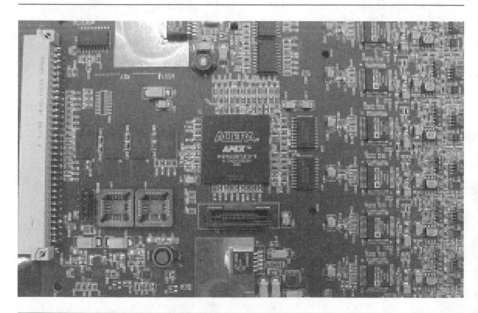

Source: Phoenix Designs, Inc.

"It seems to me," the woman observed, "that we are repeating ourselves at the macro and micro levels. Yet we refuse to consider the possibility that this is not random coincidence, but a broader principle. Let's look at a few more examples." She displayed yet another semiconductor comparison (Exhibit 15.3). "I think you will find, as I have discovered, that you will begin to see them everywhere, once you recognize the similarities."

Then the teaching assistant told a story about getting lost on her summer trip to the University of Washington in the suburbs with her two small children and a guide who spoke very little English.

"All we had was the woman's map," she said, and an enlarged version of the map appeared on the wall of the room. "Everyone in my family laughs when they see the university map. However, if one considers the preceding view of the Xilinx Place and Route diagram, a simple map seems suddenly more significant somehow." (Exhibit 15.4)

EXHIBIT 15.3 *Place and Route Diagram*

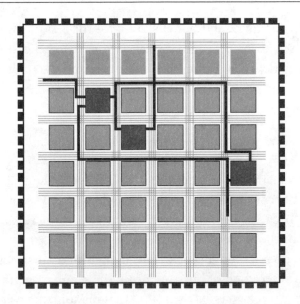

Source: Courtesy of Xilinx Design Systems.

EXHIBIT 15.4   *Map of University of Washington*

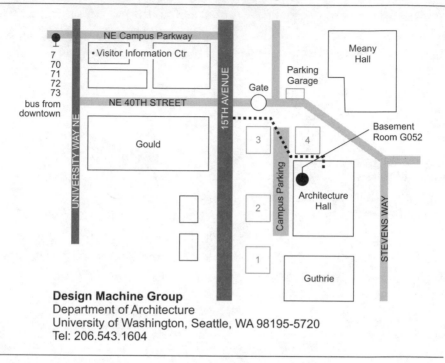

Design Machine Group
Department of Architecture
University of Washington, Seattle, WA 98195-5720
Tel: 206.543.1604

The images remained in Rachel's mind for the rest of the day; indeed, she began to see abstract similarities everywhere that she looked. Rachel was startled by her recognition of similarities, and the underlying theme of abstraction, as *when a child learns a new word and suddenly seems to find it everywhere.*

Programming instructor Elliot Anderson accepted the teaching assignment, in part because of the company's policy of Paid Volunteer Time, and in part because he thought it might help him regain his initial enthusiasm for the essence of engineering, which was to solve problems elegantly. To do so, there needed to be a balance of abstraction and detail, and he wanted each of his students in the seminar to appreciate that balance. As the weeks passed, he found that his students were composed of two types of individuals, those that preferred the conceptual view and those that preferred the pragmatic view. Each week, he struggled to find assignments that would help his students understand the necessary compromise in any successful technology solution—in their labs, in their internships, or in business.

"It is not enough to solve the problem quickly," Elliot said to Rachel's late afternoon class. "Anyone can write a software program that functions correctly."

"Aren't you asking a bit much from us?" one of the students complained. His name was Tyrone, and he was always voicing the seminar's unspoken thoughts. "I'd be satisfied to write a simple program that doesn't generate error messages."

Elliot looked around the small room. Everyone was waiting for his response. He wondered if it was possible to teach complex theory to beginning engineering students, but he knew that the world was filled with inadequately trained programmers who did not think beyond the specified requirements. Thus the world was filled with software that was inflexible, rigid, and needed constant maintenance in a changing environment. He could lecture them about learning how to do things correctly. He could provide stern warnings for what would face them when they enter the workforce.

In the back of his mind, hiding behind an odd collection of impressions and memories like an imp that had just decided to poke his head up above the pile, Elliot remembered his class on James Joyce and the odd confluence of meteorology and text. He realized that he wanted to be the person these students remembered years from now, not simply someone who taught them that $2 + 2 = 2 \times 2$.

"Let's see if I can help you discover this from your own lives," Elliot said, improvising. "Forget the equation for a moment and think about getting up from bed and getting out of your house this morning."

Again, the small group of students stared blankly at him, like the silent crowd at a local comedy club when the comedian on stage was the only one laughing.

"You may all have very different lives and backgrounds, but there's one thing all of you did before leaving your home."

"Brushed my teeth."

"Fed my cat, Magritte."

"Told my roommate to take out the garbage . . . again."

Elliot waved his hand, and told them to think about something that all of them did, not the unique actions, but the action that was common to all.

Rachel was the one who first understood the answer, and as her mind moved quickly from one recognition to the next, she began to comprehend Elliot's lesson. "We all got dressed."

"That's right," Elliot said. "Everyone in this room is wearing clothes. Now, those of you who know taxonomies know that 'clothing' is a general category that covers a wide variety of specific types . . . for example, Tyrone's knitted cap, Emily's striped stockings, Rachel's torn jeans. Now, if you were writing a code to animate your morning rituals, the beginner's inclination would be to embed the cap directly into the your architecture. But that would only apply to today's Tyrone program. Tomorrow, he would have to rewrite the program to include one of his other hats, and so on . . ."

"Your point is . . ." said Tyrone, unsure if the attention to his haberdashery was a compliment or a criticism.

"OK, let's look at one of the examples from the book I've asked you to read." Elliot said, adding, "I know some of you weren't able to find copies, and that's fine."

Rachel pulled the Hunt and Thomas book from her knapsack, spilling her music across the floor, and Tyrone leaned over to help her gather the sheets, whispering "Cool, a musician." He had been flirting with her since Day One.

"In the book," Elliot explained, "they give an example of writing code that calculates the price of the product at the check-out lane. This year, the sales tax is 7%, and if we are in a hurry, we simply include the current sales tax rate into the code itself. After all, the answer will be correct."

"Abstraction," Rachel said out loud, thinking to herself that it was the third time in one day that someone had mentioned the term, too coincidental to be believable if it were in a novel, but this was her life, and coincidence always seemed more relevant when it was real.

"Yes," Elliot said, "you have to consider the overall architecture, however small, of your program, and understand that sales tax rates or hat choices change. Therefore, you should abstract out the detail that is volatile and store it externally as meta-data. Then, as the detail changes, you need only update the database and not alter the essential code."[3]

A great and lively discussion erupted as the students debated how one knows, in advance, what information is likely to change and what elements are constant. Everyone understood that they changed clothes every day, because they had been doing that for years, but they were beginning programmers, and it seemed, in the absence of experience such as Elliot's in the business world, that it was simply a matter of guesswork.

"It feels like guesswork," Elliot admitted. "I had a manager, in my second year at the firm, who insisted that the new user interface include a blue background because the company's logo was blue. He actually signed the requirements document that no changes would be allowed. But my intuition told me that colors were a personal preference and subject to great volatility over time. The color did change, several times, before the final project was approved. My advice, and I'd really suggest reading the book because the authors describe it much more usefully than I can, is to err on the side of detail. Your core chunks of functionality should be as simple as you can make them."

Rachel raised her hand, and everyone laughed, as if they were still in high school and she needed permission to speak. In fact, it was a high school memory she wanted to retell.

"I remember my sophomore English teacher explaining how to diagram sentences," she said, "and her advice was exactly the same. The baseline of the sentence should be reduced as much as possible, and everything that can be subordinated diagonally should be subordinated."

Rachel remembered the woman quite well, not only because she was a compassionate and funny woman with a real interest in her students, but because she had helped Rachel think through the many issues that had overwhelmed her when she learned about her father's handicap. On the wall of that English classroom was an immense poster of one of literature's longest prose sentences, 958 words from the translated works of Marcel Proust, fully diagrammed in such a complex, nested fashion that, from a distance, the image of the diagrammed sentence looked like a complete USA roadmap from AAA.

As Rachel recalled, there were only 7 key words on the baseline of the diagram. The remaining 951 were considered details.

Several miles away, in her rented cottage shared with Avie, who had long since fallen asleep at the kitchen table, face down on his closed laptop, Rachel nestled beneath the quilt her mother had given her for her 14th birthday. With an unnamed PBS special flickering in the background, her TV muted, she logged onto her private blog that she used much like a journal and tried to capture the essence of her day.

> Many young writers—sixth grade journalists, college romantics, weekend poets—construct their stories and poems without ever knowing about the existence of *the suspension of disbelief*, the act of an engaged reader who without resistance accepts the written premise. It was only after many years of reading that I learned from a fellow student that the *suspension of disbelief* was a critical component of the partnership between reader and writer.
>
> Similarly, many programmers—web designers, gamers, hackers, analysts—construct their software programs without knowing (or needing to know) about *the leap toward abstraction*, the hiding of information, objects, or scripts in the design of their programs as they contrive a system to engage their end-users. Many technologists have been gainfully absorbed in their computational efforts throughout their careers without once formally recognizing the importance of the Leap toward Abstraction they are not only allowing to occur, but creating, and, in some ways, are dependent on.
>
> Suspension of Disbelief = Leap toward Abstraction

She paused for a moment as a noise from another part of the cottage momentarily distracted her thoughts. It was only Avie, waking on the hard surface of the kitchen table and lumbering clumsily toward his bedroom.

For some of her fellow students, it seemed adequate to create an artful user interface (short story form), build objects in a database (characters in a chapter), link objects to other objects (plot), and transfer them onto production servers and networks (thematic architecture).

She began again.

> For me, the intrigue lies in what has been learned by the effort, in order to attempt one's own applications, based on this knowledge. From the molecular perspective, solid objects are abstractions. From the cellular level, our bodies are abstractions. The presence of the Abstract is quite common—it is our ability to comprehend those levels, and move to the next, that should define our efforts.

NOTES

1. From http://www.xml.com/pub/r/1008. Music and Lyrics Markup Language (4ML) is an XML application for music description. Rather than being an abstraction of music notation, 4ML is an abstraction of sound itself. This approach is intended to lose less information between translations, while having fewer limitations when dealing with non-Western music systems or alternate tuning styles. The language is also able to reuse groups of notes, saving work for the user by taking advantage of the repetition in music. 4ML is designed to be a platform-independent solution for musicians and programmers, with applications for writing songs as guitar tablature, playing music over speakers, producing Musical Instrument Digital Interface (MIDI) files, or displaying lyrics dynamically.
2. Portion of Circuit Board; Copyright 2005, Phoenix Designs. www.phoenixdesigns.com
3. For additional information on Abstraction and Detail, see http://www.artima.com/intv/metadata.html, March 24, 2003.

CHAPTER 16

INSUBORDINATION
AS AN ASSET

"Daddy, why are you sad?" his daughter asked as Henry pulled on his trench coat and leaned over to kiss her goodbye.

"I'm not sad, honey," he lied, "I've just got a lot of work to do today."

He waved to his wife who was on the phone in the kitchen, and picked up the worn leather briefcase that had been with him since the early days in Silicon Valley. Together, they drove in silence to the office.

Lately, the concept of Enterprise Search made Henry Feldman uneasy.

It was not the complications of search algorithms or the variety of file formats to be indexed, nor was it the political implications of exposing private or dated information for everyone to read. It was Henry's position in life that bothered him, the road he had followed, his circuitous path from radical college "genius" to middle-aged corporate employee. Search, for Henry Feldman, was a reflection of his own qualms about getting older in a world of technology that valued the Next Big Thing more than the wisdom born of experience. His was an uneasiness of midlife disappointments, missed expectations, and promising opportunities gone awry.

Henry was not unhappy with his new position at the company. In fact, for more than two years he had lobbied for the creation of his job, and it was considered by many to be a personal and professional triumph when the executives approved the new title and pay scale. In the past, technologists had had no career path except management, which had led to the all-too-common business constraint of managers who understood C++ but knew little about people. The creation of Chief IT Architect, a staff-level technology track position reporting to the company's CIO was the first step, many believed, in the long overdue process of rewarding technical growth for its own sake.

As the Chief IT Architect, Henry was responsible for the "big picture," which meant understanding how all the pieces (servers, routers, switches, firewalls, databases, applications, interfaces) fit together, as well as monitoring the evaluation of emerging technologies. Thus Henry was perhaps the only person in the entire company who could comprehend how a new puzzle piece fit into the jigsaw that was their technology environment, the risk/reward equation of their implementation. He was also the only technical staff with a personal veto of new projects.

He enjoyed his work. He was well compensated and respected throughout the IT organization, and many of the business executives had come to trust his judgment, so much so that they often wandered by his office to ask what type of computer to buy their children, or whether the iPod was just a fad.

The only arena that caused Henry uneasiness was the topic of Enterprise Search.

"Hello, Harry," Henry said when he arrived at the front gate.

"G'morning, *Doctor*," Harry Claymaker sang in return, pressing the button for the gate to lift. Claymaker had been the company's security guard for almost a decade. The friendly old man removed his cap, scratched his balding head with one bony finger, and replaced the cap in the exact position it had been in for ten years. "Have a good day, sir."

Henry's PhD was in Linguistics, and his thesis (widely quoted in the early 1990s) was entitled "The Promise of Universal Network Information Retrieval." The paper was a landmark study of various automated "find" utilities, back in the days when the possibility of locating information anywhere on the Internet by entering keywords and Boolean terms (And, Not) was the objective of many research teams around the country. For the purposes of his doctoral thesis, Henry had written a program that "crawled" various networks, created text files of relevant documents, created a master file noting the exact location of each word in every file, indexed that master file, and created links from the master file back to the originating source documentation. When he first wrote the program, to address information security concerns, Henry had embedded a secondary query into the search algorithm that pinged the machine where the search was located and delivered the results only to that machine, where permissions could be locally verified.

There were two problems in those days. The first was finding the correct file on the network, and the second was determining whether the seeker was authorized to read or change it.

In those days, Search and Retrieval was complicated; there were no standards for document formats and little appreciation for the intricacies of needle-in-haystack compilers that parsed All Possible Combinations and listed them for the seeker's consideration. It was groundbreaking stuff in those days, and Henry felt as if he was personally responsible for one dramatic step in the adoption of the Internet as a useful research tool.

In the decade that had passed, Search eventually became a commodity. One could simply purchase a Google Appliance and install it with the one-page instructions packaged with the server. Within an hour, all the files on the company's network were retrievable, with relevance ranking and advanced search built into the standard product. What had required more than eight months of engineering, expensive software licenses, and five Unix servers, ten years before, could now be purchased for $40,000 and was fully functional within one day.

Some heralded this as evidence that the Internet bubble was not a waste of money, but rather an immense investment in technologies that have now become commonplace in our lives.

When he reached his office, Henry Feldman looked at the Google Appliance User Guide on his desk, and he felt old.

"Excuse me, Henry," a woman said shyly.

Henry was temporarily using the CIO's office while she was away on medical leave, so they could repaint his new office and put in the additional networking that he required. This also meant that the CIO's secretary was at his disposal, and although he insisted upon managing his own calendar and meetings, he enjoyed the fact that someone in the company was looking over his shoulder.

"I thought you might want to know," she said. "Company e-mail is down."

Damn it, Henry thought to himself.

". . . and Jeannine would like to see you in her office at 10 a.m. She said it was urgent and that I should cancel your afternoon appointments," the woman added with an appropriately serious tone.

"Damn it!" Henry said out loud. He nodded appreciatively and asked her to contact Katya on her mobile phone.

Henry didn't need to speak to the Help Desk to know what had happened. He didn't need to log in as an administrator to review log files, because he knew what he would find. The symptoms were clear. Nonetheless, good crisis habits were second nature, and he logged onto the R&D network then onto Katya's Sandbox machine, where he reviewed the processes that were running.

There it was, as plain to him as smoke is to the firefighter.

Process 142.

He immediately changed accounts, entered the password for "super-user," and then in the command line that was blinking in his shell, he entered:

kill –9 142

Everything on her machine stopped immediately. Henry asked the secretary once again to call Katya on her cellphone. "Immediately, please."

Katya Sarinsky loved her job.

She left St. Petersburg, Russia, with a Master's Degree in Computer Science, one suitcase of clothes, and a picture of her family. At the airport, she said a possibly permanent and tearful goodbye to her family. In Chicago, she felt she had been lifted on the wings of God and delivered to a higher plane of existence: winter was warmer than spring in St. Petersburg, she had her own room in an apartment with two other women who worked downtown and taught her about the trains, and she was being paid more money *in one week* than her fellow students could earn in a month in Russia.

"I do not understand the difference between Republicans and Democrats, it is very confusing," she wrote her mother at the end of her first week in the United States, "but Chicago is heaven, and my work is a great joy."

From her cubicle on the third floor, Katya could see Lake Michigan swell and surge, immense waves curling in that infamous wind and spraying high arcs of crystal droplets across the lakeside docks that reminded her of the Black Sea. Sometimes she would carry her lunch (they called it "brown bagging") to the Field Museum several blocks away and spend her time in the corridors of that amazing building. Everyone else seemed to be impressed by Sue, the immense *Tyrannosaurus rex* in the lobby, but Katya's favorite exhibit in the museum was Bushman, an immense gorilla that had lived in the Chicago Zoo for many years.

Her work was exhilarating. She was assigned to the Sandbox Group, a four-person team responsible for evaluating new technologies and making recommendations to the Architecture office of the IT organization. She did not initially understand the term "Sandbox." Finally one of her colleagues explained that American children play with toys in sandboxes, and she eventually understood that her group did much the same with their emerging technologies: they could install and play with various types of software, run performance tests, analyze data integrity, validate security protocols. The Sandbox itself was a lab with five networked servers disengaged from the corporate network (except via the company intranet for communication), minimizing risk to the various production systems used by everyone else for company business.

For Katya, it was the perfect job, with one exception: though she loved the experimentation, she struggled to write her summary reports and was not comfortable with her written English. Phrases that were ubiquitous in the company were difficult to translate, and she needed her manager's help with even the simplest corporate communications.

"What is this," she asked, holding a printed copy of an e-mail with a phrase circled in red. "Core versus Context?"[1]

Her manager tried to explain the phrase that had become part of the company's lexicon; it meant that certain tasks were important to the company and others were less important.

"Our job is not core," her manager tried to explain, but Katya remained true to her belief that her job, in her life, was the very center of the universe.

Two days before the e-mail servers failed, Katya was given a new assignment. A scientist from the University of Tuscaloosa in Alabama had written a search algorithm that was apparently unique, and the IT Architect asked Katya to install it in the Sandbox and test the search program.

She first installed it on a stand-alone machine, to verify that there was no "malware" in the program. After testing it on several directories containing complex documents and graphics, all of which were rendered gracefully by the new program, her manager stopped by the Sandbox and casually suggested that the next interesting idea would be to test it on the corporate intranet itself. "Perhaps we'll do that," he said, and then her manager said good night.

Katya did not realize, from her manager's indirect language, that she should not proceed with the testing until he had considered it more thoroughly. She was also honestly curious about the outcome, so she carefully edited the configuration file in the new program to search only the home pages of each department in the company, 20 to 30 various web sites.

Google did an excellent job of displaying the results and she was anxious to compare the new index with Google's result. Katya initiated the program and waited; unlike her original tests, this program continued to run—in fact, it ran for almost 40 minutes. Katya looked at the logs to determine what had gone wrong; there were no error messages. So she decided to allow the program to continue and check the logs again in the morning.

After all, it was only a test.

Katya understood basic search algorithms. And she understood the corporate intranet.

What she did not know was this: one home page of the company's Software Product Management Group included customized scripts that automatically checked the Customer Support and Contracts databases directly, presenting the latest Customer-Reported Bugs in HTML to the engineering team, as soon as they were entered into the databases. At first, this did not seem unusual; in fact, it seemed innovative.

However, unknown to anyone, the new search engine had the capacity to traverse hyperlinks, following each link to its source and indexing the related sources of information. By initializing an experimental search, she had inadvertently triggered a rogue utility that continued to gather and index every element in every Oracle table accessible via those unofficial links on the Engineering home page. The search traversed subnets following the Internet for URL resolution, leapt the Sandbox firewalls, which were accidentally configured to prevent access inward, not access outward via the intranet, and within three hours of execution, it had created a self-replicating index that flooded the network with traffic. The number of file exchanges, and the apparently infinite relational elements cross-referenced in the Oracle databases, caused a situation very similar to Denial of Service attacks triggered by hackers—only this was triggered by internal software, on a subnet not normally monitored by IT in the data center.

At first, no one noticed the surge in network traffic. Then additional traffic spikes, origin unknown, began to appear on the Data Center monitors. (It was the second spike that would later lead Frank Sorriano to phone Dorian at home and report a crisis.)

As her test program continued to expand its scope and size, slowing the related databases and servers practically to a standstill, Katya was at home, writing her mother another letter about the wonders of her job, about the unusual phrases that seemed like village colloquialisms inside this American company, and about the glorious Bushman in the museum, whose immense knuckles curled beneath him, withstanding the weight of the world.

That night, in his dreams, Dorian bought a farmhouse as a surprise for his partner's 30th birthday.

Although he had never expressed an interest in country life, Dorian was giving him a tour of their new kitchen with expansive pantry space, cabinets with hinges half a century old, and broad windows that looked out across an acre of land—their land—where he envisioned serene plantings and statuettes in place of the weeds that covered the property. In the dream, one sunflower stood tall in the sun, its huge head bowing toward the earth from the weight of 1,000 seeds adorning in its face.

Somewhere in the background, perhaps from the neighboring farm, a barely discernable alarm could be heard. In his dream, Dorian ignored this annoying infringement on serenity. He walked out the screen door at the end of the kitchen, across the weeds and toward the sunflower, hoping to taste a seed, the small sweet kernel inside its shell that, for him, represented their new life.

In the dream, he was several steps into his journey toward the sunflower when, beneath his left foot, a small rumbling reverberated through his shoe, and in the split second that was required for him to look downward to the source of the vibration, a tiny explosion of smoke and soot burst upward into the air. Startled, Dorian moved to his right, and another explosion smoked upward, scalding his right hand. He jumped backward, retracing his steps to the kitchen door as he observed several other small eruptions, like little volcanoes bursting up over the yard and burning the weeds around them, dozens of midget volcanoes—none too dangerous by themselves, but together creating a hazy landscape of risk.

"Dorian!" the man said, shaking his shoulders.

Dorian slowly retreated from his dream, the aroma of smoke still in his nostrils. "Get up, Dore, now. They need you at work. *Frank* is on the phone."

Frank Sorriano was the Help Desk Supervisor for The Company's IT division. He was covering the graveyard shift they always instituted at quarter end. Frank was talking fast: *multiple systems down*, and Dorian was thinking *Damn It, Damn It, Damn It* as he pulled on his jeans and thrust his arms into a wrinkled flannel shirt snatched from a drawer. He strapped on his watch—6:41 a.m. Frank quickly reviewed the series of machines that were not responding.

"Exchange1 and Exchange2," Frank listed, and there were others.

As Dorian rushed out of the apartment all he could think about was *quarter end*, when 70% of the company's revenue was recorded. Quarter end, when every executive was focused on meeting their numbers. There was never a good time for systems failures, but quarter end was the worst time imaginable. Careers teetered on the edge of the abyss. Dorian only hoped they could find the hotspot, get the systems rebooted, and have the company ready for business by 9 a.m.

"We have two hours," Dorian said to Frank from his cell phone as he sped out the driveway of the condominium complex, around the new concrete islands that the city had recently planted with gardenias, through the congested morning traffic. "I'll be there in 20 minutes."

Dorian knew that Frank would not have called before trying all the standard emergency response scenarios. Frank knew the systems better than Dorian, which meant that Dorian was needed for political reasons—to deal with the dozens of sales teams that would not be able to communicate, the numerous contracts that would not be retrievable by midnight, and an entire executive team that would demand a complete explanation of the unexplainable. Frank's team could handle the servers and networks, but Dorian knew that most problems could be traced to human error.

> Human error happens for many reasons, but in the end it almost always comes down to a mismatch between a human operator's mental model of the IT environment and the environment's actual state. Sometimes this confusion arises from poorly designed status feedback mechanisms . . . but other times the mismatch simply arises from a lack of experience on the operator's part, or worse, to quirks of human cognitive processing that obstinately steer even an experienced operator toward the wrong conclusion . . . people are simply too good at finding unanticipated ways to make mistakes.[2]

Frank's team would attend to the systems, and Dorian's job was to be the apologist, if the crisis could not be contained by the time the executives arrived. *Wrinkled flannel shirt*, Dorian thought to himself, *the perfect uniform for an unexplainable morning.*

His two-hour buffer was reduced to fractions of seconds when he pulled into the parking lot and noticed the CEO's car already in its spot, at 7 a.m. Dorian raced up the back stairs beside the loading platform, hoping to get to his office unnoticed, but they were already waiting for him when he arrived at his door. Standing beside George Latham, the CEO, was the new Vice President of Sales, and Jeannine Hope-Swee, Chief Financial Officer. They were arranged like a squad of prison guards and pastor ready to walk a condemned man to the electric chair.

"We're here to *help*," the CEO said quietly as Dorian unlocked his office and walked inside. Lights turned on automatically and the trio entered on cue.

"We've got very good people working on this, sir," Dorian said.

"We've got *very good people* in the field offices who need their *e-mail*," the Vice President of Sales mocked. His name was Lambert, *Pete or Paul, which was it,* and Dorian had not met him until that morning.

Damn it, Dorian thought to himself.

The CEO raised his hand, quietly gesturing for calm. He asked Dorian to sit down for a moment with them, so they might help him understand the gravity of the situation. Dorian already knew the gravity, he could feel it pulling him down, down even as he reached for air, but he was in no position to send the executives away without first listening to their laments. They spoke in slow, moderated tones, the voice a concerned parent uses when his child has been caught stealing for the first time.

Jeannine explained that a conference call with the Wall Street analysts was scheduled for 9:30 a.m., and her staff was unable to receive any of their financial data from the new Oracle system.

The Vice President of Sales, arms crossed and face frowning, said they had only two more hours to register U.K. business, given the time difference. "Two hours until London *closes for the weekend*," he repeated. His implication, unspoken but very clear to everyone in the room, was that recognizing European revenue depended upon the company's e-mail system.

"I'll get a report to you as soon as I have a chance to meet with my team and review the situation," Dorian said.

Latham, the CEO, reached across the table and put his hand firmly on Dorian's arm. "We don't want a report. We need the systems to be running. Don't come upstairs until you have good news."

The threesome left the office as the midnight Help Desk team stood in the hallway outside the office. Dorian waved everyone inside, cleaned off his whiteboard, and took a deep breath.

"All right, tell me how bad it is," he said. "Frank first."

Frank distributed a one-page memo detailing the series of failures that had seemed to cascade, one on the other, beginning at 1:30 in the morning when the backup servers did not complete their standard batch process. Upon reviewing the logs to determine what systems had not yet been backed up, his team realized that the e-mail servers—both the primary system and the failover system—were not responding. The Unix team had determined that a power unit in one system had failed, perhaps from a surge.

"What about Exchange2?" Dorian asked.

Frank explained that the Unix team was unable to determine why the backup server was not responding. One theory was a failure in the RAID[3] systems, which had recently been overhauled. This would also account for poor response from the Oracle databases.

"Those systems are supposed to *prevent* downtime," Dorian said. He was telling the group what they already knew. "What's the ETA for the power unit?"

The team was cannibalizing equipment from engineering and might be able to have the power unit replaced by 10 a.m.

"However," Frank added, "there is no estimate yet for whether or not e-mail has been lost. They are in contact with the London team to trace sent messages, but until the power unit is installed, and the RAID systems are corrected, there is no reliable way to determine if messages have been successfully queued."

"We'll do the postmortem when e-mail is back," Dorian said, postponing any additional guesswork on root causes. "In the meanwhile . . ."

Dorian calmly stood away from the table and walked to his desk for the company's Business Continuity Plan. He knew what the next steps were, but he wanted the team to see that there was some order to be found in the chaos.

"We'll need a dozen Yahoo accounts," Dorian said. "The plan calls for individual Yahoo accounts for each of the executives and one for each field office. Use the name of the company as the password."

The room was silent. Finally, Frank spoke the unspoken.

"They won't use public e-mail accounts to transact confidential business, Dorian," he said. "I know that's what we recommended, but they won't use them."

Dorian told the team that everyone in IT needed to project a sense of confidence. They needed to follow the Disaster Recovery plan that had been approved six months before. "Whether they use the accounts or not is their choice," he said.

"There's something else, Dorian," Frank said.

Dorian suddenly remembered a brief snapshot from his dream, the sense of panic as little eruptions burst underneath his feet, first one and then another. As quickly as the vision appeared, it was lost in the sudden clatter of voices, everyone speaking at once.

"We're observing extreme compute levels on the Oracle servers—98% capacity, but we don't know why there is so much traffic coming over the network to account for the poor performance."

Dorian sat down again, thinking *Damn It, Damn It, Damn It* as he listened to the litany of problems.

There was no obvious connection between the failures and little explanation for the peaks in transactional systems. For the moment, they needed to address them as separate problems. He assigned the eight people in the room to form four teams, each with walkie-talkies. He wanted a floor-by-floor assessment of systems in each of the buildings and a cage-by-cage assessment in the data center. He knew they had been working all night, and they needed him to provide guidance, direction, something to give them a sense that the crisis was being managed.

"Meet in the corner conference room in 30 minutes—I want the full list of public e-mail accounts and each team's assessments," Dorian said. "Frank, stick around for a minute."

When the triage teams left to begin the assessments, Dorian shut the door and asked Frank the "underneath question," the one that had been simmering below the surface when the entire team had been in the room.

"Who worked on the RAID overhaul?"

Frank nodded his head. "Paul was supposed to be there for the final testing but he called in sick—remember last week's food poisoning? The contractors signed off on the test plan, and we haven't seen any issues for six days." He paused when he noticed Dorian's severe distress. "Look, Dorian, we wanted to implement Byzantine fault tolerance,[4] but *they didn't give us the money for it.* We wanted mirrored systems in the London data center, but *they didn't give us the money for it.* And the VM[5] project is *still* in the planning stages."

Dorian waved his hand—he too understood that it was impossible to obtain funding when the systems were functioning correctly, and it was almost impossible to prevent failures without appropriate funding. A classic Catch-22 recognized by any IT professional with even one year of experience in a corporate setting: bread-and-water budgets, followed by blame when the patient died of starvation

"Someone should write a book," Frank said.

"Yeah," Dorian agreed, "but no one important would read it."

He smiled, unable to imagine how such a book could communicate the unexplainable. Then he showed Frank the infamous page about Finance Operations from their Business Continuity Plan. "They've got to go back to *paper*," he said quietly.

"Oh God, they're going to *love* that."

"I know. I won't ask you to tell Finance. I'll go upstairs and deliver the news. But I need you to get back in touch with Geraldine and the U.K. team to explain that all reports and contracts *need to be faxed*. She'll complain, but this is how they used to do it before the Oracle systems went live. After the United Kingdom, get in touch with Japan and tell them the same thing."

"Paper," Frank said.

The company had spent millions of dollars implementing state-of-the-art systems around the world to automate their business during the past ten months, and the solution IT was going to propose was to return to paper to close out an entire quarter's business.

"It isn't pretty," Dorian shrugged, thinking *and someone is going to take the fall when it all settles down. Probably me.* "But at least we can get through the next two hours until the power unit is tested."

Frank went to the door, then turned back and asked, "Are you going to call her?"

Dorian was already reaching for the phone when Frank closed the door, dialing the Lakeview Medical Center's Surgery Unit. The company's Chief Information Officer was on medical leave for a torn ACL from a skiing accident three weeks before. Her surgery had been two days earlier, but Dorian knew that his boss would want to know about the crisis and what they were doing to recover. He also needed some guidance about the new VP of Sales, who would surely blame the IT department for any lost business. Dorian didn't actually need the advice, not yet, but it seemed the best way to warn his boss that things were coming apart.

A nurse answered the phone. Only after serious pressure from Dorian, and a partial lie that he was part of her family, did she finally hand off the phone to her drugged patient.

"I'm sorry to bother you, Barb," Dorian began, "but we have a situation, and I thought you would want to know."

He explained the loss of e-mail, the visit from the executives, the possibility of lost contracts from London. She was laughing by the time he finished, her morphine-induced euphoria providing just enough buffer to give her a different perspective.

"Tell them I *told you* to go to paper," she said, slightly slurring the words. "I'll blame it on the morphine."

Dorian appreciated her willingness to take the blame, and in the modest moment of relief following her statement, he remembered one additional question he needed to ask, even in her diminished state.

"Our policy is that only you and our CFO can call a Crisis Management Response Team meeting," Dorian said. "I was wondering . . ."

She laughed again, and Dorian felt a bit of jealousy that her inebriation allowed for a sense of humor at a time when everyone else, including himself, was becoming overwhelmed by corporate anxiety.

"*Call the meeting.* You have my permission . . . no, let's make it more formal. I'm instructing you to call a meeting and institute a war room. How's that? Oh, and by the way, you better get in touch with Henry before they do."

Henry, he thought. The one person he had forgotten to call.

Dorian penned an ad hoc list of his morning volcanoes:

- Boss in the hospital
- VP of Sales and the Blame Game
- Multiple servers down, e-mail and Oracle
- Possible loss of data, extent unknown
- Critical moment for revenue, one hour until analyst call
- Overworked staff troubleshooting blind
- Bad shirt day

He thought about phoning his partner, but before he had the chance to dial, a woman burst into his office, screaming: "What *asshole* decided that we are closing the quarter on *paper*?!"

Dorian asked her to take a seat, saying he'd be glad to explain their approved disaster recovery scenarios, but the woman had no patience for logic, waving her arms and loudly warning that she was taking the issue *upstairs*.

"I wouldn't want to be *you* in the next thirty minutes," she barked on her way out the door.

Dorian didn't even know her name.

Frank spoke to three people in Sales Operations—in the elevator, in the bathroom, and in the walkway between two buildings—before he remembered to call his wife, who had been expecting him for breakfast.

"Lilly, honey," he began, speaking on his cell phone as quietly as possible in the event someone important walked by and thought he might not be taking the crisis seriously. "I know . . . I know . . . Honey, it's my job, and it's been a very bad night, so let's not . . . I know . . ." Frank looked at his watch. She had a piano student in a few minutes, so he knew she wasn't really looking for a longer conversation. "Lilly, honey, I'm sorry I missed you this morning . . . No, I have no idea when I'll be home . . . Yeah, me too."

Frank Sorriano spent the next 30 minutes on two separate but equally important tasks: first, he communicated the fallback strategy to the field offices, including Geraldine in the United Kingdom, who took the news surprisingly well. He didn't have the time to think about her unexpected response, as he also began gathering data from the four teams that were moving through the data centers and networking closets, using the time-proven strategy of identifying the problem by determining all systems that were in perfect working order. His team was very good at this kind of binary deduction. (The problem is either in A or in B, so once you determine that B is not dysfunctional, you focus on A, where the problem is either in A1 or A2, and so on, reducing by 50% your investigation until you have found the exact location of the problem.)

It was their version of Occam's Razor, but he didn't talk about that with his Help Desk team. They just followed the steps in his triage process, because they knew it worked—they had always found the problem, although sometimes it required time, lots of time.

Within the hour, however, it was becoming clear to Frank that what the company had experienced at 4:30 a.m. was not triggered by a single failure, but rather at least two concurrent problems with independent causes: the failure of the backup servers' power unit and the still incomprehensible surge in network traffic. This, of course, meant that Occam's Razor would require hours to detect specific causes, and it also meant that Dorian had a much more complex series of issues to translate into English for the executive team.

Geraldine Lofgren had worked in the company's London office for almost ten years and was second only to Harry Claymaker in seniority. She began as a part-time salesperson when they opened the tiny, one-room office on Gallant Square, and when she was promoted to Manager of Sales Operations, she oversaw their move to the suite in downtown London, overlooking the Thames.

Frankly, Geraldine hated selling their product—it was overpriced and unreliable, and it never met the customer's expectations. When she had the opportunity to move into sales administration and let the other unfortunates work on commission, she embraced the promotion with a zeal not unlike that of a missionary among the natives.

Geraldine was organized and unflappable. She had a photographic memory that gave her absolute recall of even the most minor clauses of old contracts. She ran the office with such outrageous efficiency that other field offices complained they didn't have the resources to keep up with the United Kingdom. Every year, Geraldine got her bonus, whether the salespeople made their numbers or not.

Nonetheless, Geraldine liked coming in first. Until the current quarter, her efficiencies kept their sales region in front of every other international site. However, the new Vice President of Sales in the United States was changing every process and procedure, alienating even his own sales teams. During her tenure, The Company had hired and fired three sales executives, and she wondered how long the new VP would remain.

She knew the current financial quarter was going to be different. Weeks before anyone else noticed the slowdown, Geraldine began to notice the symptoms of a bad pipeline, and she had long since prepared herself for the reprimands that were sure to come when they finally announced that their two key contracts for that period had been rejected. It would take weeks to rewrite them to the customers' satisfaction, and they did not have weeks, only hours. In fact, she was ready to prepare the "bad news" e-mail message to her new VP when she received the call from Frank Sorriano, indicating that the corporate e-mail servers were down. She would have to resort to spreadsheets and fax machines until the close of business that evening.

"I know this is a huge burden, in the eleventh hour," Frank said sympathetically. "If there is anyone in the company who can pull this off, it's you, Geraldine."

She liked the sound of his voice, the way his sincerity underscored every word.

"That's jolly nice of you to say, Franklin," she said in return. "But I'm sure everything will be fine over here."

Geraldine had never liked computers. The way she saw it, computers were just a faster way to make mistakes, and she had continued her habit of keeping up-to-date financial records in her ledgers. She preferred the days when they faxed contracts at quarter end, and this simply gave her permission to return to her old way of doing things.

However, when she hung up the phone, she also realized that the perfect storm in the IT group also provided her with the perfect smokescreen.

None of the executives would notice that the U.K. region had missed their numbers, because everyone would be upset about the downtime. It might be weeks before the accounting staff would learn that the real reason behind their bad quarter was not the e-mail failures, but that there was simply no business to be finalized. By that time, with any luck, the Pfizer and Rolls Royce deals would probably be signed, and everything would be back to normal.

Yes, she had a slight twinge of regret as she considered how difficult this would be for the IT group in the United States. They would surely be blamed for The Company's nightmarish results. But Geraldine was, first and foremost, a survivor and a competitor. It was, after all, only a minor moral issue. If the United Kingdom missed their numbers, she might not receive her bonus, whereas if she could be seen as heroically responding to a crisis that someone else had caused, the bonus might even be increased. For Geraldine, who was struggling to pay for her stepdaughter's Stanford tuition, this was not a serious dilemma— obfuscating the truth for her own benefit seemed like the right thing to do. However she imagined it, the scales always tipped in the same direction, and she finally set her qualms aside.

One very long hour later, Dorian took the elevator to the top floor and exhaled once, loudly, as the doors opened into the executive suite. He smiled weakly at the CEO's secretary, Debby or Donna or Diana, he couldn't recall. When he glanced into the main office, he saw Henry Feldman in a serious conversation with the CFO.

He knew he should have phoned Henry. *Damn it, Damn it, Damn it.*

Minutes before, the CFO had welcomed Henry into her office overlooking Lake Michigan and asked if he would like a bottle of water or cup of coffee. Then she shut the door.

"What's going on, Jeannine?" Henry asked, to the point.

Jeannine smiled. She and Henry had known each other for several years, and she had personally sponsored his promotion to a staff-level executive position in due acknowledgment of his brilliance—that and the fact that the company did not want to lose someone of Henry's talent to their competitors. She liked that he always moved straight to the point in their conversations.

"We have a difficult situation, and we're hoping you can help us resolve it," Jeannine said. Henry recognized the euphemism for "We have to fire someone."

"I'm not sure if you're up to speed yet on our IT problems this morning . . ." she began, and Henry interrupted.

"I'm well aware of the issues," he said, preferring brevity when an executive was in termination mode. "We've identified the problems, and will soon have fixed all of them."

The woman stared out the window, across the landscape of white-capped lake water and passersby whose overcoats were blowing in the Chicago wind. Henry knew that she was uncomfortable with what she was about to say.

"I have been instructed to remove Dorian from all management responsibilities," she said quietly. "With Barb in the hospital, I have no one with enough seniority to take over the IT organization until she returns, and I am hoping . . ."

Henry cleared his throat, and Jeannine turned to face him.

". . . actually, I am *assigning* you that responsibility, and the task of firing Dorian, until her return."

Henry returned her steady look with one of his own; they both understood the hypocrisy of the assignment. The two of them had just completed an extensive revision of Human Resources policy that had created a technical track for senior engineering employees. Now, within two weeks of its approval, she was assigning him direct management responsibilities. The looming disagreement filled the air of her office with a fog of tension.

There were two other reasons why Henry did not want to accept the assignment.

First, Dorian, Frank, and Katya were performing their duties exactly as they were supposed to, and Frank and Dorian were doing them heroically. To suspend Dorian's management privileges in response to this situation would be to undermine the morale of the entire IT organization. Instead of stabilizing the situation, which Henry assumed she meant to do, she would be introducing a layer of mistrust that would take many months to undo.

In addition, and most importantly, Henry believed there was a specific principle to be adhered to, a fundamental concept about IT organizations in a net-based society. He had described it in his thesis, had observed it in every position he had held since graduation, and knew—with absolute clarity—that this principle was operant that morning as the company struggled to respond to the crisis. The principle, an underlying theme of knowledge-based systems, was this: *hierarchical responses to matrix problems would only lead to additional problems*. Henry knew, deep down, that Jeannine's edict "from above" would cause harm. He intended to do no further harm.

"I'm sorry, Jeannine," Henry said finally.

"Excuse me?"

He didn't recognize the gracefulness of his response until he spoke the words. "In my current capacity, I have the authority to test emerging technologies, and my charter specifically allows for risk. When you gave me my new role, you noted the obligation the company has to allow for mistakes."

"I don't see . . ."

"This was *my* error, Jeannine. A rogue process in our Sandbox unit jumped the firewall and brought production systems down. It was not Dorian's responsibility, or Frank's. I'm aware that there are problems in the United Kingdom, but the office of the Architect is responsible. Blame rests here."

"I'm not sure you understand . . ."

"I understand, Jeannine, and I am refusing to accept this new assignment. Furthermore, I will not support any personnel action for this morning's unfortunate events," Henry said with a firmness that surprised him. "I will take the action item to deliver a postmortem analysis of the downtime, and I will make recommendations for ensuring that it doesn't happen again. Anything beyond that is out of the question."

The woman was stunned that Henry was "taking the arrow" for Dorian. Furthermore, there was little she could do about it, given her very vocal support of his position at the executive level, only two weeks before. In the old organization, before the creation of his new post, his response would have been classic insubordination. However, simply by changing his single role in the system, a whole shift had occurred; unseen dominoes were falling one after another, and power had been transformed in a way she had not recognized when she signed his promotion. She only realized it fully at the moment Henry stood to leave her office.

"Perhaps we can review the IT budget now," Henry said, "and make the right investments to ensure that this doesn't happen again?"

"*They* aren't going to be happy with this," she said.

"The watchword should be *resilience*," he said on his way out her door, "not termination."

In the hallway, his eyes met Dorian's. Henry put his arm around him and led him back to the elevator, down and away.

NOTES

1. Geoffrey Moore, *Crossing the Chasm* (New York: HarperCollins, 1998).
2. Aaron, Brown, IBM Research, "Error Recovery," *ACM Magazine*, November 2004.
3. RAID (Redundant Array of Independent Disk) systems are often implemented to reduce the risk of a single failed disk from interrupting operations. In most cases a single failed disk can be replaced and data replicated without interruption.
4. A sophisticated backup and recovery methodology that reduces both temporal (time lapse) and spatial (physical) data loss during failures.
5. VM (virtual machine) technology allows automatic snapshots to be taken periodically and quickly reactivated to restore a system to its near-actual state, further reducing human error and data loss.

CHAPTER 17

THE CONSORTIUM

"Frankly, your claims are unbelievable."

Gillian paused to look at her Swiss Army watch, a gift from Jonathan, and shifted restlessly in her conference room chair. The leather cushion burped quietly beneath her, and she grimaced at the thought that the sales rep had heard the sound.

". . . I don't mean to be rude," she continued, "simply candid. I've been in Tech Services for many years. Some would say too many." She glanced at the members of the team sitting beside her, most of whom were smiling to themselves. They enjoyed watching her dismantle a new vendor, particularly when the vendor's claims were beyond the realm of possibility. "The proposition that you can reduce additional staffing expenses by 50% and double, or even triple, the productivity of the group . . . Well, we've heard these promises so many times that we've all become a bit cynical."

The man standing in front of them was wearing a very expensive wool suit with a subtle shirt and tie combination of pale blue stripes. His gold-and-onyx cuff links suggested that he was either very successful (the image he surely intended to portray) or that he spent every penny of his income on clothing. Gillian thought he was overdressed the moment he stepped into the room, but he had a firm handshake and looked directly in her eyes when he spoke, so she asked him to continue his presentation, in part because she wanted to hear his response. She also knew it was good for her junior staff to witness these candid exchanges with salespeople, a skill she wanted them to learn before they became executives themselves.

"I've always believed in testing the metal of an idea by banging on it," Gillian said, "and I mean no ill will. Please continue . . ."

The rep's name was Ben Goldman. He was the CEO and Managing Partner of a small consulting firm, The Consortium, specializing in building alliances. That was the only information her CFO had given Gillian when he asked her to meet with the man. (Apparently, the two attended the same gym and their families knew each other well, often skiing in Tahoe together during the holidays.)

"It sounds like he's got a good idea," her athletic boss had said to her earlier in the week. "Check out his presentation, and let me know what you think."

Gillian was always pleased to entertain vendors introduced by the executives who were more willing to fund a special project later if they had been the one to provide the introduction. However, more often than not, a referral from other executives in her company produced little of real value.

"Of course, I'm aware of the incredible nature of our claim," Goldman explained. "But when you understand the model we are proposing for you, I'm sure it will make sense." He then turned to the classic "community of communities" image Gillian's team had seen over the past few years in every legitimate IT publication in existence (Exhibit 17.1).

EXHIBIT 17.1   *Collaborative Alliances*

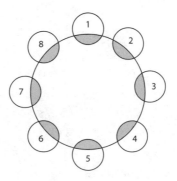

Source: Maggie Law, The KM Conundrum, KMERA Corporation, 2003.

"I'm sure you've seen this image before, or something similar to it," Goldman observed. "I believe it originated as a metaphor for the various distinct offices within a company, located around the world, with a common requirement to share information."[1]

"Yes," Dorothea said, suddenly interupting. "I've seen that in a recent journal about collaborative technologies . . . not Rheingold's book, maybe Denning's . . ."

The rest of her group groaned. Dorothea was known for two things in her team: her prodigious capacity to keep up with the latest industry literature and her insistence on reminding everyone of it, whenever she had the chance.

"To your point," Gillian said, redirecting the conversation to the man at the end of the table.

"In this context, I'd like you to consider the diagram as a cluster of various products and services, a community of technology partners, each with their own businesses, projects, organizations, and priorities. For instance, in the semiconductor industry, an example might be that Company #1 is Motorola, Company #2 is Synopsys, Company #3 is Flextronics, Company #4 . . ."

"Supply chain partners," Gillian rightly observed.

"Yes, but it can be any type of business alliance in which there are individual IT organizations," the man explained, "medical cooperatives, research firms, even software user groups."

The group around the table seemed to understand his method of grouping companies, and each of them nodded in recognition.

"More often than not," he said, "IT organizations such as yours have little to do with the IT organizations of your alliance partners. Usually, these partnership contracts are marketing or revenue driven. However, let's look at an example of an existing customer of The Consortium and see the possibilities when their alliances were augmented with our methods."

He moved the presentation forward to a slide that included logos from so many companies that it was hard to read the page. They were all partners of Consortium's client, and all of them had allowed their logo to be used for promotional purposes. Every sales presentation that Gillian had seen over the last ten years had included a slide like this one—Microsoft, IBM, Hewlett Packard, Cisco Systems, Symantec, EMC. She had come to hate the alliance slides, because they actually meant very little of any value.

"Reed's Law, which describes exponential returns from trusted networks, suggests that even the most modest coordination between these separate groups could yield impressive results,"[2] Goldman said. "So, we applied this to the notion of technology partnerships: the IT organizations would work together whenever it was useful, to achieve their various objectives."

Gillian stared back at him, still unsure of what he was proposing.

"Imagine this scenario: your IT organization is suddenly faced with an urgent project—a network hub needs to be replaced, or some data corruption has occurred in your sales database that needs to be scrubbed, perhaps something as simple as an executive decision to move from Notes to Exchange."

The entire group groaned at the mention of the latter example. Each of them had their own experience of decisions made outside IT that had the potential to make their lives miserable.

"Now, imagine you had an agreement with a dozen other IT organizations to share resources in specific situations," he said, adding, "and let's imagine that your alliance arrangements provided that staffing for no additional cost."

"You're suggesting that I might ask a partner company for the use of their network architect for three days?" Gillian asked, doubtful but intrigued.

"Absolutely."

Everyone in the room stared back and forth at each other.

"Let's take that example. Your team is completely focused on a new security architecture. A network closet goes down, and you unexpectedly need to upgrade and test the new hub apparatus. What do you normally do, in such emergencies?"

Gillian said she would work with the executive team to determine the impact on other projects. If it were possible, she would bring in one or two contractors to do the additional work or backfill the project so her team could address the emergency. "Pretty standard sourcing strategy," she said.

"Yes, it is. Let's consider that approach. First, you meet with your execs. That takes a week or so to arrange. Then you calculate the budget impact. That's another few days. Finally, you engage a consulting team to determine the resources needed. The team provides a Statement of Work. (This is on the chance that the team is already an approved vendor in your Procurement System.) Several weeks might have gone by at this point."

Gillian nodded.

"Now, imagine if you could simply pick up the phone, or, alternatively, log onto the secure RSS (really simple syndication) feed between the partner companies and quickly identify qualified staff who have done this very task before. Then further imagine that you could obtain the services of one of their senior network administrators who could be on your premises the next morning."

"It would save us a lot of thrashing around," Paul said to Gillian. He managed the system administrators, and his team would benefit most from the approach. Everyone else seemed to agree with him.

"Isn't this pie in the sky?" she asked. "I mean, who has the resources to lend another company casually? Really, I'd never have extra staff to loan away. We laid them off a long, long time ago."

Ben Goldman took off his tailored suitcoat, and sat in one of the chairs nearer Gillian and her team. Then he removed his cuff links and rolled up his sleeves. It was his calculated now-we're-getting-serious gesture, but even if it was overly theatrical, it worked. Everyone's attention was glued to what he was about to say.

"You're telling me that Perkins Global never has anyone who's about to go on vacation and therefore isn't assigned, in those last few days, to any particular project? Or that you never complete a project and have perhaps a week before all those engineers are deep into their next assignment? Or that one of your Indian engineers has never traveled back to India to get married, and during that month-long period, has never sent an e-mail to his friends here at the company, offering a bit of his time?"

"Of course, these things sometimes happen." Gillian agreed.

"Exactly. According to our studies, they happen frequently. When you calculate the number of staffing hours available among a partnership of 20 technology partners, as many as 1,000 engineering hours a year could be better utilized." Ben Goldman sat back in his chair, pleased at the impact of his number—1,000—on the faces of his audience.

"One thousand hours of engineering time . . ." Paul repeated, half out loud, imagining what he might be able to accomplish with all of that extra staffing

Goldman stood up, turned to the next page of his presentation, and began to describe an actual case study. In his experience, at this juncture an audience was just about ready to hear a real-case scenario of The Consortium approach. At the center of the slide, like the midpoint of an hourglass lying on its side, was a mechanism called "the resource broker," which was used to locate available resources rapidly and map them to current (real-time) requests (see Exhibit 17.2).[3]

"Of course," Goldman deferred, "your staff will recognize the basic architecture of an service-oriented architecture engine, in which system requests are managed in real time. All we have done is extend that analogy to include the human element."

From Gillian's perspective, it seemed as if he was describing the creation of a consulting firm—composed of the combined IT resources of the participating companies—and that everyone's "bench time" could be made available to other partners, upon request and with the right series of e-mail–based approvals. Suddenly, she understood the concept, but not without concerns.

"It's a trusted professional network," Gillian said, resting her forehead on her palm. "Sometimes you provide resources, sometimes you request resources . . . My guess is that you have an optimal number of

EXHIBIT 17.2   *Virtual Resource Brokerage: Number 1*

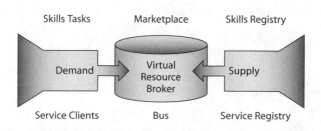

Source: Based on information from the IT teams at Credit Suisse First Boston.

participants, so that the number of potential staff is high enough to provide a reliable response, yet not so large that the tracking becomes bureaucratic . . . but this would require rather sophisticated skills assessment, resource tracking, and time allocation software."

Ben Goldman nodded and showed the next slide, a financial summary of the number of staff hours provided (multiplied by the ramp time for timely responses) and the projected savings obtained by not having to seek, and compensate, outside consultants to do the work.

"As you can see," he said calmly, "every one of the participating companies recorded a substantial increase in work, accomplished without an increase in expenditures . . . and three of the companies recorded such a remarkable return over the course of our six-month trial that we have now formally established their consortia."

> I didn't believe it would work when we started the pilot with The Consortium, but I am simply amazed at the ease with which it was administered, and the equally amazing cooperation among the partner companies. We, conservatively, saved more than 150k during our six-month test. We're convinced.
>
> —Stephen Vourajilos, VP of IT and Operations
> Techtonica Industries, Columbus, Ohio

"Reed's Law," Alec remembered, "isn't that David Reed? It's based on Moore's but it's exponential."[4]

"Yes," Goldman said, adding "and in response to your observation about skills tracking and management, our Consortium has developed an open-source marketplace engine that can be connected to any of your existing Active Directories or Human Resources systems, with a request disbursement tool that can be customized by your team to accommodate any internal requirements, whether it is authenticated access, stylesheet–based design, or logging for compliance reasons. Then he closed his laptop and unplugged the projector. Another group was already forming in the hallway for the next scheduled meeting.

"Reed calls them Group Forming Networks, or GFNs, and we believe they can be established very easily with IT organizations that are already partnered with your institution, as well as with others that may have already joined The Consortium. This is why I felt comfortable proposing the ROI (return on investment) that I stated at the beginning of our meeting. I expect you could derive even higher returns, if you spent the right amount of time establishing a trusted link with those organizations and an accurate skills registry."

Gillian now understood The Consortium. The only question that remained in her mind was their business model. "And just how does The Consortium itself stay in business?"

Goldman smiled, for he understood that when a prospective client asked this question, it had been a successful meeting.

"There is an annual tiered membership model for Consortium partners," he explained briefly, "and very modest fees, based on utilization, not unlike the public utilities. If I may be so bold, I would propose to you that this is how all tech resources will be managed, a decade from now. We're simply the first that I know of to move in this direction actively."

Gillian knew what her next step should be.

"Ben," she said in a confident whisper that quieted the entire room, "I have someone I'd like you to meet."

That night, Jonathan wanted to stay in his father's room at the center a bit longer, perhaps to enjoy a moment of quiet with him after the old man's prolonged outburst. Gillian was glad to excuse herself to the nursing home's cafeteria for a cup of coffee claiming to be cappuccino that was composed of water and powder mixed by a machine.

"That'll be $1.40, ma'am," the woman said from behind the register. She was wearing a pink uniform to simulate nursing attire.

"Is there any difference between the regular and the cappuccino?" Gillian asked.

"I think they add some powdered milk, ma'am," the woman said.

Before she had the chance to reach inside her pack for a wallet, a familiar voice behind her offered to pay for the coffee. She turned to see an old friend.

"Linwood!"

She hugged Linwood Eddy like the long-lost friend he was, for she hadn't seen him since coming to Perkins Global several years before.

They had once worked together and became friends; their spouses became friends too. Now their fathers-in-law were living in the same facility.

"I'm *so sorry* about Adrienne," she said in an attentive and sincere tone. "I know you must be devastated."

Linwood smiled a faint smile, practiced and disengaged, and then artfully sidestepped the question, gesturing for Gillian to join him at the table. He was lunching by himself, waiting for his own father-in-law to complete physical therapy upstairs. Gillian brought her coffee to the table and they sat down.

". . . and you still come to see him every day?"

"Every day," Linwood said. He reached to close the magazine he'd been reading, but Gillian asked to see the article.

"Just something I'm trying to understand," Linwood said nervously, "about how one particle's experience can alter the experience of another particle." He knew it was a description of the science behind quantum entanglement, but he also knew it sounded uncomfortably close to the Divorce topic he wanted to avoid.

Gillian looked at the article by Dave Jarvis, apparently a layman's tutorial on quantum physics.[5] Gillian knew Linwood Eddy well and therefore knew that Linwood was drawn to illustrated explanations of complex topics for a very good and very private reason. The page with a dog-eared corner included a diagram of two independent waves (particles) exerting an influence on one other (Exhibit 17.3).

"I still think it was one of the most courageous acts I have ever known," Gillian said, turning the article over on the table. "I really do, Linwood."

Gillian was referring to Linwood Eddy's decision, after more than 50 years of private struggle, to tell his supervisors—and his daughter—that he could not read. The revelation of his lifelong illiteracy was stunning, partly because he was an executive of a very large financial firm and had thus navigated the labyrinthine pathways of corporate behaviors without any of the useful tools everyone else takes for granted. Gillian had realized that Linwood must have been a tactical genius and possessed awe-inspiring tenacity to accomplish what he had in his career with such an overwhelming "disadvantage." It was at that point that he had also

EXHIBIT 17.3   *Interference Pattern*

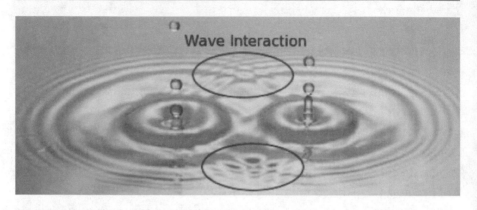

Source: Copyright 2003, Museum Victoria.

decided to try again to learn how to read, finally exposing his personal challenge to everyone. She wondered which had been more difficult, learning to read, or admitting publicly that he couldn't. But his genius and bravery were largely unappreciated by his family, particularly his daughter, who had thought for years that her father simply didn't think it was important to read stories to her at night, or help her with her homework. They, too, were estranged, and Gillian felt sorry for him.

"How *are* things with Rachel?" she asked.

Linwood stared into the distance, past Gillian's shoulder and through the window behind her, his gaze settling somewhere between a shrub and a dented garbage bin with a toxic hazard sticker covered by graffiti. The bin had been tagged by the neighborhood gang, and Linwood knew it was the 59th Street Posse because he recognized the symbols. He was gifted in the area of pattern recognition, as are many who did not learn to read in school and who had found artful and elegant workarounds in the Army, in corporate America, in sports, or just in daily life.

"Did you know I can translate graffiti faster than I can read English?" he said, joking his way around Gillian's personal questions.

"Okay," Gillian acquiesced. "Maybe it's safer to talk about *work*?"

Linwood laughed out loud. "I don't think we're allowed to talk about *that*, either, Gillian!" Then she laughed, too, at the irony.

Because their companies had announced their merger intentions, still in the "quiet period" during which the SEC formally investigates the companies for monopolistic aspects of a combined entity, employees were not officially allowed to speak to each other. No "insider information" could be exchanged during this period, although, because they were IT professionals, any exchange of information could only be beneficial to both companies. The quiet period had long been a source of exasperation to Gillian. Major system conflicts were discovered too late in the process to be financed as a cost of the merger, and the impact on IT capability was long range and deleterious.

"I've always thought someone should write a primer for mergers and acquisitions," Gillian said, sipping from a cup of what she quickly learned was scalding-yet-utterly-tasteless cappuccino.

"Yes!"

"It could include all the questions that executives never think to ask until valuations are completed, and *then* they learn about incompatible networks, competitive e-mail, and calendaring vendors . . . not to mention *financial applications*."

"By the way, I understand you're an Oracle shop." Linwood said with a smile.

Gillian knew they shouldn't be discussing such things, but she also realized that the two IT organizations might be able to establish relations, within a certain framework, even during the quiet period. She spent the next few minutes explaining The Consortium to Linwood, the notion of temporarily lending resources within an alliance, their brokerage utilities offered in the "Software as a Service" model. Her own executives might approve a project with The Consortium as facilitators, and in this way, the two IT organizations could begin the task of getting to know each other's infrastructure and each other's employees.

"I like it, Gill," Linwood said, "especially if your CFO is supportive. He asked her to have the CEO of the company give him a call, and when she told him the man's name, Linwood blurted, "Ben Goldman? I've known him *forever*. Last time I heard, he was having heart surgery." Before he could explain his "small world" connection with Goldman, Gillian's husband approached.

"I'm ready to go home, Gillian," Jonathan said, appearing beside them with the weariness of someone who had just completed a marathon of emotional calisthenics. "Oh, Linwood, . . . hello . . . how's the family?"

Gillian quickly shushed her husband away from the taboo subject and gave Linwood a hug with promises that she would e-mail Ben Goldman's contact information. Arm-in-arm with Jonathan, she walked back to their car. As she opened the passenger side door to step in, she glimpsed the bright yellow and red graffiti on the garbage bin and thought once more about Linwood's private wrestling match with life and how lonely he must be, now that Adrienne and Rachel had pulled away.

"He still visits his father-in-law every day," she said as she shut the car door with the familiar thud of Volvo doorframe engineering serving as an exclamation point to her day.

Ben recalled every detail with uncharacteristic precision—the sounds, the conversations, the color of his pulse on the monitors—remembered with a clarity that remained vivid, weeks after his coronary surgery to correct a blocked artery.

Perhaps it was the excruciating pain that framed the moment with significance.

Perhaps it was the expression of fear on his wife's face when the nurse explained the procedure: a tiny camera would be inserted into a vein in his upper thigh, dye would be diffused to help portray the arterial system for the doctor, a little "balloon" would be used to expand the blocked area, and a stent, a tiny, curlicued wire, would be placed at the weakened area to keep his blood flowing normally.

Perhaps it was simply his sense of sudden vulnerability, the realization that everything he had worked for during his life, everything he had accomplished, everything that had lifted him to the pinnacle of success could have been erased instantly in that unexpected clench of pain.

It was pain like none other in his life. Broken arms, torn ligaments, the fish hook embedded in his palm on a fishing trip with his father— none of these seemed as meaningful as that sudden surge of agony, first in his left arm and then in his shoulder and chest.

Please make it go away, he remembered saying as they rushed him through the banging doors, *make it stop*.

Lying on the table, diazepam and morphine dripping steadily through the top of his hand, bright green blips roller-coastering across the monitors above him, he recalled the warmth as they unfolded a second blanket over him. He recalled the assistant's apologetic tone as they inserted the tube into this thigh. "This is going to sting a bit, like a bee," the man said. "Then it will get very warm; that will be the local anesthetic."

The sting was nothing, a tiny candle in comparison with the fireworks in his chest the night before, and he remembered saying *I like bees* to the attendant, who laughed beneath his mask. Ben remembered the way the mask blossomed out and back with the laughter.

"You're Ben Goldman," the doctor said. Ben nodded. "I'm Doctor Hilton, and I'll be performing your angioplasty today."

I thought I'd be knocked out by now, Ben remembered saying to the bespectacled doctor who was snapping yellow gloves tightly onto both hands.

"No, you'll be awake and you can watch everything we do up there," the doctor said.

Remember this moment, Ben thought to himself. And he did remember it, weeks after the surgery, long after he had returned to work as the new CEO of his company. On his first day back his secretary Elaine (which was also his wife's name) hugged him hard and said, "Have you made any decisions about your life?"

Yes, Ben said to her with the memory of that moment still crystalline and exact in his mind. "I'm going to build a new house. Elaine has wanted a new house since our kids left, and now that we can afford it, I'm going to build her that house, just the way she wants it. I made the decision right there on the surgical table, watching my heart expand and contract."

"By the way, I also decided to change the way we do business here."

His secretary was pleased for Ben's wife, who had always been kind to his employees. She had worked for Ben for 15 years, followed him up the ladder through reorganizations and mergers, and now that he was the Chief Executive, she also had achieved status, as chairwoman of the executive assistants. Ben knew, though he didn't say it, that she had been worried that he might undergo a life change, reduce his stress, even retire.

Retirement had never entered his mind, although he remembered a conversation with a night nurse who was giving him another dose of morphine a bit ahead of schedule because he couldn't sleep. She had asked if he wanted to make any changes in his life. "A lot of people do, at times like this," she said as the morphine announced itself by tickles that spread across his face like bits of sand in a sudden wind.

I think I like my life, Ben told her that night, *I think I like things just the way they are*. Then he added, *except for this*, pointing to his left shoulder.

"You're a lucky man," she said, rubbing his forehead with her soft hands. She had very soft hands. "In that case, you should do something to celebrate your good fortune, because this surgery will keep you alive another 30 years."

It was at the exact moment that they inserted the tiny camera into his vein and began the ascent to his heart, as he felt the warm blanket on his chest and the pinch of the intravenous tube taped to his left hand, as he heard the doctor say with no alarm, ". . . and there it is . . ." that Ben decided he was going to take some of his new salary and build a house in Danville, a house that was going to be exactly what his wife had wanted since they first married and moved into their Montclair home, the same home where their children were born, where they learned to drive, and where they said goodbye when they left for college.

I'm going to change the way I do business, and I'm going to build a new house, Ben said to the doctor. The doctor laughed, mask moving out and in with the laughter, and then he said "Let's fix this little problem first, and you can start on your personal transformation next week."

"What do you *mean*, release our software as *open source*?!!" Celeste exclaimed in her usual cynical tone. She was the company's VP of Technology. Her team had built the product and improved it. If she had been completely candid, she would have said they *owned* the code. "Actually *give it away*?"

"Great," Marcus said, throwing his hands up in mock despair. "I'm going to tell my *sales force* that, from now on, their commissions are a percentage of *something we're selling for free!*"

Incredulous and chaotic whispering filled the room in a rapid pianissimo. Ben knew that some of his staff were convinced that a side effect of his heart surgery was insanity and that he had lost the ability to captain the ship. He imagined one of them sending a wireless e-mail, appealing to the Board of Directors with an argument of "diminished capacity."

When the tumult had subsided, Ben explained that the concept was one he had proposed to the Board of Directors more than two months ago. It was one of the reasons they had selected him to replace the outgoing CEO, who remained as Chairperson.

"This is *not* a result of my surgery," he insisted, "nor a whim I just concocted over cocktails last night." He stood from his chair and began circling the room, so that he could make eye contact with each of the executives in the meeting. "This is a very carefully considered change in our strategic business plan."

The room was suddenly still.

"Think about it." Ben began the list of reasons from his remarkable speech to the Directors, after they had identified him as one of the three finalists. "We sell our product—a good one—which is used *once*, so we have few creative licensing options open to us to increase revenue. We cannot transform our company into an enterprise software giant, which is the direction everyone else in the industry seems to be going, because the product does not help every employee in our customer companies, only the architects in IT. Anyway, everyone in the room knows how I feel about the term *enterprise*, which has become literally meaningless."

"I'm with you, Ben," their CFO said. Tom had been with the company for less than a year, yet he knew well that their projections were not exciting. He had attended the meeting at which Ben had convinced the Board of his new approach, and he wanted to help the others get past their anxiety. "Perhaps you should tell us just where the revenues *will* be coming from."

"Revenues," Marcus said, "as the Sales guy, I would be *very* interested in where the revenues will be coming from. I've got *numbers* to meet this quarter."

Ben thought about his new home, and what an immense project it had become—a good idea that had morphed into a monster within weeks. He wondered if he was reaching too far—attempting two massive transformations in his life at the same time. Yet they were intertwined, because his new position, with its substantial bonus, had given him the confidence to build the house. Without one, there would not be the other.

"There are many issues to discuss, and we will be having an extended meeting later in the week to review all of them," Ben said, "but let me address these two now, since Marcus has raised them."

Marcus nodded deferentially. He had been one of the other candidates for the CEO position, and Ben hoped they would be able to continue with some accord, although he had never approved of Marcus's aggressive tactics with potential customers, or his incessant pressure on the field organization, as if they were galley slaves expected to work seven days a week for his glory.

"First," Ben explained, "I believe that the professional services opportunity has been sadly ignored in the past two years. We've lost a lot of business to our system integration partners, who come in, just after we close a deal, and reap the rewards that our product makes possible."

Ben looked around the table, noting which faces were engaged and which were filled with cynicism. Since his surgery, he had little patience for cynicism. "We will be jumpstarting a campaign to recruit an alliance of technology organizations that will, over the coming months, be capable of taking over most of the business we now give to those partners. We'll remain with IBM Global Services and Hewlett-Packard Technical Services, because they are good channels for the product, but we have more than 50 other small companies, in every geography, that bring in much higher revenues than we do. The idea is to create a consortium of highly skilled partners who, with the assistance of our software as a brokerage, will be able to respond within days to most of the IT challenges our customers face."

"A services organization," Tom explained to the rest of the execs. "Our projections, by the end of Year One, would be, conservatively, ten times what we now recognize as revenue."

Ben then turned to Marcus and addressed all the previous projections, including the current quarter's numbers (the goals they must meet in order to be granted their annual bonus payments, which in Marcus's case was double his regular salary). "Everyone will receive their bonuses this year, regardless of their numbers," Ben said calmly. "I have negotiated an additional $500,000 in discretionary funds, to reward those employees who make extraordinary contributions during the transition. In other words, we are going to reward the ability to change course."

Ben could tell from their reactions that several of his current staff did not understand the concept, nor would they actively support The Consortium. He did not expect them to remain his staff much longer. No longer than necessary.

Ben was pleased to hear Linwood Eddy's voice on the phone. They jumped into a conversation as if they were still working together, Linwood as Ben's corporate MBA sponsor and thesis supervisor, so many years before.

"So what's this I hear about a new business model?" Linwood asked.

Ben told Linwood about his surgery and about his epiphany as the doctors began to traverse his veins with immediate television support. "The old notion of selling overhyped intellectual property that rarely works as advertised just didn't appeal to me anymore."

"As I recall," Linwood said, "I don't think it ever really appealed to you."

Ben knew that was true. Though he was an exceptionally capable manager of executive teams and knew how to run a technology company, he had never enjoyed Selling to the Customer. It seemed contrary to his beliefs in shared value.

"Linwood, it seems to me that the greatest attribute of Open Source is the community of well-intentioned and very smart people around the world who are sincerely dedicated to improving each other's work, 24 hours a day, 7 days a week. Someone will always answer your question, usually within minutes, and they are always right. I'm interested in tapping that abundant resource of technical talent."

"Go on," Linwood said, remembering the day, so many years before, when Ben Goldman came to him with an idea for building a software engine that, in concept, could replace almost every product on the market because it was designed to be so accessible to personalized use.

Ben continued. "It also seems to me that the greatest threat to Open Source is the basis of Capitalism, our inherent and undeniable addiction to property. This is mine, you can't have it. In the playground of the world, populated by wise caretakers, young parents, adolescents with a disregard for authority, and the elderly sitting on the benches and wondering where their lives have gone, we are the little children in the sandbox, throwing a tantrum because someone just touched our yellow plastic shovel."

Linwood had to agree. His own boss, for all his strengths, was the living epitome of sandbox tantrums.

"Our corporations are addicted to ownership," Ben continued, as if he were lecturing a graduate class on the risks of Capitalism. "Their value is determined by the intellectual property, both real and imagined, that they valiantly guard, protect, and share only if given large amounts of money. They support their addictions by convincing others to become addicted, an entire national economy fueled by addictive behavior and the consequent behaviors of those who profit from the ever widening audience of addicts. You cannot profit from something that is free and shared; therefore, it is not only valueless, but dangerous and perhaps even morally bankrupt. After all, if you let everyone be a member of your country club, what would be so special about it anymore?"

"*Exactly.*"

Ben smiled, and imagined Linwood smiling too. They had always been businessmen of a different mold.

"Well, Linwood, it seems to me that this model is lumbering toward its demise, and any company that continues seeking to support itself in this manner is also lumbering toward an unfortunate end. What we are trying to jumpstart, with The Consortium, is a marketplace of technically talented people available to assist each other on projects of common interest, supported by a Software Commons to which they all have access and to which they all contribute."

"Ben," Linwood said, playing the same devil's advocate role that he had enjoyed during Goldman's MBA work years before, "just how is everyone compensated? After all, we have mortgages to pay, tuitions to support, parents in need of care."

"Oh," Ben said, "I'm sorry I didn't ask sooner. How *is* your father-in-law?"

Linwood said *fine, just fine* and told Ben not to change the subject.

"Our intention is to create an SaaS[6]-structured repository, into which all the developers would place their work product, the code, the documentation. It would be time-stamped in just the same manner as source code control, with one exception. Everyone in the The Consortium will have access to the code, and each variation (if an engineer in Company #2 modified an applet originally created by Company #1, for example) would be checked in as a related branch in the system. As part of the shared Commons agreement, remix would be allowed in all cases except those involving material gain. In those cases, the material gain would be shared. As managers of the Software Commons, we will charge a fee for use, in addition to membership dues that, over the course of time, will pay for most, if not all, of our operational expenses."

"I've heard of the Science Commons," Linwood said.

Ben explained that Creative Commons licenses, and the actual notion of the Science Commons, was to allow for the reuse of intellectual property while maintaining the essential ownership. "Creative Commons applauds efforts by universities to make scientific and scholarly research more widely available," Ben said, "by adopting policies that encourage faculty to retain some publication rights and to exercise those rights to post their research in open digital repositories. Other Creative Commons licenses may be better suited to authors who retain only partial rights to their work. Through its Science Commons division, Creative Commons also is developing technological tools that make it easy to deposit research articles into digital repositories."[7]

There was an awkward silence on Linwood's end of the line, so Ben tried again. "Really, Linwood, we're not creating a public library for software, we're simply following a similar model so that our members can easily avail themselves of each other's resources, whether those resources are technology products or human assets. We have a rather unusual engine, a brokerage really, that will enable us to link requests with responses, track the utilization, and regularly incorporate new and changed work. As for the Creative Commons itself, I am hoping to use their licensing structure . . . negotiating it is on my list, as soon as I complete my management team."

Linwood liked the idea, but he liked Ben's energy even more. The man had become reengaged with his wife, his life, and his business following a brush with death, and he was quite happy—though more than a bit jealous—of Ben's transformation.

Ben moved to his desk and tapped at the keyboard for a moment. He told Linwood to look at the file he had just e-mailed. When Linwood opened the attached document, he saw a familiar design unfold (Exhibit 17.4).

"Each of the clusters may be different companies, but to the Consortium partner, they simply become a team that can come together collaboratively to address a problem."

"Flash teams," Linwood said.

"Excuse me?"

EXHIBIT 17.4   *Virtual Resource Brokerage: Number 2*

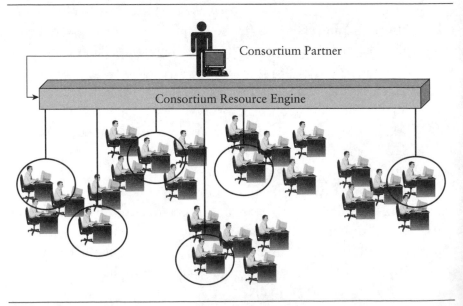

Source: Based on information from the IT teams at Credit Suisse First Boston.

"*Flash teams* and the creation of the *Trans-Firm*," Ben's mentor said, and the ex-MBA student knew he was about to learn something he should have known previously—he recognized Linwood's instructive tone of voice.

"Linwood," Ben said quietly, "is there something I need to know?"

Linwood thought about his meeting with L.M. Tooms weeks before, how he had tried to explain the notion of multienterprise resource markets. It wasn't an easy sell, even if the audience was intelligent and understood the analogy. The missing ingredient was trust. Perhaps the notion of an alliance provided such a framework, something he hadn't previously considered. It was the governance issue that underscored many of the earlier efforts toward communal ownership of intellectual property.[8]

"No, I think you're on the right track," Linwood said. "So, how can I help?"

NOTES

1. Maggie Law, *The KM Conundrum*, April 2001, summarizing the findings of a joint session between KMERA Corporation, a knowledge management vendor, and the San Francisco team of IDEO (www.ideo.com).
2. "As the scale of interaction grows more global via the Internet, isn't it possible that a combination of social capital and GFN capital will drive prosperity to those who recognize the value of network structures that support free and responsible association for common purposes?" From "That Sneaky Exponential—Beyond Metcalfe's Law to the Power of Community Building," by David Reed, 2002, http://www.reed.com/Papers/GFN/reedslaw.html.
3. From the innovative research of the IT Research and Development team at Credit Suisse First Boston in New York, "Service Oriented Development," September 2005.
4. See note 2: "As Francis Fukuyama argues in his book *Trust*, there is a strong correlation between the prosperity of national economies and social capital, which he defines culturally as the ease with which people in a particular culture can form new associations. There is a clear synergy between the sociability that Fukuyama discusses and the technology and tools that support GFNs—both are structural supports for association.

5. David Jarvis, "Quantum Entanglement": ". . . the information passed between particles in an entangled system must remain a secret." http://www.joot.com/dave/writings/articles/entanglement/.

6. Software as a Service; networked applications hosted on another company's infrastructure that one would lease (the pay-per-drink model) rather than purchase. See Salesforce.com for further information.

7. From the Science Commons web site, July 13, 2005: http://sciencecommons.org/literature/ccoastatement.

8. Stephen Weber, "The Success of Open Source," Institute of the Future. Principles for organizing distributed innovation require that we "create a governance system that sustains the process." www.hup.harvard.edu/pdf/websuc.pdf.

CHAPTER 18

THE EVERYSPHERE

"Hey, Maimon, what's that story you tell about the potato?" asked a disembodied voice from a cluster of colleagues in the hallway. The speaker was on the way to becoming very drunk.

The "story of the potato" was one of the Professor's favorite anecdotes in social settings, where, without good conversational devices, he was not as adept or glib as his students imagined him to be. On these social nights at the beginning of a new term, when the full faculty gathered at the home of the Vice Chancellor to welcome the new instructors, the Professor was, more often than not, asked to tell his potato story, so that his colleagues could quietly gauge the newcomers' sophistication by their responses. The new faculty did not know it was a status test—not until it was their time to judge the next set of newcomers. It was a parlor game, a professorial hazing of the intellect, and he was oddly pleased to be included in the tradition. Otherwise his colleagues paid him no attention at all during the rest of the semester.

"In his Nobel lecture," the Professor began, and the faculty around him quieted to listen, "Carl Jung tells a story of his very first patient . . ."

According to Jung, the woman came to him with a severe anxiety, triggered by a specific event. Ultimately, he came to understand that, when the woman was a young girl, her father was a potato farmer and she would often help him dig for potatoes when she was not in school. One day, while looking for potatoes, the eight-year-old girl lost her baby ring—a gold band with her initials engraved inside. Years later, while having dinner at a Munich restaurant, she cut into her baked potato—there was the ring she had lost 40 years before.[1]

When the Professor paused, there was a quiet gasp, as there almost always was—someone in the crowd had fully envisioned that moment from the woman's point of view.

"Synchronicity," one of the newcomers said.

"What?"

"That's what Jung called it, synchronicity," the man repeated. "He believed there was an *acausal principle* behind such meaningful events."[2]

The man's name was Jonathan Moore, and he was a new instructor in the Humanities Department. Moore was just completing a book to be published by John Wiley & Sons. He had only three more chapters to write, but he'd elected to return to academia, so he wouldn't run the risk of being stuck on a speaker's circuit without a university credential. When the Professor explained that the anecdote was a parlor game, the man laughed.

"My favorite party story," he said, without showing a bit of discomfort that he'd just been subjected to an adolescent trick by grown-up men and women, "is the one that Stuart Brand asked Gregory Bateson, you know, *what color a chameleon would be if it was standing on a mirror*. It's the title of one of our new museum exhibits, yes?"

"Your focus is on psychology?" the Professor asked.

"No, actually," the man said, a bit chagrined. "I'll be taking over High-smith's course on organizational theory, in the sociology department."

The Professor refrained from stating his narrow-minded view that sociology and psychology belonged in one department, not wanting to insult a newcomer's profession.

"I'm supervising a graduate thesis from someone in your department," he said instead. "Her notion is that the capability of humans to innovate is increased as they automate the other areas of their life. She's doing some funny things with our data center team."

"You're in information systems?" Jonathan asked. He hoped that his dinner table knowledge of that discipline, what he'd gleaned from Gillian's career in IT, would carry him through the evening's conversation.

"No," the Professor said, appreciating the irony of their dialogue, "I teach modern American poetry . . . but I seem to be dragged into the University's computer problems every semester, like it was a minor. Big advocate of network theory."

The two men sauntered through the stone hallway and into the Vice Chancellor's immense living room, one of three gathering rooms in his 9,000-square-foot house. It was owned by the University and had often been given to one of the chancellors in lieu of high salary over the years. The living room was paneled in a beautiful light oak in immaculate condition. The same wood outlined the windows and French doors, and several paintings on loan from the Art Museum hung on the walls. The Professor had often wondered if everything in the Vice Chancellor's life was on loan. He whispered that notion to Jonathan as they neared an almost perfect half-circle of their peers, who were listening to Jacob Ordman, Chairman of the Department of Physics, discuss his recently published paper. The Chairman had proposed a new law, naturally named Ordman's Law, that governed the coincidental exchange of energy between two photons, called Entanglement.

"We haven't yet been able to explain some of these quantum behaviors, though we can replicate them easily in laboratory settings. So, I'm doing my part to move the conversation along. Ordman's Law," the man orated, as if it was already an accepted principle in quantum physics, "states that the exchange of energy between two statistically independent particles, one influencing the other without rational explanation, is similar to the exchange of information between two quantum computers, where information becomes energy and can be seen as entangled *qbits*."

"Interesting idea," Jonathan whispered as the twosome weaved their way toward the cocktail table for refills.

The Professor hated to admit it, because he thought Jacob Ordman was the quintessential Pompous Ass, but Jonathan was right. The idea of information as energy, which therefore allows for rules of information exchange to be applied to particles and rules of energy exchange to be applied to bits of information, led his mind to a further leap—that the subjectivity of the observer, which is the basis for eventual determination as a wave or a particle, is like the subjectivity of a reader for a story that can/does have multiple meanings. Everything began to resonate.

". . . it is the collapsing of possibilities," Ordman was still booming from halfway across the room, "In the moment of perception, all the possibilities collapse into a single reality. Ordman's Law concerns the nature of that collapse, when the infinite becomes finite."

"Is he always so caught up in himself?" Jonathan asked as he reached for his fresh glass of Cabernet.

"We all are," The Professor admitted.

This time, it was Jonathan's turn to engage with the Chairman's proclamations. He had always been fascinated by the precise moment *before* recognition, the moment just before the observer sees a particle, when it had the potential to be either one. Like Bateson's *uncommitted potentiality for change*,[3] Jonathan wanted to believe that each moment in his life offered the structure for a wide (perhaps nonmeasurable) array of possibilities. Subsequently, if his perspective *was* the governing factor, might he not be able to adjust his perspective, and, therefore, observe an entirely different life?

"Now you're the one who's distracted," the Professor said, elbowing the newcomer in the ribs. He liked the idea that there might just be one member of the faculty with whom he could be friendly, exchange pleasantries, discuss current events without being judgmental.

"Sorry," Jonathan said. "I was just thinking of my father."

The Professor didn't push any further. He believed that people would provide personal information only if they wanted to, and they needn't be encouraged by an intrusive question. His ex-wife, whom he had just noticed coming toward him wearing the slinky black dress she saved for such occasions, always believed in exactly the opposite. It was somehow rude if you didn't inquire about a colleague's personal life, didn't show interest or convey a sense of concern.

"Hi," was the only thing he could think of saying when she appeared beside him, looking beautiful.

"Ben, you should introduce me to your new friend," she said with a degree more comfort than the Professor wanted her to show. He always felt awkward at faculty gatherings. Why didn't she?

"Ah," the Professor said, "yes . . . well, yes. This is Jonathan Moore, newbie in the sociology department . . . Jonathan, this is Dahlia Maimon, my . . ."

". . . his *ex*-wife," she said quickly. "How do you do, Jonathan? Welcome to this august gathering of people who are just too damned smart for their own good."

The Professor thought she looked too damned attractive in that dress.

He offered some hasty and unexpected goodbyes, retrieved his over-coat from the immense walk-in closet, and moved toward the stone entryway, out into the jasmine-scented night. Outside, the evening fog shrouded the maple trees, magnifying the sound of his footsteps. He could hear echoing voices from a neighbor's open kitchen windows and a man's barely audible lecture from Peters Hall.

Perhaps it was the musicality of the lecturer's voice, or perhaps it was simply the Professor's desire to distract himself from any further thoughts of Dahlia's social energy. Whatever the reason, he stepped inside the open doorway of Peters Hall, just as the visiting lecturer began to read selections from a recently published book.

The Professor was only half listening as he entered the room and found a seat in the back. It was only as the silver-haired speaker—in a highly verbose manner—explained the topic of his lecture that the Professor's attention was suddenly and completely diverted to the front of the auditorium.

"In deference to this evening's mixed audience, that odd but familiar combination of engineering students alongside those who prefer fiction, I'd like to read a portion of my chapter that addresses Quantum Entanglement, which, as some of you surely know, concerns the uncanny yet verifiable exchange of energy between two otherwise unconnected and diffuse photons, a behavior that scientists of other generations have described as a 'jumping together' of objects and still others, decades before us, might have described as an example of 'consilience,'[4] though, for our purposes tonight, I will discuss only those aspects pertaining to particles of information and the exchange of information between them."

It was an uncanny coincidence. The Professor wondered what the esteemed Dr. Ordman, at that moment only two city blocks away from Peters Hall, would say if he knew there was someone else on campus with the same interests and expertise.

"For those of you in the audience who truly prefer direct reference to sources, and for those who require definitions of the most technical terms, it would be useful to interrupt this narration with a glance at the bottom of the page to read the many relevant footnotes provided for just that type of reference and further edification, which the author has whimsically dismissed to footnote status. However, if I were to interrupt the 'flow' of this chapter with half a dozen footnote interruptions, we might never reach the end of what I sincerely believe is a simple and memorable example of tonight's subject. For those of you who desire credible references, I will pause but a moment to suggest that both groups in our audience tonight would enjoy investigating the work of the late (I'm so sorry to say) Professor Stephen Jay Gould, whom I once had the honor to meet on the speaker circuit and actually share a dinner with, a truly generous fellow. The other author I'd recommend investigating in this regard, if references are important to you, is the honorable William Gass of St. Louis, for those in the audience more interested tonight in the unfolding of the prose, which is unfolding, you must admit that, it is, at long last, unfolding.

"As you may know, or hopefully soon will know when you buy an inscribed copy of this book on your way out, one of the central propositions of this 'mutant business manual' (*New York Times* Science Editor), this 'elegantly confused collection of short stories' (*San Francisco Review of Books*), as you may already know, one of the central propositions of the book—get ready, get your pencil, you'll need to put this in your status report tomorrow as proof that you attended and were actually listening. Ready. One of the central propositions of the book, which is really a collection of short prose works that one day became a book, a central proposition is the similarity—yes, for purposes we can study and draw conclusions from—for purposes of underscoring a most important theme that weaves throughout the book itself—we can draw conclusions from the similarity of chapters, of particles, of database objects, of nodes on the network, and of people at work in the organization supported by that network.

"Two independent particles, or data objects, or network nodes, or two team members exchange information in similar fashion when they do so, and they also behave in similar fashions when they exchange no information whatsoever, for those of you tracking that level of detail (p. 200)."

The Professor didn't like the speaker's self-referential approach or his annoying inclination to digress for the sake of digression. However, the man's central comparison between those who write software programs and those who write narrative prose was intriguing, a reinforcement of his own recognition of their similarities.

"In accordance with our central proposition, this chapter—tonight's reading—considers the energy of information exchange as well as its absence within the corporation. Yes, for the purposes of discussion, our case study is, indeed, a software engineering team at this very institution, and though our conclusions will apply to them, they can also be applied, with an open mind, to any organization in conflict.

"For those of you who do not have an engineering background and are not sitting next to a talkative engineer whom you could listen to (really, he or she will enjoy the fleeting moment of attention), for those of you interested in prose for the sake of prose—yes, you three in the back row with black . . . god, everything's in black, look, even their fingernails, excellent. For you three, I will apologize for the absence of a Glossary to quickly locate definitions for those silly engineering acronyms (which became SEA, Silly Engineering Acronym) because it would be easier for you, I know, to keep up with this bloody reading if you could just check a definition or two. I can only offer, in compromise, that the book itself does indeed have a Glossary, my homage howsoever small to our nonengineering reading public who, bless them, may find characters and plot and moments of life that change, transforming them all.

"But for today, I will omit the definitions, if only to minimize the risk of losing the engineering audience's attention, engineers who would, as surely as they balance their checkbooks once a week, find the literary analogies flighty or tedious, so much so that we risk losing their attention. And as everyone knows who has ever spoken to an engineer, once you lose their attention, if only for a moment, you allow that purebred engineering mind to wander and then you have truly lost them, lost them to their more fascinating internal algorithms, those secret pockets with little pencil nubs and folded bits of paper scribbled with equations."

The audience was amused by the speaker's overgeneralizations about two very different professions, but the Professor resisted the man's allure. He also recognized that professional pride might be at the root of his resistance. After all, he was preaching the Gospel according to Maimon.

"So we have elected simply to define the important terms, one of which will be defined in just a moment. They will be defined in context, which turns out to be the more memorable way to learn a new term. Yes, a Glossary would be a wonderful addition, but such a contrivance will only delay the beginning of this chapter, a chapter that concerns the exchange of information between two groups of people."

Then came the story, entitled "The Chameleon's Mirror."

Too much coincidence.

It was now clear that the man was well aware of his audience and was intentionally creating what he believed was a "significant event." At this point, the Professor could no longer determine whether the man's work was fiction or nonfiction, whether it should be considered academically or creatively, or whether it was all an artful facade. Though the Professor enjoyed blurring the lines between one discipline and another, he found himself entirely uncomfortable when someone else was doing it.

He tried to be inconspicuous when he stood to leave, his second impulsive exit of the evening.

Outside Peters Hall, connecting the auditorium with the nearby museum, was a long curtained pathway—white linen stretched between aluminum poles, leading from one building to the other. As he entered the museum, he realized that the synchronization of subject matter had been intentional, as if the entire campus had been programmatically arranged to celebrate the theme, and he was the only fellow on campus who was unaware of the preparations.

The Milton Fisher Museum of Art and Natural History was the youngest building on the immense campus. With an arching glass entry many stories in height, and winged sections of the museum constructed in concentric arcs, like the trajectories of water sprinklers frozen in stone, and a central room designed by the artist Andy Goldsworthy that exaggerated the symmetries in a refined and seemingly unending series of crystalline curves, the museum was elegant and welcoming.

The Professor did not know Milton Fisher, nor his family, and had no idea when the man lived or died or what he did for a living, but if all he

had done in his entire existence was provide a legacy for such a building, it was more immortality than most could hope.

The museum was open for another hour. Unsettled by his sudden exits
from the party and the lecture, and not ready to return home, he stepped
into the glassy entryway to see the newest exhibit, which was placed in
the very center of the Goldsworthy arcs so that one's attention was
directed in that path. Of course, the title of the work was "Chameleon
and Mirror," continuing the debate that began with Stuart Brand and
Gregory Bateson in the 1970s.[5]

The sculpture was poised on a polished wooden pedestal that appeared, at first glance, to be the corner of an immense oak desk with
intricately carved drawers and knobs and dovetailed joints so precise
that the Professor could not determine if they were true joints or mere
simulations. The sculpture itself consisted of two polyethylene hands,
poised above a computer keyboard, one hand's extended finger touching the "c" key and the other resting on the "h." The two fingers were
the only support for the suspended hands, which were reminiscent of
Escher's famous Drawing Hands lithograph.

The Escher print, along with dozens of other photographs, surrounded
the central sculpture, each a variation on the theme of our physical interface with digital forms. The sculpture itself, positioned as if it were the
high priest at Stonehenge, was the quintessential three-dimensional reflection of the two-dimensional photos that surrounded it.

The computer was the mirror, the plastic human hands were the feet
of the chameleon, and the debate was echoed in each of its photographed
"reflections" (see Exhibits 18.1 and 18.2).

"What do you think, Professor," came a familiar voice from behind
him.

Esther carried several books in her crossed arms and her hair
was pulled back into a loosely braided tail. He didn't see this coming,
as if the narrative of his story turned in an unexpected direction, and
he was always intrigued by unpredictable developments. "Well," he
said, improvising ideas based upon the Brand-Bateson anecdote that
he'd heard only an hour before, "I've always believed that the
chameleon could only portray the color of the hand that had placed it
on the mirror."

EXHIBIT 18.1   *Hand and Keyboard (Digital and Digital)*

Source: Photo courtesy of Maximilian Fuery-Robbins, photographer; Hands by Isabel

"So you're in the Quantum school," she said, half respectful and half mocking. "We cannot remove ourselves from our observations; we are not *spectators*, but *participators*, is that it?"[6]

Now she had done it. She had touched intelligently on his central question, his prime mystery, the one that lingered behind every story and poem he had ever written, like the scarlet curtain in old theaters. "Exactly," the Professor said. "I am convinced the same theory applies to the reader and the text, that the reader is not an observer but a participator, but I haven't found a way to . . . a link that . . ." He paused, searching for the right words.

". . . that proves the theorem," she said, finishing his sentence.

"Exactly."

The two stood in silence, lost in thought.

EXHIBIT 18.2   Drawing Hands *by M.C. Escher*

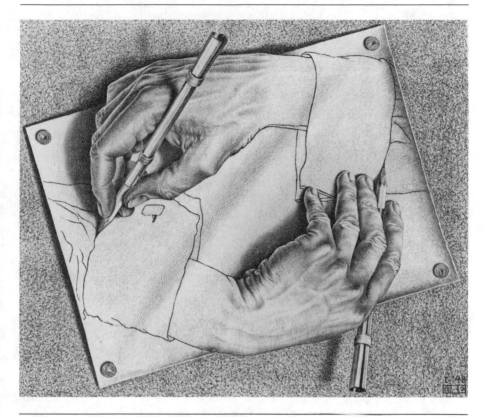

Source: The M.C. Escher Company, Baarn, Holland

"There is one principle that is irrefutable," the Professor suggested. "Everything is connected with everything else. The scientists have proven as much with nuclear identities, and the subjectivists indirectly agree."

"I'm not sure I follow you, Professor."

"Think of it this way: if you are simply a reflection of certain optical, neural, and psychological projections of mine, and my world is simply a broad and immense surreality that cannot be objectively ascertained, we remain connected only within my subjective imagination."

"In fact," he continued, "from this perspective, the principle that everything is connected survives one of the traditional theoretical tests— Occam's Razor, Bishop Berkeley's kicking of the rock and feeling it, Jung's notions of archetypes—because everything is equally possible from any point of view. It is only the *why* upon which we may radically disagree."

Esther was sorry that she could not linger to discuss the *why*; she explained that she needed to get back to her studies. They parted with friendly goodbyes.

Soon after her exit, the Professor also left the museum and moved toward the longer sidewalk, away from the museum entrance. The evening's linear progression of events had presented more than the usual provocations, and he knew he would be awake all night, at his typewriter, archiving as much of the evening's vocabularium as possible.

The notion of the chameleon and the mirror stayed with him.

He considered it in relation to his own thoughts about the network as narrative, that each interface/metaphor is a bridge between disciplines. He thought about the reader and writer, and their interface in the text. He thought about the programmer and the people who use the programs, and the computer-human interface whereby they interact. And he thought about the many ways by which we, as citizens, as teachers, as authors, as readers, have undermined the cross-fertilization that would be otherwise be so simple to use in our work and in our lives.

It was just as he thought about the absence of metaphor in our marriages that the Professor noticed a familiar form in the distance. Long black hair, a graceful gait. It was Esther, again, on her way home.

Should he call out to her, offer her some company in the dark night, suggest that he walk her to her off-campus home?

He decided instead to simply follow her home, thereby assuring her safety without any inappropriate connotations, and it was this simple decision, driven by complex and not entirely knowable (to the character, to the writer, to the reader) reasons and impulses, this simple decision that led to a moment that would alter the Professor's world dramatically, causing him to question the entanglement and the mirror, although not the connectivity of all things, which by its proof only added to his distress.

He turned up his collar to protect himself from a breeze that was lifting brown leaves into spirals and partially obscuring his vision of Esther as she cautiously made her way home. Fortunately for him, the wind and the leaves also muffled the sound of his footsteps. The leaves swirled, the chilling wind numbed his ears, the tip of his nose, and the index finger of his left hand where a small hole had appeared in the worn leather of gloves he had purchased long ago, on a vacation with Dahlia, in another cold winter, in another life.

The Professor was not surprised that Esther was heading north, away from the campus, because most of the graduate students had long since moved away from the dormitory clusters around the museum and library complex. When she turned right on Vermilion Street and continued eastward—in the direction of faculty housing—he assumed she was taking a shortcut to her destination. He thought about calling out to her because they were now heading in the same direction, and they could easily have crossed paths with only coincidence as the gravitational force. Nothing inappropriate about coincidence.

Esther was several blocks ahead of the Professor, a slice of a shadow in a windswept landscape, when she greeted someone with an embrace that indicated deep friendship. They seemed to be close to his own home, but the wind and the rustling leaves made distances difficult to gauge. The two figures in the distance moved to a nearby car whose motor had been running. Smoke was curling from the exhaust pipe in wisps that quickly adopted the motion of the leaves in the wind. As the car moved away, the Professor watched the two familiar red eyes of the tail lights disappear into the distance.

His nose was nearly frozen by the time he reached his porch, and he didn't see the piece of paper tucked into the door frame right away. He was intent on one thing, getting into the warmth of the house and warming himself with a whiskey. He turned the key in the lock as he had a thousand times before, a process memory that now repeated itself without conscious thought, so that he could think of other things as he came home each day.

It was only as he turned to shut the door, as the last gasp of the wind blew into the house, that the piece of yellow paper whipped past his face and onto the floor of his entryway, battling the many cardboard boxes for floor space. He picked up the note with one hand as he rubbed his nose with the other. The handwriting was familiar.

Sorry to have missed you. Wanted to speak with you about the book. Will call in the morning, not too early. I know you like to sleep in.

Dahlia.

Dahlia. He smiled at the imagined scene, his ex-wife knocking on his door, an acknowledgement that she knew he'd been uncomfortable at the party. She wanted to reassure him. Dahlia.

Only then did he realize, deductively, that it was Dahlia who had met Esther in the street, it was Dahlia and Esther who drove away, into the night.

Dahlia and Esther.

The Professor slumped into his office chair, knees pressed into the curve of his desk to prevent him from sliding to the ground, balanced his glass on one knee, and stared at the poster on the opposite wall.

> ". . . the physical wiring of collective human consciousness. The idea of connecting every mind to every other mind in full-duplex broadband . . ."[7]

What would the eminent Mr. Barlow say if, in his mind that was always connected with other minds, he realized that his daughter was somewhere else, with one of his close friends, and that the three of them— by the very definition he himself had proposed—were intimately connected in a manner that was not unchaste yet was quite difficult to articulate, a bleak version of post–de Chardin consciousness that he could not escape.

Who had not, at some moment in his or her modern career, stated that everything was connected? It is becoming our modern cliché—but in the many times that the interconnectedness of molecules and network servers had been demonstrated, had anyone ever noted that this was not a moral imperative? Had anyone admitted that his or her connections were becoming problematic? Had the admirers of the multiple universe theory confessed that some futures were better than others?[8]

Among his numerous impressions of the multi-verse, the Professor had stumbled upon one that he didn't like, he didn't like it one bit.

NOTES

1. Carl Jung, *Synchronicity* (Princeton, NJ: Princeton University Press, 1973).

2. Ibid., p. 96.
3. Gregory Bateson, *Steps to an Ecology of Mind: Essays in Anthropology, Psychiatry, and Epistemology* (New York: Balantine Books, 1972), 396.
4. Stephen Jay Gould, *The Hedgehog, the Fox, and the Magister's Pox: Mending the Gap between Science and the Humanities* (New York: Three Rivers Press, 2004), 258.
5. Kevin Kelly, *Out of Control: The New Biology of Machines, Social Science, and the Economic World* (New York: Basic Books, 2004), 69–70. "Stuart Brand posed that riddle to Gregory Bateson in the early 1970s. . . . Brand published his chameleon koan in his Whole Earth Catalog, in 1974. Writes Brand of his riddle: "I asked the question of Gregory Bateson at a point in our interview when we were lost in contemplation of the function, if any, of consciousness–self-consciousness. Both of us being biologists, we swerved to follow the elusive chameleon. Gregory asserted that the creature would settle at a middle value in its color range. I insisted that the poor beast trying to disappear in a universe of itself would endlessly cycle through a number of its disguises." In a 21st-century society wired into instantaneous networks, marketing is the mirror; the collective consumer is the chameleon. What color is the consumer when you put him on the marketplace? Does he dip to the state of the lowest common denominator—a middle average consumer? Or does he oscillate in mad swings of forever trying to catch up with his own moving reflection? Bateson was tickled by the depth of the chameleon riddle and passed it on to his other students.
6. F. David Peat, *Synchronicity: The Bridge between Matter and Mind*, (New York: Bantam, 1987), 37.
7. John Perry Barlow, "The Great Work," *Communications of the ACM*, January 1992.
8. "*What if* time is like an ever-branching tree with countless possible futures? If each decision we make affects the future then there must be an infinite number of futures. In the river-of-time concept the future is immutable. If, on the way to work in the morning, we decide to take the bus instead of the tube and are killed in a bus accident, then that death was predestined. But if time is ever-branching then there are two futures—one in which we die in the accident and another in which we live on, having taken the tube. It therefore follows consistently, or at least consistently to a science fiction author's mind, that if there are an infinite set of futures-there must then be an infinite set of pasts as well." Harry Harrison, quoted in *The Entropy Exhibition*, http://www.novymir.com.au/terminalcafe/natverse.html.

CHAPTER 19

Q NARRATIVES

In a moment of unusual candor, Dieter Kahn, the company founder, admitted that his original design for their business was an error. Furthermore, Dieter explained, it was a Fundamental Attribution Error.[1]

The individual most stricken by this pronouncement, at the beginning of an otherwise ordinary staff meeting, was Daniel Skeet, Vice President of Engineering and the company's cofounder. Daniel was a graduate of MIT with advanced degrees in Computer Science and Industrial Economics, a quiet man who rarely demonstrated emotion and was even more rarely surprised by anything his long-time partner said to the other executives. For Daniel, a business problem—like any engineering problem during his days at MIT—was simply an equation to be solved.

Daniel understood the significance of Fundamental Attribution Errors (FAEs). These were the most difficult engineering problem to solve, because the error occurred *at the very outset* of sequential events. In simple terms, if a software program was viewed as a complex sequence of zeroes and ones, each binary set leading to their consequential steps, an FAE is an error that occurs at the first pairing.

Instead of beginning with zero, the FAE begins with one.

The challenge of discovering an FAE is that every single binary choice after the initial step can be profoundly correct, each properly leading to the next in a complex series of branching choices, yet, because of the initial error, one arrives at a destination exactly opposite of the intended goal—180 degrees in the wrong direction. Discovery and diagnosis is often expensive and sometimes impossible, because, as you work backward from the end point (incorrect outcome), you will find only correct elements, one after another.

"A faulty assumption," his Advanced Algorithms professor once explained, "is most dangerous at the very beginning of your project. You may never recognize the mistake until it is much too late to fix."

Dieter's candid confession did not immediately register on the faces of any other executive, and his colleagues would not have noticed anything untoward about his statement had not Mirna, their Director of Talent—the woman responsible for executive training sessions and the most socially perceptive person at the table—observed Daniel Skeet's grimace. Daniel was sitting exactly opposite, and she was perfectly positioned to observe his uncharacteristic reaction. Daniel seemed to be in sudden pain, a kind of intellectual angina.

"Our taxonomy is incorrect," Dieter said to the silent room of managers, each of whom began to experience anxiety about their salaries, their mortgages, and their children's education, if only because of their CEO's serious tone.

Taxonomies were once a simple affair; every piece of data was classified as customer information or employee information. This was the standard two-factor taxonomy that most businesses used, though certain manufacturing companies had developed a three-factor data classification: customer, employee, and product.

Dieter had finally realized that each of the company's major challenges, some of them caused by bad judgments and others by more complicated technical constructions, could be traced to his original decision to organize their efforts using the two-factor taxonomy for the company. His PhD was in information sciences, and he had finally come to the understanding that modern taxonomies have no base factor. Customers can also be competitors. Competitors can be acquired and become employees. Employees who buy their product are also customers.

"Our identities change from one moment to the next. Who we are, as a company, is temporal, and I didn't design our framework with enough flexibility," he said.

If this were a novel, it would focus on Dieter's profound personal transformation as he began the arduous journey of reevaluating his life. If it were cinema, the camera would slowly move from one distressed face to another in that paralyzed moment. However, this is an allegory of business during a moment of change, and therefore it is the woman's response that launches our tale.

"I hate awkward silences," she said, hoping to break the ice. "Imaginations can go wild. Can you tell us what you plan to *do*, now that you have recognized the error, Dieter?"

It was bad news, but he knew he must not leave it unspoken.

"First of all, I'm afraid that the possible acquisition of our leading competitor will not be possible," he said with the kind of sadness one reserves for funerals. "As you remember, it was our only hope of keeping this company solvent."

Dieter found himself feeling overwhelmed. "Mirna, I can answer your question fully only in a much longer meeting, so our agenda for this weekend's offsite meeting will have to change. Can *you* suggest a next step?"

If this was the garden of forking paths, then the executives were poised at the quintessential juncture. How they managed to move forward would determine the outcome, many weeks ahead. Mirna knew that yet another fundamental error would be disastrous. On an impulse guided by more than a decade of organizational development, she suggested an improvised agenda for the following weekend.

"We can break into working groups, led by the respective vice presidents. On Day One we can brainstorm alternatives, on Day Two we can present them, and on Day Three we can make decisions. We've handled big problems before."

And that was how the eight executives of a struggling company in the midst of a struggling economy planned to gather at the rustic San Dolores beachfront conference center. She told everyone she would have a specific agenda and logistics by the end of the day, and apologized to everyone for the sudden change in plans

"And Dieter," she said, "I believe this should remain confidential."

One Set of Rules

The phrase was printed on a large placard and hung on the front wall of the conference room where the executive team was scheduled to meet later that morning. Long after midnight, Dieter had suddenly understood one of the central reasons for the imminent failure of their company. Despite detailed planning by Human Resources staff, who had a very specific agenda for the day, he decided to play the role of *unpredictable boss who says one thing and does another* and create a detour for his team.

"Good morning, Dieter," Mirna sang as she made a boisterous entrance, carrying a box of props (markers, Post-Its, index cards, pencils, tablets, company shirts) and exhaling loudly as she placed it on the long table. "You look like you didn't get any sleep."

It was true, his shirt was all wrinkled and he was unshaven. He could have been Einstein or a mental patient. She tossed him one of the T-shirts, still in its plastic bag. It was white, with the company's blue logo on the left sleeve. Dieter disappeared into the nearby men's room to change. He threw some water into his hair, transforming himself from genius/hobo to New York Hip.

Back in the conference room, as he was wedging the wrinkled shirt into his briefcase, Daniel patted him on the shoulder and asked him about the placard on the front wall.

"Yes," Mirna echoed, "I was wondering about that myself."

"Little surprise for everyone," Dieter said, with a modest air of mystery. "I'll wait until everyone is here, so I don't have to repeat myself."

"You always repeat yourself," Daniel laughed.

Mirna glanced over at Dieter to see if he was amused. He was, so she laughed too. She missed the moment by several seconds, however, and her laughter seemed like a lost balloon.

The rest of the management team arrived and made themselves comfortable around the table, each with their own little routines to begin a long and probably arduous meeting. Elizabeth had the Starbuck's travel mug that went everywhere with her, in addition to the ubiquitous bottle of spring water. Ackerman (his first name was Allen, but everyone had been calling him by his last name as long as they could remember) changed seats three times before finally choosing one in the exact middle of the room. Naomi Li was attending for her supervisor, who was on extended leave after knee surgery. She waited until almost every other team member had selected a seat before she took hers. Finally, Sal Romano, Vice President of Sales, took his seat. Sal was a cynic whose expression told everyone he was not happy about being forced to attend an offsite instead of closing new deals.

"You're one of those people who change their seats a dozen times before the movie begins, aren't you?" Mirna said to Ackerman, and he admitted that it drove his wife crazy.

"If I can say a few words before we begin . . ." Dieter said, two degrees louder than the room's conversation. His team was well trained; they fell silent immediately.

"Mirna will explain the rules of engagement for the meeting in a few minutes," he said, walking toward the front of the room, "but I realized something last night that I wanted to get in front of you, first and foremost, because it should be our guiding principle for the day."

"I thought our guiding principle for the day was going to be the Darwin quote." Mirna said, perplexed. "It's already on everyone's agenda."

The rest of the team looked down at the agenda in front of them. In very bold letters, on the pale blue topsheet, was a statement paraphrasing Charles Darwin that Mirna had discovered during a recent conference on "Getting the Best from Every Employee":

> It's not the strongest or the smartest,
> but those who can adapt to change . . .

"It's fine, Mirna," Dieter said reassuringly. "I'm just being one of those bosses who changes things at the last minute."

Mirna slumped in her chair. "I'll adapt."

Dieter waited until everyone's attention returned, and after an initial bout of whispering about the possibility of another reorganization, the room became quiet.

"One set of rules," Dieter said. Then he waited.

When no one asked for clarification, he underscored the thought with another phrase.

". . . for *everything*," Dieter said firmly.

"Everything?" Daniel asked.

"Yes," Dieter said, as expansively as he was capable of expressing himself, "*One set of rules for everything.*"

The group was quiet for a moment, and then Ackerman posed the next question. "I suppose you mean in the company—for instance, between Engineering and Finance?"

Daniel was amused at the thought of running his engineering teams with the precise mechanisms of the accounting team, but he decided not to speak out. He knew Dieter was going somewhere, somewhere specific, and he was willing to let the man run in an open field. There would be plenty of opportunities later in the day to play Gadfly.

"Yes, but it's more than that," Dieter said.

"Perhaps he's . . . you know," Naomi Li said quietly, "talking about our customers and our partners."

Dieter waved his hand impatiently. It was going to be a long day, and he had spent most of the previous evening sleeplessly outlining the new mission statement. He knew underneath that the group wasn't ready, but he made an attempt to move forward more quickly.

"Everything. Everything," he said loudly. "*One set of rules for everything.*"

Mirna walked to the whiteboard at the other end of the room. She reached for a black marker, double-checked that it was erasable, took off the cap with deliberate seriousness, and reached for the board, poised to write whatever came next. She stood there, arm upraised, for an entire minute before Dieter exhaled and apologized.

"I'm sorry, everyone," he began, "but I've been up all night putting my own thoughts together on this, and I realize I have to play catch-up with you . . . Daniel might be comfortable with my leaps of abstraction, but I know it's too much to ask of the whole team."

Mirna remained poised at the board, arm upraised like Lady Liberty.

"This is what I came to understand last night, as I was thinking about why we have arrived at such a difficult state of affairs—not just our own company, but countless others that are stagnant in a dull economy, trying to reconcile innovation with productivity with cost reduction with compliance with growth."

"Not a pretty picture," Daniel said.

Mirna wrote: Innovation, Productivity, Cost Reduction, Compliance, Growth.

"No, it's not, Daniel, and I've realized that the reason we're stuck, both as a company and as an industry, is because we've taken ourselves down a certain path—let's call it the *business evolution* path, the *survive or perish* path. Now we find ourselves lost and unable to get back to where we need to be."

Ackerman asked the question, "And where do we need to be?"

Dieter removed a legal tablet from his briefcase, the top page of which was covered with arrows, boxes, and captions, all surrounding a familiar graph (Exhibit 19.1).

It was a picture that the entire team had seen before, each time Dieter had explained his vision to customers or investors or a new employee. (He particularly liked showing it to new employees.) In the diagram, the entire technology industry could be seen as moving from a hierarchical, linear type of business to a multidimensional, unbounded cycle of clustered business interactions.

His favorite example, though he had many and could often be heard in the hallways presenting the latest to anyone willing to listen, was

EXHIBIT 19.1   *Q Transformation*

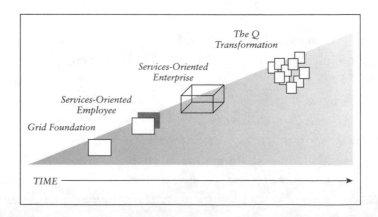

Domino's Pizza. "Until today, who knew that Domino's did not deliver its own pizzas, but outsourced the responsibility to UPS, who could do it better at less cost. UPS uses a Domino truck, or a Domino logo on their own vehicles, and follows a pizza the same way it tracks packages."[2]

Everyone knew the example, but they all pretended to have heard it for the first time, and Dieter laughed.

"Okay, so you know our basic business premise: we have always believed that our products need to be aligned with the type of business in the upper right-hand corner of the chart.

"This is where we went wrong," Dieter said, and he drew a big arrow beside the list of stages (see Exhibit 19.2).

"We should have begun to decouple ourselves from Darwinian business (*survive or perish*) to quantum business (*from the many comes one*)," he explained. "But we haven't . . . yet."

Daniel finally lost his patience with his friend's conceptual approach and raised his hand. He didn't wait to be recognized, he merely wanted Dieter to know he was about to interrupt.

"Look, Dieter . . ." their chief technologist began, "I've known you long enough to believe that this makes sense to you, and I'll further speculate that you are actually on to something very important . . ."

Dieter nodded his head.

". . . but it seems to me that, if you want the rest of us to absorb this, if you really want us to be one team with one set of rules by the end of the day, then you need to break this down into parts. I'll start. Can you

EXHIBIT 19.2   *Q Corporation*

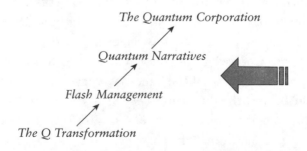

explain what you mean by 'Q Narratives' in simple language? That would be a good beginning."

Dieter was silent. He knew he was lost inside his own explanation. He also knew that he was asking them to make an illogical leap, one that does not necessarily come from better explanations.

"I'll begin with one very technical piece of information that I reread last night," Dieter explained, "because it will help you to understand what I want to do with our company."

He looked at the faces sitting around the conference room table. With the single exception of his Vice President of Sales, who was always cynical about changes in strategy, everyone's eyes were on him—open, alert, ready for him to give them direction. This was the poignant moment of leadership, an almost palpable sense that his team was starved and that only he could assuage the hunger and cause the company to prevail.

"You've all heard about that piece of physics saying that a wave is also a particle," Dieter began. Several heads nodded in assent.

"There are other, equally important discoveries in physics that I believe play a critical role in our understanding of human behavior. I won't lay them all out, because I already hear Daniel complaining that I'm still being too theoretical."

Someone laughed. Daniel relaxed into his seat.

"Last night, I read about a man named John Wheeler who worked at the Institute of Theoretical Physics in Austin, Texas. He conducted an experiment in order to prove that reality is not fixed but is defined by the perspective of the 'observer.' He designed what is called a gravity-lens interferometer. I won't bother you with a detailed explanation of what it does or how it works, but I *will* show you what he ultimately validated."

Dieter paused to reach for the black marker, erased what he had written on the board, and drew a diagram (see Exhibit 19.3).

Dieter went on to explain what Wheeler had proved. Depending on where the observer places a phosphor screen used to observe the photons of light, the movement of the light may curve along either position A or position B, and the curvature *cannot* be physically known *independent of the observation*. Therefore, though the source of light itself may have occurred billions of years ago, and the light itself exists,

EXHIBIT 19.3   *Two Places at Once*

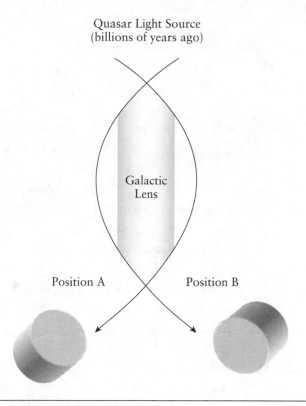

Quasar Light Source
(billions of years ago)

Galactic
Lens

Position A   Position B

Source: Based on Nick Herbert, *Quantum Reality: Beyond the New Physics* (New York: Anchor, 1987).

traveling along its curved arc, the *actual path* of the light is entirely dependent on the position of the observer.

"Wheeler's delayed-choice experiment seems to show that the past is not fixed but alters according to present decisions."[3]

"And just what does that have to do with company revenues?" asked their Sales cynic. He seemed quite frustrated with the meeting and with his visionary CEO.

"It's a fair question, Sal," Dieter said, sitting down at the end of the table and folding his hands. "Give me five more minutes to answer it, and if I don't, you can come over here and smack me in the face."

It was the first time Sal had smiled all morning.

"All of this is to explain that thought changes the material world[4] and that our point of view (in Wheeler's case, the position from which the light was observed) changes the thing being observed."

Dieter stopped to check his team's attentiveness. Ackerman was taking notes. Naomi Li, in her first exposure to "the executive level," seemed overwhelmed. Mirna was watching Dieter's every move, as was Daniel.

"*This* is where we made our mistake. We did a terrific job of creating a 'flash environment' for our R&D teams, but we didn't adjust the rest of the company to reinforce it. We couldn't. And *this* is where Q Narratives come into play—here's my answer to Daniel's question at last . . ."

Everyone except Sal applauded. Sal simply tapped his watch, to remind Dieter he was taking the "five-minute warning" seriously.

"Quantum Narratives, or Q Narratives, are *stories*. They are not stories based on a fixed reality of the company, because the company grows and changes over time. Each one of us should have our own individualized point of view about the company's direction and our very specific role in it. Our problem is that we have not articulated our stories, our Q Narratives, very well, and they've become muddled. If, however, we can develop our narratives—each a different story but all based on a common underlying theme that is our company—then we can move the company forward."

"You have 90 seconds before I come up and slap you," Sal said with a deadpan expression that left everyone in the room convinced that he intended to do so.

"Sal," Dieter said in response, "what do you do when you arrive at a new customer site?"

"What do you mean, exactly?" the man asked.

"What do you do when you're standing in front of a roomful of executives who know very little about our product or our company?" Dieter knew the answer, but he hoped he could lead Sal to it.

"I have a standard presentation, it's our corporate deck—you know the slides, Dieter," Sal said with an odd inflection.

"I know, Sal," Dieter said, "and what does our presentation convey to a new customer?"

"It's our vision, our history, who we are and what we do, why we can be trusted to solve their problem."

"It's a *story*!" Mirna blurted out.

". . . and Mirna, what do you do when we bring in new employees, on their first day?" Deiter was in full Socratic mode now, slowly trying to move each person at the table toward a common understanding.

"Orientation," Mirna said, ". . . company policies and procedures, how they fit in . . ." then her face lit up. "Oh, a *story*!"

Dieter congratulated her. "And Daniel," he continued in rhythm with the moment, "what is the single most complex issue facing our operations, the item that most concerns the Board?"

"Besides revenue?" Daniel asked. "Our business processes, or lack thereof."

"Exactly," said Dieter, "and what is a business process other than our narrative of how certain procedures should be completed within the company? There is a business process, or story, for generating sales leads. There is a business process, or story, for recognizing revenue. There is a business process, or story, that supports the software development lifecycle. There is a business process, or story, for how we terminate employees. In well-written stories, you all have your favorites, one scene flows to the next in a manner that seems perfectly logical for you. And you are also aware of stories that just don't make sense because something seems to be missing. If you're a good reader, or even if you're just watching a movie, you can identify the place in the story that needs to be fixed. If we approach our business processes with the same attention that we listen to stories, we will know which ones work, and where the broken ones need to be fixed."

He went on to point out that everyone in the company had a different story—what they tell their investors, how they report their earnings, how they train customers. The combination of all of these narratives composes the entity termed Hypothekon.

"Therefore," he said to Sal, hoping to meet the self-imposed deadline, "our narratives *are* the company. If we are to change the company's direction, first we must all understand the theme and how each story reflects it, how each of our stories is changed, so that they all make sense."

Ackerman smacked the table with an open hand. "Business processes," Ackerman repeated, almost to himself.

Dieter didn't say anything, waiting for his very senior General Manager to tie things together.

"You're talking about business processes!" the man said with absolute confidence. "And you're *right*, we need to articulate them much better than we have done, and you're *also* right that if those processes—particularly our key performance indicators—are not integrated, they can slow down the entire enterprise. Narratives are processes."

"... and what happens if your narrative is not synchronized with Sal's sales narratives?" Dieter asked. Even Sal knew the answer to that one.

"We miss our goddam numbers," he said loudly.

"All right, Sal," Dieter said, "here's the punch line, and if it doesn't resonate with you, I'm ready to get smacked."

Mirna and Ackerman leaned forward in their chairs. Either way, the next few minutes would be fascinating.

"Business potential is the target of each Hypothekon narrative. The challenge of the modern corporation is to predictably convert business potential (our projections) to business reality, information that is observable, measurable, and real. How we observe those narratives plays a huge role in our ability to meet the challenge. There is an exponential range for our potential growth, and the boundaries are limited only by our narratives, our stories, our business processes."

"You're saying that we are talking about the *wrong things*," Sal said.

"Remember the Fundamental Attribution Error Dieter described in our staff meeting on Monday?" Daniel said to everyone. "It means we *have* been talking about the wrong things. Yes, Sal, that's exactly right. And even when we came close to talking about the right things, there were pieces that were missing, like a missing clue in a mystery without which the ending makes little sense ..."

Ackerman seemed disappointed. "No slap?"

Everyone laughed. Then quiet descended on the room as each of the attendees realized the seriousness of what Dieter was asking them to do. He was asking them to radically change their view of the company and their own roles in it.

"This is the true challenge of leadership," Dieter said. "If the stories in this conference room are confused or contradictory, the company's path cannot be changed. But if our stories do fit together, they become a larger lesson that has tremendous gravitational pull."

Daniel smiled at the sudden memory of their first discussion about leadership, when they filed incorporation papers and founded the company. They had been trading ideas and analogies all day and were exhausted. Dieter was standing behind the desk and Daniel was at the keyboard when he found, on the NASA website, an image that made sense.

The principle in question was called "Frame Dragging," and it concerned the influence of large gravitational forces on light, an influence so great that light actually bends in proximity to the force exerted by immense bodies, such as Black Holes (see Exhibit 19.4).

"I believe that leadership functions in much the same way as gravity," Daniel remembered saying to Dieter that day, long ago. "The influence is so dramatic that everything around it is affected by its presence. There are also certain individuals who, by their sheer intuition or imagination or conviction, create similar patterns." It was a fond memory, and Daniel was pleased to know that Dieter remembered it, as well.

"No, Daniel," Dieter said with the tone of an inside joke being told in public. "I'm not going to explain the details of Frame Dragging to everyone. I think Sal has had enough of my physics for one weekend . . ."

EXHIBIT 19.4   *Gravity Field: Frame Dragging Example*

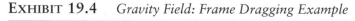

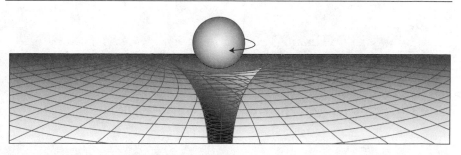

Source: National Aeronautics and Space Administration

Mirna returned to the whiteboard with the marker she'd held on to for the entire morning, finally ready to facilitate a brainstorming session.

"I think Dieter wants us to begin with "One Set of Rules." Right, boss?"

Dieter nodded, and they began the hard work of changing themselves by changing their narratives, one at a time.

NOTES

1. From the *British Journal of Social Psychology*, September 2004: "It has been argued above that our connection with the world is first and foremost practical. We ask what elements in the world, including other people, can do for us or to us. We wish to know what we can use for tools, protection, to entertain us and capture our imagination, and who will help, harm or interest us. This engagement is pre-reflective—we do not have to spell things out in an internal dialogue. The nature of our embodiment is such that we quickly and pre-reflectively read other people's intentions, the way they connect to the world. We are equipped to do this without conscious thought, although we may reflect on this engagement, being able to capture the process to the extent that we have available the necessary vocabulary and syntax. We read the other's intentionality directly—it is an intersubjective understanding, and not due to a process of cognitive inference, for which, quite literally, there would be no time. When assessing another's intentionality we are less concerned about the reasons or causes for their behaviour than with their project (Sartre, 1969) or care (Heidegger, 1962), that is, their principal concerns or objectives in the world." Darren Langdridge and Trevor Butt, "The Fundamental Attribution Error: A Phenomenological Critique," *British Journal of Social Psychology*, 359.
2. Thomas L. Friedman, *The World Is Flat: A Brief History of the Twenty-First Century* (New York: Penguin, 2005), 84.
3. Nick Herbert, *Quantum Reality: Beyond the New Physics* (New York: Anchor, 1987), 167.
4. http://www.sff.net/people/doylemacdonald/r_flight.

CHAPTER 20

LEAVING FLATLAND

How shall I make it clear? When you move straight on, does it not sometimes occur to you that you could move in some other way? . . .

—E. A. Abbott
Section 14, *Flatland*
1884

O n the edge of her unmade futon bed, the young woman looked over her shoulder as she tucked wisps of shoulder-length red hair behind one ear. Delicate hands performed the two-fingered tuck-and-curl, a gesture repeated countless times over the years.

He had watched her do it as a child, too.

She was entirely absorbed by his presence in her room that morning, looking at him with disbelief (and perhaps hope) again and again as if she didn't entirely trust he was there, sitting in the corner of the room. She was wearing the elegant blue satin robe her mother had given her on her 18th birthday, and thick white socks were cuffed at each ankle. More like a little girl in a playground swing than the college sophomore she had become, her feet kicked back and forth slowly, like sprinklers in the garden outside, first one, then another, sometimes both.

She was wearing two platinum earrings, little cages with small birds in-side, and they glinted in the sunlight as she turned to ask the unanswerable question. The silver-haired man in the overstuffed velvet chair was sitting in shadows, almost outside the reach of the sunlight. Between his thumb and forefinger, a Kennedy half-dollar played a slow hide-and-seek. The coin also shimmered when it was exposed to the sunlight, and it seemed to him that the light bounced between his hand and her earrings, a momentary connection with extreme velocity, then gone. Her question reached across the room with a similar speed.

"Why did you wait so long?"

Linwood had wanted to tell her 100 times before.

He had wanted to tell her when she was 6 and needed help with her Language Arts homework, when she was 11 and reading on the Internet about Christopher Columbus. He had wanted to tell her the day the acceptance letter came from the art school in Maine, the summer before she went to college. A thousand and one times throughout his experience as a father Linwood had wanted to tell his daughter that he could not read, yet he did not.

Of course, there was shame. Shame "came with the territory" of being functionally illiterate. As a younger man, Linwood did not know that many successful executives had reading disorders, and he had found himself unable to admit his problem to his only child as she was growing up. By the time he tackled the issue (again) in his fifties and, with the help of *Hooked on Phonics* and a very patient wife, finally taught himself to read, his daughter had long since become estranged. After so many years of unexplained rejection, their relationship seemed to be beyond repair.

As he sat in the deep, comfortable chair in her cottage bedroom, Linwood silently remembered each one of those poignant and painful scenes. *I would give everything I have to answer that question adequately*, he thought to himself.

She hadn't expected his visit that day, though she had sometimes imagined it, only to scold herself for remaining connected to the image of a father who had so consistently avoided telling her the truth. But something was different that morning. The sun bathed her in warmth, and one question after another came to mind.

"I don't even know how you came to be an exec," she said, wishing to hear the many stories other children heard from their parents when they were young. "What did they do when they found out you couldn't read?"

The world changes, then we change, he wanted to say. *But it should be the other way around.*

> **Nothing was visible, nor could be visible, to us, except Straight Lines. —E.A. Abbot, Section 1, *Flatland,* 1884**

This was the story he wanted to tell . . .

Linwood had a remarkable ability to recognize patterns. So quickly could he locate an out-of-sequence punch card, back in the days when punch cards were the best way to transfer data from one machine to another, that Frank, his supervisor, had promoted him to first-line management. In his first week as a junior supervisor, he helped the team revise the inventory processes on the shop floor, removing three steps in the path from shipping dock to operations and eliminating two hours from the schedule, every day of every week. That single decision saved the company $140,000 a year.

It was not genius, just intuition. An awkward moment in the flow of tasks grabbed his attention, appeared to him like an orphaned orange in a crate of apples, but rarely did the people around him notice the rogue task until he pointed it out to them. This was how Linwood succeeded in business, if not in his troublesome personal life. It was as if he had a special cornea that highlighted aberrations in sequences; he simply saw things differently.

Subsequently, Linwood made most decisions very quickly.

Someone had once told him (and it bothered him that he could not remember who it was) that good executives are successful because they can make the correct decision with only 10% of the information available to them. It seemed as if Linwood's mind moved from A to B to Z because, once he had ascertained the pattern, the end result was quite obvious to him. His challenge, in the business world, was not simply to be correct—that was the easy part. The challenge, rather, was to find a way to articulate his decisions for those around him, those who did not have his capacity to observe and decide quickly.

By the time Rachel entered Stanford as a freshman, Linwood was spending many more hours each day among people—at meetings, in conferences, on the telephone—and he sorely missed the society of the machines that had been, for so long, his closest friends.

It was a kind of homesickness, not for a place but for a time, a time of his life when he had learned to be confident and enthusiastic, a time of his life when he had learned to prevail over seemingly insurmountable limitations. His relationship with machines had unshackled him, and he felt a bit lonelier with each day that he went to work among engineers and secretaries and managers and customers. Linwood's loneliness was pervasive, and it was not easily assuaged.

I was simply trying to survive, he wanted to say, *but they thought it was something more, and they kept promoting me.* His only concern, at the time, was supporting his wife and daughter financially, paying the tuition and the mortgage.

Rachel turned sideways on her bed, propping her head on one hand and pulling at the bedspread with the other for warmth.

She wanted to know everything.

It was as if the entire world was founded on an assumption that she suddenly understood was incorrect. So many pieces of the puzzle begged for re-examination. Fundamental Attribution Error.

"It must have been so hard," she said, imagining a life without reading, without words. "Jesus, how did you survive?"

The honest answer was that he had not survived. For some reason, Linwood remembered a particular scene involving his longtime employer, L.M. Tooms, who was an authoritarian nightmare for many other employees, hence the belief that his initials stood for Little Mussolini. But Linwood had always been able to talk to the man; he had always had a knack for identifying a factor his boss had not seen, a new perspective, a different solution, an alternative view of the working men and women who depended on him for their livelihoods.

Tooms sat behind his desk with a royal and somewhat despotic air. However, in all his meetings with the new exec of the company,

Linwood hadn't noticed a single moment when Tooms's reputation as a slash-and-burn turnaround specialist was evident. It was as if Linwood, in their first meeting, had earned a special insider privilege, someone Tooms trusted, someone who thus had the opportunity to alter the man's dreaded impact on the company.

"Your idea, please," said L.M.

Linwood's pulse quickened as if there was a chasm yawning at his feet.

"My idea," Linwood said, "is to keep a job for everyone in the company. God knows how to part seas, but I don't have such tricks; all I can do is plead their case."

L.M. winced with disapproval.

"I don't believe in God, Mr. Eddy."

Linwood smoothed a wrinkle from the blue Armani tie that Adrienne bought for him a long time ago. The company's newest Chief Executive continued his unsmiling introduction. The way he saw it, people needed a god in order to have someone to blame when the sufferings of their lives grew too vast to be blamed on the usual villainies.

L.M. Tooms clasped his hands behind his back and walked thoughtfully by the conference room table to the windows. He glanced down to the corporate parking lot below. For a moment, the room was noiseless except for the hum of overhead lights. Then he turned back to Linwood and added, "Of course, when I was young, I wanted to believe in God, any god would do, but since those sad days I have come to believe that there is no underlying moral order. It is all a struggle, simply to prevail against the usual villainies."

"Yes, sir. May I suggest that a layoff is the usual tactic," Linwood continued sidestepping the theological debate, ". . . something everyone in the industry expects. Everyone is doing it. Outsourcing. Reducing costs. Instead, we could announce that we are spinning off an entirely new company—our entire engineering and manufacturing group—and that the new entity would be responsible for all product development and delivery. This new company would receive seed funding from us in the form of a long-term loan, and the original company could take a full write-off this year for the investment."

Linwood stopped to catch his breath, adding, "I believe the loan itself could be considered a business expense, in addition to the numerical reduction in costs that would, by themselves, meet the Board's criteria sufficiently . . . but we would probably have to check that with . . ."

L.M.'s interruption was sudden, yet his concentration was vigilant. "A spin-off as a deduction?"

This was good, and this was bad. Tooms was intrigued.

Tooms moved to the small refrigerator and silently offered a chilled bottle of water to Linwood. Then he took one for himself. "*He is an insatiably thirsty man,*" Linwood thought to himself.

"I've read some of the literature on networked organizations, all the new jargon about The Trans-firm," he said between sips of water. "I understand the proposition that cross-functional initiatives cannot be managed hierarchically . . . but I'm not sure it's true. I believe very strongly in the accountability that hierarchies ensure."

"Accountability," Linwood repeated.

"Yes," Tooms said, with a lilt at the end of the word as if it were a question, or a melody.

Linwood Eddy walked over to the refrigerator and retrieved the bottle of water he had earlier declined. It was a delaying tactic, and he knew that Tooms knew it.

"Tell me, Mr. Tooms," Linwood said, changing the conversation and feigning a kind of confident calm that befriended him during such moments. "In your various pursuits, have you ever known someone who simply did not want to hear what you were trying to tell him?" Tooms glared.

". . . or her . . ." Linwood quickly corrected, but sexist grammar was not the source of the man's distress.

Tooms leaned forward, elbow on one knee, water bottle in the other hand, which he now waved at Linwood like a judge's gavel or a conductor's baton. He asked if Linwood was mocking him.

"Mocking?" Linwood asked. "No sir, I was simply . . ."

"Because if you're not mocking me, then perhaps you're a highly intuitive fellow," Tooms said, more relaxed with this option.

The CEO stared up and to his right, the direction where people stare when they are lost in thought, or remembering something from their childhood, or debating a fine point with their conscience.

"You see, Linwood, when I was a boy, I suffered from a serious case of meningitis that rendered me entirely deaf. Entirely. Years went by. I was forced to learn to sign and to read people's lips. Fortunately, an-other unfortunate event occurred years later but, as an indirect result, I regained my hearing—or, just enough of it to truly treasure the sound of people's voices. So when someone suggests that I might not be hearing what they have to say . . ."

Linwood, stunned, now understood why Tooms' remarks in large meetings were often short, staccato-like pronouncements, why he pre-ferred meeting with individuals rather than groups, why he was drawn to companies whose products reproduced sound.

". . . that person is either mocking me," Tooms said, "or he has guts, real guts."

Linwood started to apologize. "Well, sir, I was certainly not aware of . . ."

Tooms waved his empty bottle dismissively.

"Fine, fine . . . no matter. I think you were right, Linwood, I am so immersed in merger details that everything I hear comes through that filter." Then he observed that Linwood was the only senior manager in the entire company to challenge Tooms on anything. The only one.

"They are worried about losing their jobs," Linwood explained, although as soon as he spoke the words, he understood what Tooms would say in response.

"Their worries are the reason why they *will* lose jobs . . .," Tooms said, "and you're not worried?"

Linwood worried more than most, because his marriage was a strug-gle, his relationship with his daughter was a struggle, simply navigat-ing the grocery store was a struggle. His job was his only source of stability. From the time he entered the parking lot in the morning until the time he left his office late at night, he felt a balance that did not exist elsewhere. He was *present*, and he very much wanted to stay *present*.

"I have other worries, Mr. Tooms, but that is another story . . ."

Tooms nodded and the meeting was over, but not before he had instructed Linwood to try out his ideas on the other executives. "If it works, I can take credit for it later, but for now, let's have them think-ing this is coming from you. I want to see how they will react without the shadow of Little Mussolini hovering over them."

Linwood understood the tactic and actually agreed with the approach, but he was startled by the Mussolini reference. He couldn't imagine how the CEO knew his company nickname.

"You'd be surprised what you hear in the bathroom," Tooms said with a sly smile, "when no one thinks you're listening . . ." Then he looked at his watch and cursed.

"Work on the numbers tonight," L.M. said. "I'll need to see the business case by morning—four or five slides will do. Linwood, if we are going to propose this to the Board . . . well . . . we probably have 72 hours to make this work."

Numbers and text by morning.

They shook hands, and in that moment of moments, as the two men looked at each other, in that instant when personal histories were being defined, Linwood could have said what Adrienne wanted him to say. He wouldn't have needed to be specific; he could have simply said he would need help with the presentation.

Linwood exhaled a breath he seemed to have been holding since the start of the meeting and then rubbed his forehead. He focused his attention on the tiny fist of anxiety in his chest, that round ache, his very familiar cramp, breathing in and out, until it began to recede. He remained there, alone in the executive conference room, for several minutes.

It's all a battle, Linwood thought, simply to prevail in a struggle against the usual villainies.

Suddenly, all he could think about was getting out of the office. He had to get away, to be alone; he needed to find a safe place to think, to breathe.

To breathe.

"Tomorrow," he said as he left the office and quickly moved down the nearby stairwell, through the Emergency Exit and into the parking lot.

He gulped for air. It was dusk, and Linwood's chest was clenched in a knot. He loosened his tie as he unlocked his car, turned on the ignition, and hurried away from Building 1. He drove as if he were escaping an attacker, as if by leaving the company's property he could escape his anxiety. He could not go home, not yet; he could not tell Adrienne what he had done, and what he had not done, what he had not said. She was already very angry at him.

Linwood didn't remember driving through two busy intersections or past the business district where he often stopped for dinner on Wednesdays. He didn't remember pulling the car off the road, into the weeds. He didn't realize that he was at the new construction site, on the way to New Dachau, until he rolled down the window for some air, precious air, and saw, in the distance, the two yellow tower cranes. They were angled in opposite directions, forming an immense X inside the circle of temporary fencing, beside the makeshift billboard that named the construction company and the project sponsors in bold print.

He strained to read the words on the sign. Full concentration. As he focused on their patterns, he didn't see the large truck coming from the opposite direction.

> **But in writing this book I found myself sadly hampered by the impossibility of drawing such diagrams as were necessary for my purpose: for of course, in our country of Flatland, there are no tablets but Lines, and no diagrams but Lines, all in one straight Line and only distinguishable by difference of size and brightness; so that, when I had finished my treatise (which I entitled, "Through Flatland to Thoughtland") I could not feel certain that many would understand my meaning. —E.A. Abbott, Section 22, *Flatland*, 1884**

"You needn't worry about me," she said abruptly, interrupting their condolences. "I'm *fine*, just *fine*."

"Red, we're just trying . . ." Avram said as he reached to put his arm around her. She pushed it away firmly, repeated that she was *fine*, and went back to her room, to her silence, where she could try to begin to understand.

Her father was dead.

He had been struck by an oncoming truck and had never regained consciousness. Her mother had phoned with the news, though Avram had learned about it at work. It was not, all things considered, a collapse of the world as she knew it. In fact, it was surprising she was so unconcerned, even for her mother, who had to make all the preparations, deal with an estate that was surely messy, arrange the mortuary and the cemetery fees, and was probably spending that entire evening on the phone with various relatives.

Rachel was once again annoyed at her father; he was doing it again. He was interrupting her mother's life, and her own, with obligation and distress. She wanted to go to the library that night. She wanted to finish her notes for an essay on Borges. She wanted to pretend he was still alive so she could ignore him.

Avram knocked on Rachel's door and asked if she would be ready by 9:30. "Your mother is going to be here soon, Red."

She opened the door, still in her robe. "I can't do this, Avie. I just can't do this."

Avram's heart thumped once, so loudly that he thought she could hear it. At that moment, he was the only person in her world who could help her through the very difficult morning that lay ahead. They rarely touched, but he put his hands on her shoulders, and he told her to focus.

"Your black dress," he said, "the one with the lacy straps. Put that on, and you can wear my black jacket over it. Then brush your hair, and I'll meet you in the kitchen in ten. Just do it, Red. Don't think; let me do the thinking for you this morning, OK?"

She nodded and closed the door, wishing she had had the chance for one more conversation with the man who was her father.

Meanwhile, Avram went back to his room where he removed the new suit from the hanging bag and laid it out across his unmade bed. His father once told him there were three times in a man's life when he should buy a new suit: his Bar Mitzvah, his Wedding, and the first important funeral he was compelled to attend. He glanced at his watch; then he hurriedly slid the dark tie into his collar, knotted it, put on the suit (which fit him perfectly, just like the salesperson had promised), and arrived in the kitchen moments before Rachel.

"Here," he said, handing her his black jacket.

"Oh my God, Avie," she said, suddenly noticing him, as if for the first time. "You got a suit. God, Avie, you bought a suit for this."

He nodded, helped her into his jacket, and then watched as she flipped her red hair from underneath the collar as he'd seen her do so many times before with sweaters and sweatshirts. She looked absolutely gorgeous to him, at that moment, and he swallowed the urge to tell her so, because she would only have dismissed the comment as something he was saying just to make her feel better. He fully expected that eight, perhaps ten, years would have to pass before he was ready to tell her everything. Until then, his job was to remain close, protective, trusted.

The doorbell rang, and Avram met Rachel's mother as she stepped into their cottage. It was their first face-to-face meeting. "She's in the kitchen," he said. "I'll wait outside."

When the two women came out, Avram was touched by the uncanny resemblance between them, as if he was seeing Rachel side by side with the woman she would become in 20 or 30 years.

In that brief moment time was linked, and those decades, the distance between them, did not exist.

> IF OUR highly pointed Triangles of the Soldier class are formidable, it may be readily inferred that far more formidable are our Women. For, if a Soldier is a wedge, a Woman is a needle; being, so to speak, *all* point, at least at the two extremities. Add to this the power of making herself practically invisible at will, and you will perceive that a Female, in Flatland, is a creature by no means to be trifled with. —E. A. Abbott, Section 3, *Flatland*, 1884

"Would you mind driving, Avram?" Adrienne asked, and he gladly agreed, pleased with her trust. He locked the cottage door behind them and opened the back door of the car. The two women slid in without a word.

"The chapel is at the corner of . . ." Adrienne began.

"He knows where we're going, Mom," Rachel said. They hugged again as Avram started the car. He drove in silence, careful at each stoplight.

Rachel told him it would be a small gathering, and he expected a few dozen people. But as he tried to find parking nearby and had to go several blocks before locating a spot, he wondered if there might be some other event at the chapel, a wedding perhaps, or a meeting of the church elders. He had never been inside a church before, nor to a non-Jewish funeral. From the moment he entered the doors of the immense building with ornate beams in its vaulted ceiling and intricate stained glass windows on either side of the main room, he realized it was not going to be like anything he'd imagined.

Rachel was stunned by the number of people coming down the sidewalk, milling in the front hall, or already seated in the large chapel. The chapel was part of the Episcopal church where she had sung in a Christmas pageant many years before when her school auditorium was being remodeled. There were far more than a few dozen people. Hundreds of people were there. Every row was filled, and at least 50 people were standing in the back.

"Mom . . ."

"Your father had many friends, honey," she said, "and a lot of people who worked with him are here too. I see a few I recognize . . . Billy Chan, I'm so glad he's here, he struggled so with your dad at work. And there's Cicely, oh, I'll have to make sure to find her after the service, she and your dad worked together at his first company, my, it must be 20 years ago. They were together for so long." Then her mother stopped, realizing she could have been speaking about herself.

Rachel simply could not believe her eyes.

One by one, his employees came to the podium to tell their favorite Linwood Eddy story.

A retired accountant told the very funny story of his Army days, when Linwood was driving a Jeep outside Munich filled with senior officers who were very drunk. None of them remembered how to get back to the barracks, but Linwood could interpret the pattern of letters on the German highway signs, even though he didn't speak a word of German, and they all got back before the front gates were locked.

The police sergeant who found Linwood after the accident told of a late-night conversation, many years before when he was only a cop on the beat. Linwood had taught him about street art and about the different gangs' very specific tagging styles. Linwood had helped him rise above the other detective-level candidates, who never had the knack for recognizing shape and color. "He seemed like a magician," the man said, "and he taught me one of his tricks."

One of the company's college interns took the podium and spoke about the night Linwood helped her with her college studies in Random Informatics. He showed her the secret of locating your specific phone number in the long string of numbers that composed Pi.

Another man, named Henry, said only a few words. He was trying to explain that everything of value that he had learned about people had come from Linwood Eddy, but as he reached the words ". . . everything of value . . ." he could not continue and held a handkerchief to his eyes as he turned away.

Rachel just sat still, allowing the waves of paradoxical knowledge about her father to wash over her like an immense tidal surge, carrying her back to an unknown beach.

Linwood's long-time employer and friend came to the podium and began to talk about what Linwood had taught him, in a more solemn (and very prepared) speech. Rachel was still watching Henry return to his seat. He was sobbing visibly now, and a woman was comforting him who seemed familiar, though Rachel could not remember her name.

". . . but Linwood would insist that I think about every individual in the company, insist that they be encouraged to talk to each other. He had a theory—and now, I've come to the belief that he is, excuse me, *was* entirely correct. Linwood told me that our technology and our manufacturing and our accounting systems would not talk to each other if the people responsible for them were not talking to each other. It seemed too simplistic to me."

L.M. Tooms paused and then added a personal reference.

"This was not how I was raised. It was not what my own unusual childhood had led me to believe. But Linwood would remind me, by example after example, of how it was true in our company. As I stand here before you today, honoring this man who held his private worries very close but extended himself with abounding generosity to those around him, I now see that he, in fact, may have been correct about everything.

"He was right about the network of people that is as important as the network of iron and wire that fills our data centers. He was right about the value of those people which only adds to the value of any opportunity for revenue or profit. He was right about the gravity of leadership which naturally pulls surrounding objects without, at any time, commanding it."

L.M. Tooms paused again, lost in his own recollections of Linwood's genuine method of teaching his boss by allowing his boss to behave like the teacher. The gravity of leadership. Then the pastor cleared his throat in that not-so-subtle manner that is supposed to be discrete but is heard by everyone in the room.

L.M. smiled, as if remembering a private joke. "I suppose it is ironic that the two executives responsible for thousands of jobs, the jobs of many people in this room today, were most notable for being Hard of Hearing and Unable to Read . . .

I did not know about his literacy, not then. And that's perhaps the best example of what I found so remarkable in this person, because it never held him back, never stopped him from working so very hard to do the right thing. So, as a final salute, I'd like to ask everyone who believes they learned something important from Linwood at some time during their acquaintance with him to please raise your hand . . ."

One. Five. Twenty.

Rachel looked back over her shoulder, tuck-and-curl of her fingers pulling a strand of hair behind one ear. She saw a stunning image: the hundreds of people in the chapel were all raising their hands.

"Thank you everyone," said the presiding pastor, as he returned to the podium and began his own lengthy remarks about the role of special people in communities.

Rachel was absorbed in her own silent memories of a man she had known her entire life and never understood. It was simply not possible, in one day, to recompute a lifetime of mistaken assumptions. Too much new information was overloading her system.

> Does this still seem strange to you? Then put yourself in a similar position. Suppose a person of the Fourth Dimension, condescending to visit you, were to say, 'Whenever you open your eyes, you see a Plane (which is of Two Dimensions) and you *infer* a Solid (which is of Three); but in reality you also see (though you do not recognize) a Fourth Dimension, which is not colour nor brightness nor anything of the kind, but a true Dimension, although I cannot point out to you its direction, nor can you possibly measure it.' What would you say to such a visitor? —E.A. Abbot, Preface, *Flatland*, 1884

It was only the pastor's concluding words that she heard clearly as everyone stood for the final benediction.

". . . and from the Book of Job, we know that we all must strive to *find the place where the light is distributed*. It seems to me, on this day, that we are bidding farewell to a man among us who lived in that place, and understood the distribution of that light, and helped so many in this congregation today to find their piece of it."

The distribution of light.

There was something about the distribution of light, the suggestion of impossible velocities, its speed the single constraint that keeps time in positon, the influence of gravity, but Rachel knew it was not an appropriate moment to be jotting notes, and hoped she would remember this pre-idea long enough to write it down. She filed out of the chapel beside her mother, first to the ornate lobby, then to the rear of the vestry room where they shook well-wishers hands and received their well-meaning hugs of condolence as Avie waited patiently by the door like a well-trained chauffeur waiting for his services to be needed. It seemed an eternity.

Rachel felt as if she was stepping over the stick figure of a father whom she did not know, into a three-dimensional world that had more complicated rules and many more variations. His world was not as flat as she had long considered it, and she was now adjusting to the sudden existence of dimensionality, where lines were only sides of cubes, where circles were only the circumference of spheres, where linear connections became similarly multidimensional. Now dozens, even hundreds, of misunderstandings could be seen from a different vantage point.

An entire universe, and all of the planets and moons and melons and baseballs in that universe, appeared in coordinated motion before her eyes, suddenly made real by her shifted perspective.

At that moment, she wished that her father was waiting to explain it to her at last, from the beginning, as fathers are supposed to do. "Why did you wait so long?" she asked, then imagined herself back in her room, sitting in her long blue robe, the one her mother had given her on her 18th birthday, while a silver-haired visitor with a familiar face answered, out of the shadow, every question she could ask.

CHAPTER 21

WE ARE THE PLATFORM

I am aware that to explain literature is to incur the risk of explaining it away . . .

—Jorge Luis Borges, 1931

O urs is an essential collaboration, author and reader, technologist and user.

The author's role is to invite a suspension of disbelief, asking us to enter the fictional world without our biases and preconceptions, our histories of broken trust and tainted expectations. If the writer is skilled and the reader is gifted, their collaborative comprehension of the stories can be remarkable, their combined perspectives creating a unique interface into the text that expands in value with each new reader.

Books, too, have their own internal logic and structure. We are familiar with the framework: title pages, tables of contents, footnotes. We cross the boundary of a book in search of knowledge, mystery, or simple entertainment we cannot provide for ourselves. In well-crafted works, elegant and complete, we are transformed by the act of reading as the characters are transformed by the events of their narratives.

Storytelling offers more than pathos, or laughter, or the passage of information from one generation to another. It offers the opportunity to be changed by the interaction of gift and receipt. With due and sincere respect for our collaboration, now that we have the common vocabulary of shared experience embedded in this collection of stories, I offer one final example of these System/Mirror principles.

I began this project with a very strong belief in the Prime Theorem and its corollaries and an equal belief in the potential for each short story to convey, in between the lines, a truth about information technology that is best understood through the eyes of the characters in the stories.

I also believed that the book itself could mirror *the essential complexity of a service-oriented enterprise* in which a variety of distributed objects, servers, functions, and practitioners are best understood, like the Internet itself, as a matrix of relationships. The Professor's essay on the "Network as Narrative Form" was prompted by my initial correspondence with Jim Levine, my agent in New York, who asked for an overview. In preparation for the Professor's penultimate chapter, and in response to my agent, I sketched two diagrams that portrayed in the abstract what the book would ultimately become, in practice.

Exhibit 21.1 is a high-level architectural schematic of a standard net-based application environment.

In a service-oriented architecture, the applications are designed as distributed resources on the network, available for quick composition and delivery. From such a diffuse and "loosely coupled" framework of resources, we move toward this level of architecture, which is driven by the "economics of agility,"[1] which requires our IT organizations to

EXHIBIT 21.1   *Presentation Layer Schematic*

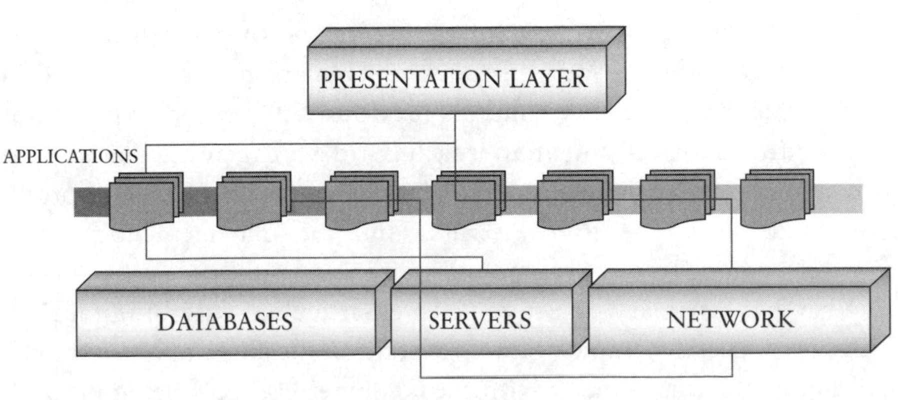

respond in *hours* rather than *months* to any request for new functionality. Then the separate "applications" become distributed behaviors that can be rapidly organized and provisioned. Functionalities such as "search," "authentication," and even the more sophisticated "virtual brokerage," will eventually be delivered as services. This, in turn, drives the most important elements of business (human innovation) *upward* toward the Presentation Layer (the computer-human interface) available 24/7 in an entirely mobile, multidevice, multilanguage mode

For our purposes, the "presentation layer" can be understood in many ways: it can be *the introduction* to a collection of short stories that invites readers to suspend their disbelief and enter into the work, or it can be a personalized avatar that leads a user through a multimedia game. In the world of IT, it is best understood as the user interface, often delivered via the browser, that assists the user in navigating hierarchies to locate the information or functionality that they seek.

In the coming decade, the presentation layer will become increasingly significant to our software interactions, because of two important trends that are impacting our world of IT simultaneously:

1. The decentralization of infrastructure, as we move toward "on demand" and "utility" computing: the actual data center operations physically exist elsewhere.

2. The globalization of the IT workforce, as we begin to take proper advantage of exceptional technical resources in Russia, India, Taiwan, Ireland, Israel, and so on.

This dual diffusion—of our infrastructure and of our workforce—is currently creating a serious dilemma for IT managers, as described in the Interfaces and Identity chapters previously. Diffusion requires not only a different management approach (Grid Management Theory) but also an increased emphasis on that which remains "local" to our provision of services: the user interface and the management/business processes unique to our specific enterprise.

What is the primary objective of a well-articulated user interface?

As introduced by Apple in the 1980s, the desktop metaphor removed us from interacting directly with the compute resources being utilized.

This was the source of Linwood Eddy's original distress, for when the graphical user interface was introduced, he lost his ability to communicate directly with machines via 0s and 1s. The desktop inserted itself, providing a layer of abstraction, a process that continues at all levels of IT: functionality is delivered to the user through an interface that serves the role of communicating instructions and responding with results. It is happening in our data centers and on our networks, as Lucid in the Virtualization chapter eventually understands.

As the IT world becomes increasingly diffuse, our reliance on metaphor in the service of abstraction increases.

Subsequently, for this book to appropriately mirror the world that it describes, it was necessary to provide a layer of metaphor, emulating the information being delivered in a manner that a) made the information more accessible, and b) submerged the technology "underneath the surface" of the reader's attention. This enforced abstraction, as the Professor notes in his essay, is an analog of the suspension of disbelief. The reader/user is invited to participate in the function/text and interact with the stories/objects, toward the overall goal of elucidating the theorem and principles that sit at the core of this effort.

Therefore, *The Prime Theorem* can be observed even at the structural level *of the book itself,* in the same manner and with the same viability that it applies at each architectural level and—the point of this example—to the very framework of this collection of short stories.

When viewed in a similar (three-tiered) model, this book can be understood as a collection of distributed objects (stories) viewed uniquely by each reader. The objects can be combined in different orders, to produce different but integrated results.

Exhibit 21.2 demonstrates the book schematically. Viewed in this manner, the principles that apply to a service-oriented architecture may well be applied to the narrative, with equal results: themes and subplots can be reordered and can emerge as different, but equally valid, organized entities.

Our sensations of linear time, and our notions of space, are challenged by this nonhierarchical and multidimensional architecture. A reader might elect to read only the chapters pertaining to Linwood and Rachel, providing a specific view into one storyline and its accompanying themes. Another reader might elect to read none of the Linwood/Rachel

EXHIBIT 21.2   *Narrative (Book) Schematic*

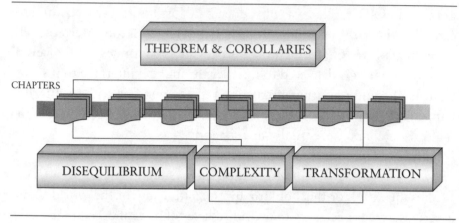

stories, preferring the individual accounts in *Virtualization* and *Orchestration*. (I am humbly reminded of Julio Cortazar's *Hopscotch*, a magical realist's experiment with stories as transposable objects. Also pertinent to this perspective is Ted Nelson's *zzstructure*, specifically his portrayal of Loose Cells.[2]) A review of Ted Nelson's work, in relation to this alternative schema, informed the Professor's chapter on the Network as Narrative Form. (See Exhibit 21.3).

In theory, other stories could be added as distributed objects (e.g., by a specific IT team to augment a particular subject area for discussion). Alternately, a new "oral tradition" could be initiated to highlight a company's key business processes, as reflected in Dieter Kahn's *Q Narratives*.

Perhaps some of the stories in this book (on this network) are components of larger works of fiction beyond the reader's scope, yet informed and enabled by that original text (source code) existing elsewhere, beyond the boundaries of this particular volume. Rachel's next story, after Flatland, has yet to be written, yet the future chronology of that story is already implied at chapter's end, as if any imagined fiction is a type of "open source" that invites each reader's modifications and enhancements.

This book, subsequently, was crafted in the fashion that Web Services are ultimately to be designed. Each module was written as an independent mechanism, self-describing and autonomous; when the modules are

EXHIBIT 21.3   *Loose Cells Structure*

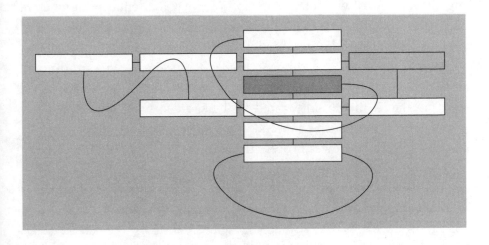

Source: Based on the *zzstructure* proposed by Ted Nelson.

collected together, however, themes emerge (Disequilibrium/Complexity/Transformation) that provide an overarching context to the work.

The analogy can be extended, beyond the architecture and development of the chapters, but to the very process of the book's production. In the final editing stages (so often occurring offstage and outside the view of the audience), an urgent marketing matter emerges. Editors confer. Author proposes a solution. In the implementation of that solution, an entire chapter in the original manuscript was eliminated from the version you now have in your hands. One or two significant passages were retained, and threaded into another chapter's narrative.

The same situation emerges, in many variations, every day in our compute environments. An important server is taken offline. A network closet is eliminated, with key routers strategically relocated in other areas of the building. A business application module, provided as a real-time service to be dynamically invoked by other applications, is removed during QA cycles. In such cases, IT staff ensure that the institution's information flow is uninterrupted, the business process (Q Narrative) continues to function.

The ultimate design goal of this book was to demonstrate the usefulness of the central metaphor—the prime theorem—at every level, where *even the demonstration itself was a mirror of its own intention*, becoming an example of what it was meant to prove, a circular path wherein the reader (like the end-user of business software) opens the book (logs on to the system) and is provided with a suite of chapters (applications, functions) that can be readily comprehended because of the traditional narrative devices employed (reusable components and a well-articulated user interface). In well-integrated systems, aided by human design, an entire collection of such chapters (applications, functions) is essentially aligned with the business process they are meant to enable.

The oversimplification is intentional.

As with any effort toward abstraction, specific details are eliminated in order to portray a larger theme that might otherwise be difficult to discern in the chaos of their heterogeneity. As Borges worried, in 1931, about explaining away literature (lest it would not have its desired effect), there is a risk in candidly providing this architectural clue to the composition of this book. Additionally, I am well aware that such an oversimplification may undermine its ultimate value.[3] However, our desire for literature gives way to the larger objective of delivering understandable business principles that explain (by means of abstraction) the very complex environment we find ourselves facing in the IT of the coming decade.

Once the system/mirror principle is understood, we begin to see episodic evidence of it everywhere, as when we learn a new word and find it suddenly ubiquitous in our lives. From such a perspective, one might wonder whether Marcel Proust was describing the Internet in 1922:

> But the truth, even more, is that life is perpetually weaving fresh threads which link one individual and one event to another, and that these threads are crossed and recrossed, doubled and redoubled to thicken the web, so that between any slightest point of our past and all the others a rich network of memories gives us an almost infinite variety of communicating paths to choose from.[4]

The system *is* a mirror, and to correct inadequacies we see in the reflection, we should not simply cover the mirror, or replace it with another. The mirror does not become overweight, or unattractive, or arthritic through the passage of time. Prudence advises us to accept the honesty of what we see and begin the more complicated work of changing ourselves in order to improve our systems. Though it is much easier to continue "buying new mirrors" until they show us the way we want to be seen, a more honest response is to recognize that part of ourselves that is insufficiently displayed—our inadequacies, our purely human limitations—and adjust our postures and styles, our organizations and processes.

Technology is not the problem.

I am convinced that we are on the verge of yet another tectonic shift in IT, one milestone of which will be the standardization of Grid Computing analogues within and beyond our institutions, until these grid networks themselves become a larger ecosystem that mirrors the ecosystem of alliances, partnerships, vendors, employees, and facilities that compose any specific corporation; abstractly, they mirror nature itself. These ecosystems, what Kevin Kelly calls "vivisystems,"[5] will be the latticed business community, grids interacting with grids.

An excellent analogy can be found in the world of environmental art, specifically in the sculptures of Andy Goldsworthy whose career has been an exploration of our relationship with nature. In the movie, *Rivers and Tides*, his sculpture entitled the *Stick Dome* is, first and foremost, an intricate dome of riverside sticks. The natural assumption is that the sculpture itself portrays the *end result* of the sculptor's efforts; however, it is only the interim phase of the project.

As the sea approaches the beach, the oncoming tide slowly lifts his entire stick sculpture, which floats independently out to sea. There, the swirling tides slowly uncurl the arrangement to create an immense, dynamic spiral that is entirely in sync with the complex water currents that support it.

Our analogy to the current service-oriented architecture and the broader field of autonomic computing is easily explained: current rigid system architectures are akin to the stick dome on the beach, which required very specific manual intervention to be constructed and to be maintained over time. The stick dome, once afloat in the sea, is our architecture that exists dynamically within the surrounding environment, responding to complex change without human intervention.

Clearly, IT management techniques for one type of architecture (rigid, manual, costly) are the practices seen in most current IT organizations:

high degrees of attention and effort being given by very senior staff to maintain the structure on its changeless foundation. IT management techniques for the dynamic state, in which the spiraling architecture is self-governing, aligned with natural forces of change, and requires little human intervention, are quite different.

Subsequently, one of the first and most important objectives for IT leaders who hope to move their organizations from the rigid and expensive paradigm of their current architectures to the more adaptive, autonomic systems in the network-based computing model is to begin the education (of their employees and executives) that a dynamic *technology* framework requires a dynamic *organizational* framework, one in which teams can form spontaneously (without formal approval structures or barriers) to solve problems rapidly, in context.

For an institution in which relationships thrive, where trust is an enabled commodity of exchange between management and the employees, these employees are capable of responding to even the most extreme problems. Their solutions will be innovative, cost effective and will be implemented quickly. Once a single institution (single system) begins to behave in this fashion, the overall enterprise (network of networks) can begin to interact in this manner.

Therefore, to influence and contribute to the ongoing momentum toward autonomic, Grid-based, pervasive computing, we must change ourselves. Only then will we ultimately change what we build. It is the essential truth of the Prime Theorem.

The consequent postulate of this logic suggests that we must engage in the more difficult dialogue (with ourselves, within our teams, among our corporations) of identifying those boundaries that have predictably limited our progress (hypercompetition, ego- and ethno-centric rationalizations) and begin to model those behaviors if we want the mirror to reflect a better view.

We are the distributed resources connected by many devices and cultures, becoming the Grid of Grids, that will become the foundation of next-generation technologies. Building block by building block, *we are the platform*, and those future technologies (bionomic, autonomous, intelligent, coevolutionary) will be built on this vibrant interconnected matrix of practitioners. With Mashing Up and Remixing, loosely coupled components are recombined quickly, in ways that are yet to be understood. But the matrix is not merely the chaotic swirl of possibilities, services to be combined with others in previously unpredicted ways to create newer services. It remains dependent on a conceptual architecture; it requires a standardized *platform* on which the chaos is no longer just chaos, but immense, potential, and widespread community-based innovations.

We are the Platform.

Our information systems will ultimately accommodate what we are capable of modeling. The compute systems within our reach today are abstractions, at the more simplified level, of what we want to do, who we want to be, and how we want to be remembered.

Technology is not the problem. We must transform ourselves.

NOTES

1. Steve Yatko in conversation with the author, Credit Suisse First Boston, 2003.
2. The synchronicity of this diagram and Ted Nelson's portrayal of "Loose Cells" in his recent work on an alternative to hierarchical approaches to data can be seen on: Ted Nelson, "Diagram of Loose Cells," 2003, http://xanadu.com/zigzag/ZZdnld/zzRefDef/
3. "Using literature to help us understand science is, of course, as dangerous as using science to understand literature"—Alice Flaherty, *The Midnight Disease* (New York: Houghton Mifflin, 2004). p. 16.
4. Marcel Proust, *Remembrance of Things Past*, vol. 7, 258.
5. Kevin Kelly, *Out of Control: The New Biology of Machines, Social Systems, and the Economic World* (New York: Basic Books, 2004).

INDEX